DONREA
2012

CHEERS

2012
NYCC

case aga

[illegible] years after he [illegible]

BY RICHARD [illegible]

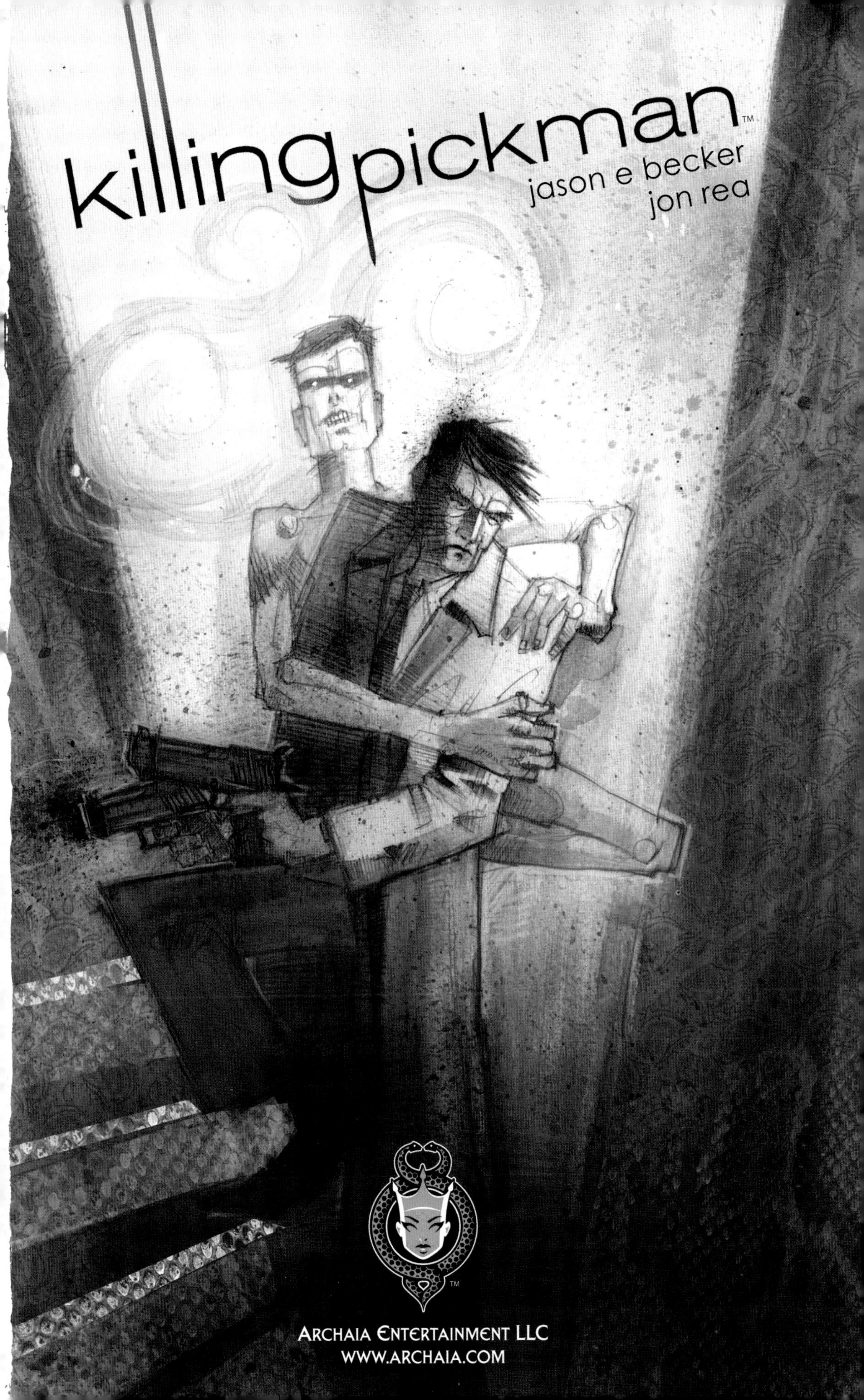

killing pickman™
jason e becker
jon rea
™
Archaia Entertainment LLC
WWW.ARCHAIA.COM

killing pickman ™

written by jason e becker

illustrated by jon rea

lettered and additional colors (page 104 to139) **by** matt talbot

Paul Morrissey, *Editor*
Scott Newman, *Production Manager*

Archaia Entertainment LLC

PJ Bickett, *CEO*
Mark Smylie, *CCO*
Mike Kennedy, *Publisher*
Stephen Christy, *Editor-in-Chief*

Published by **Archaia**

Archaia Entertainment LLC
1680 Vine Street, Suite 1010
Los Angeles, California, 90028, USA
www.archaia.com

ARCHAIA ™
NEW STORIES. NEW WORLDS.

KILLING PICKMAN Collected Edition Hardcover. October 2011. FIRST PRINTING

10 9 8 7 6 5 4 3 2 1

ISBN: 1-936393-14-X
ISBN 13: 978-1-936393-14-5

table of contents

For Mom because she watched the scary ones with me. For Poppy because he wouldn't give up until I looked out the window into the darkness. And for Fred Ward. He'll always be Lovecraft to me.

—jason

For Jim & Rhonda for patiently watering the seeds, for Jake and Maddie for keeping it exciting everyday, and most of all for Jill for tolerating the late nights and the empty bed. It took all of you.

To my tolerant friends and ersatz models: Kevin Streckewald, Jeremy Rea, Jim Rea, Jill Rea, David Margolis, Gary Deamer, Frank Pronesti, Bronagh Boyle, John Zadnik, Kevin Connolly, Jon Moore and Don Rubin.

—jon

chapter one

Of Cain

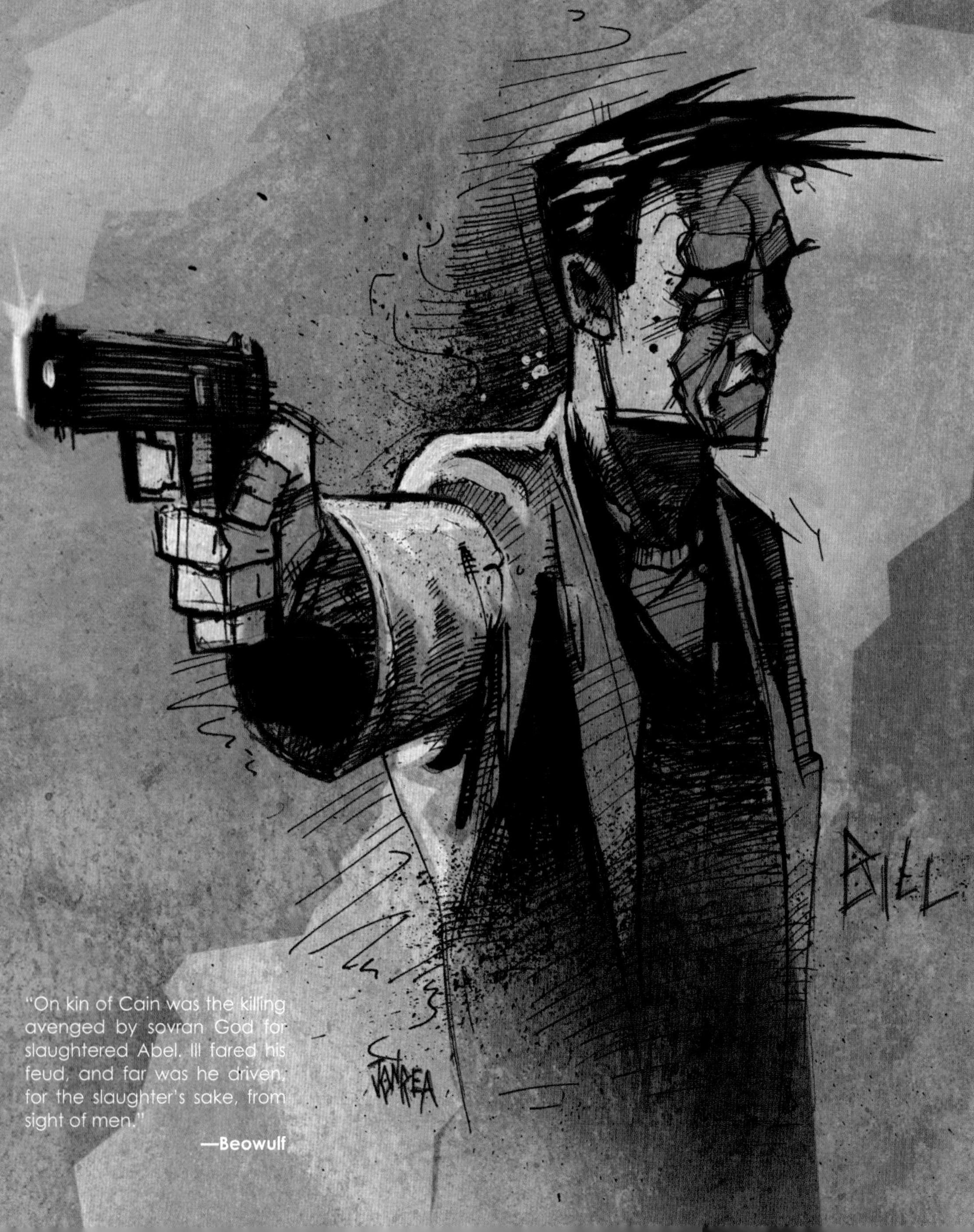

"On kin of Cain was the killing avenged by sovran God for slaughtered Abel. Ill fared his feud, and far was he driven, for the slaughter's sake, from sight of men."

—**Beowulf**

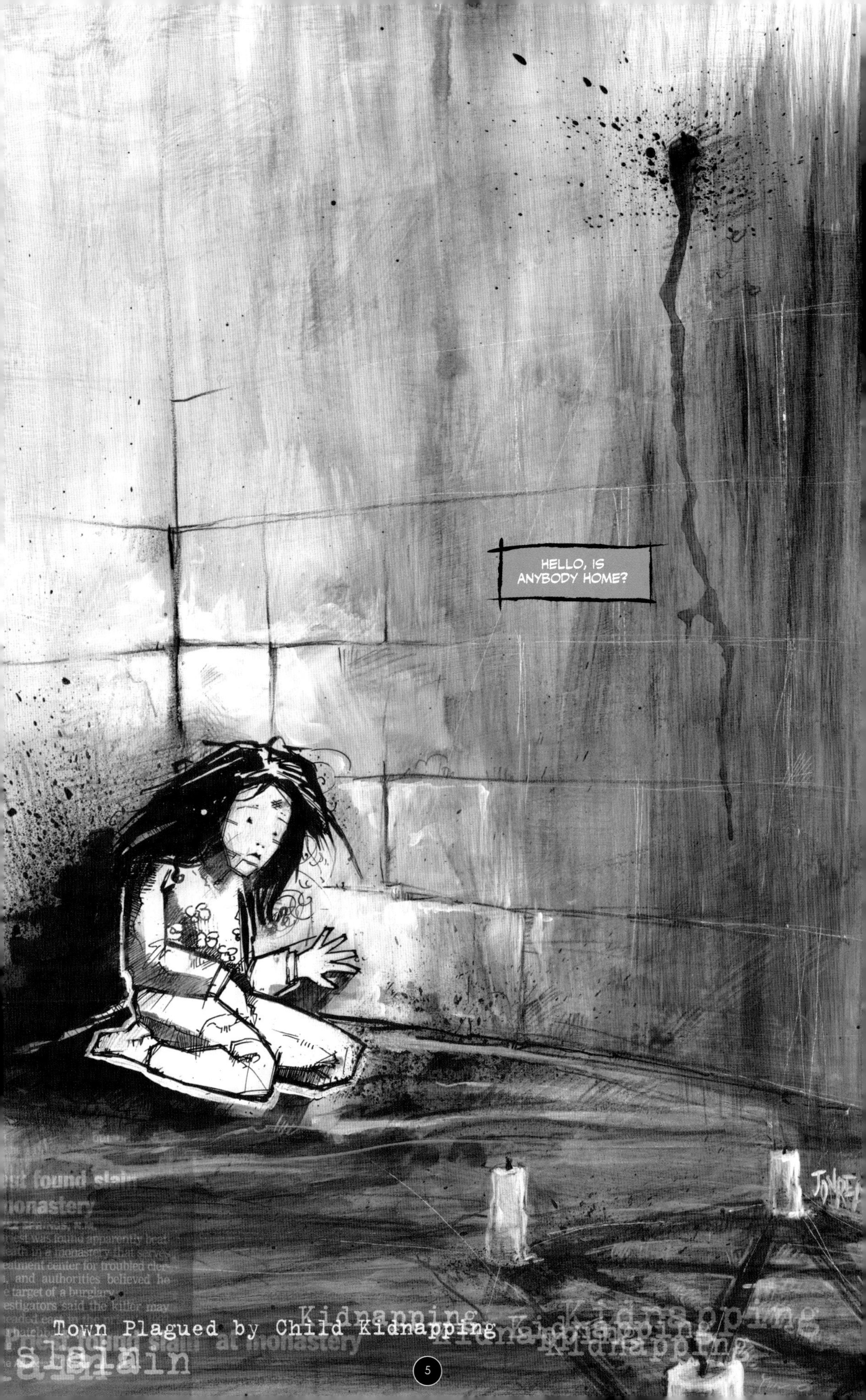
HELLO, IS ANYBODY HOME?
Town Plagued by Child Kidnapping
Kidnapping
Kidnapping
Kidnapping
slain

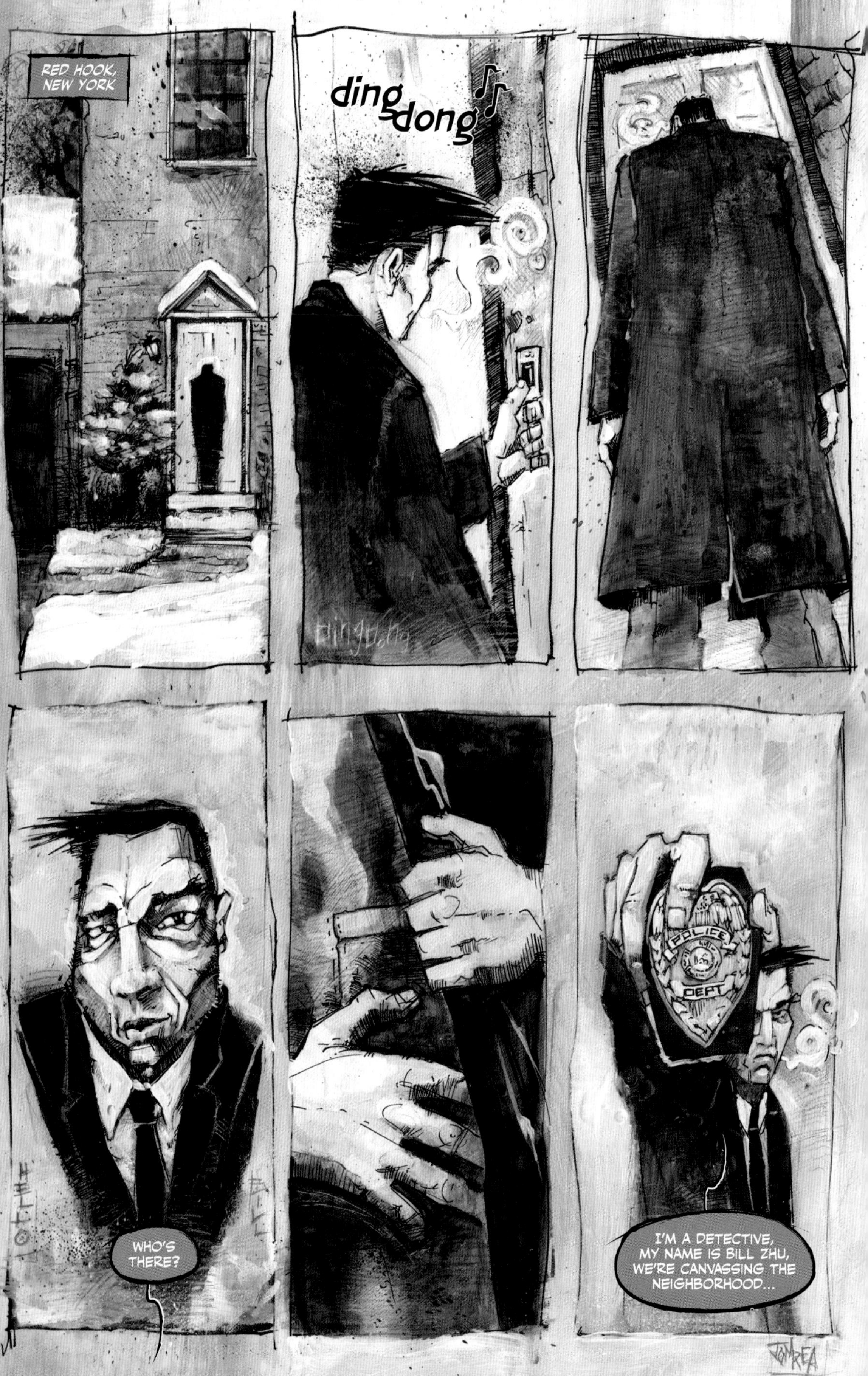
RED HOOK, NEW YORK
ding dong
WHO'S THERE?
POLICE DEPT
I'M A DETECTIVE, MY NAME IS BILL ZHU, WE'RE CANVASSING THE NEIGHBORHOOD...

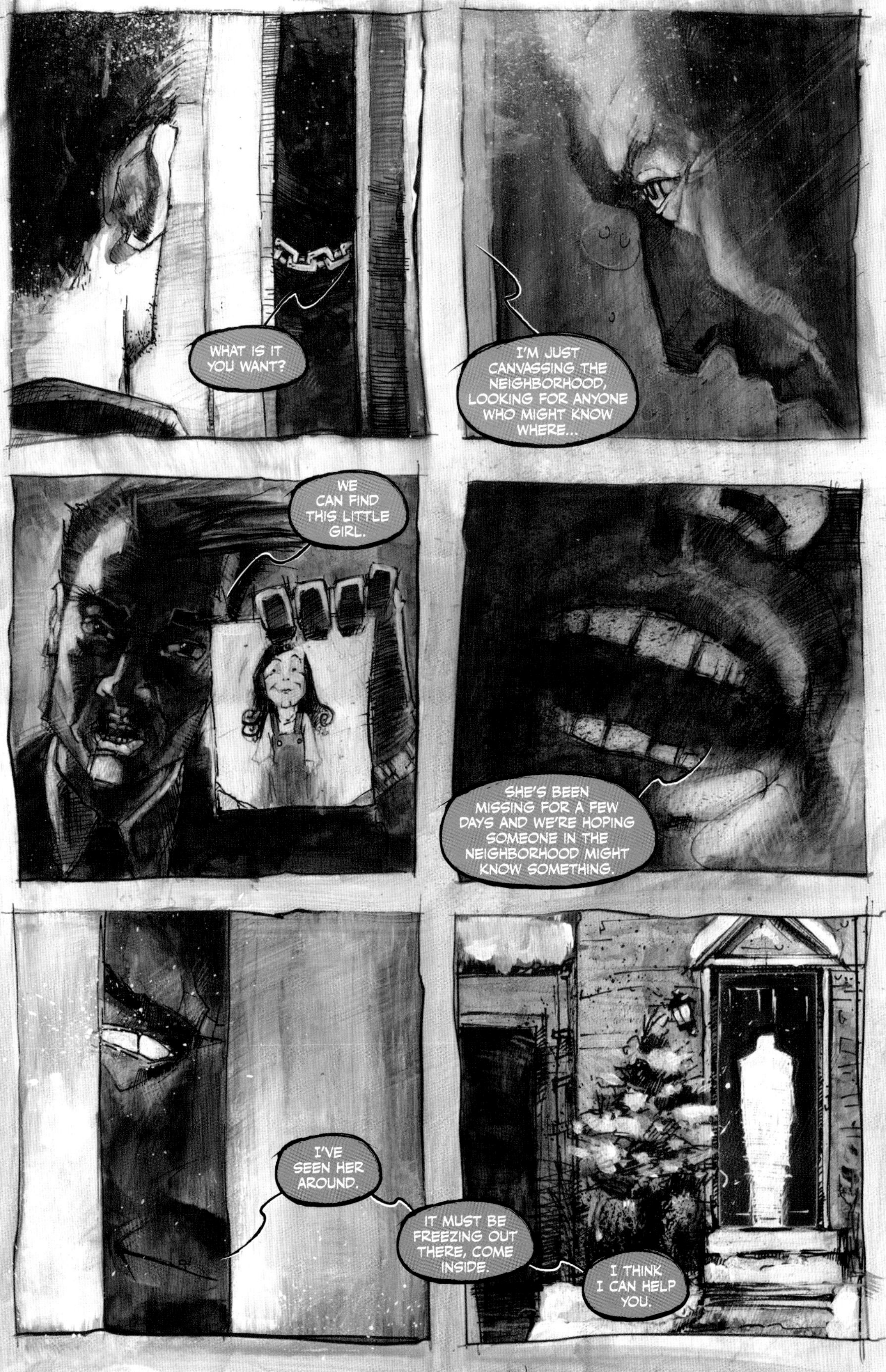
WHAT IS IT YOU WANT?
I'M JUST CANVASSING THE NEIGHBORHOOD, LOOKING FOR ANYONE WHO MIGHT KNOW WHERE...
WE CAN FIND THIS LITTLE GIRL.
SHE'S BEEN MISSING FOR A FEW DAYS AND WE'RE HOPING SOMEONE IN THE NEIGHBORHOOD MIGHT KNOW SOMETHING.
I'VE SEEN HER AROUND.
IT MUST BE FREEZING OUT THERE, COME INSIDE.
I THINK I CAN HELP YOU.

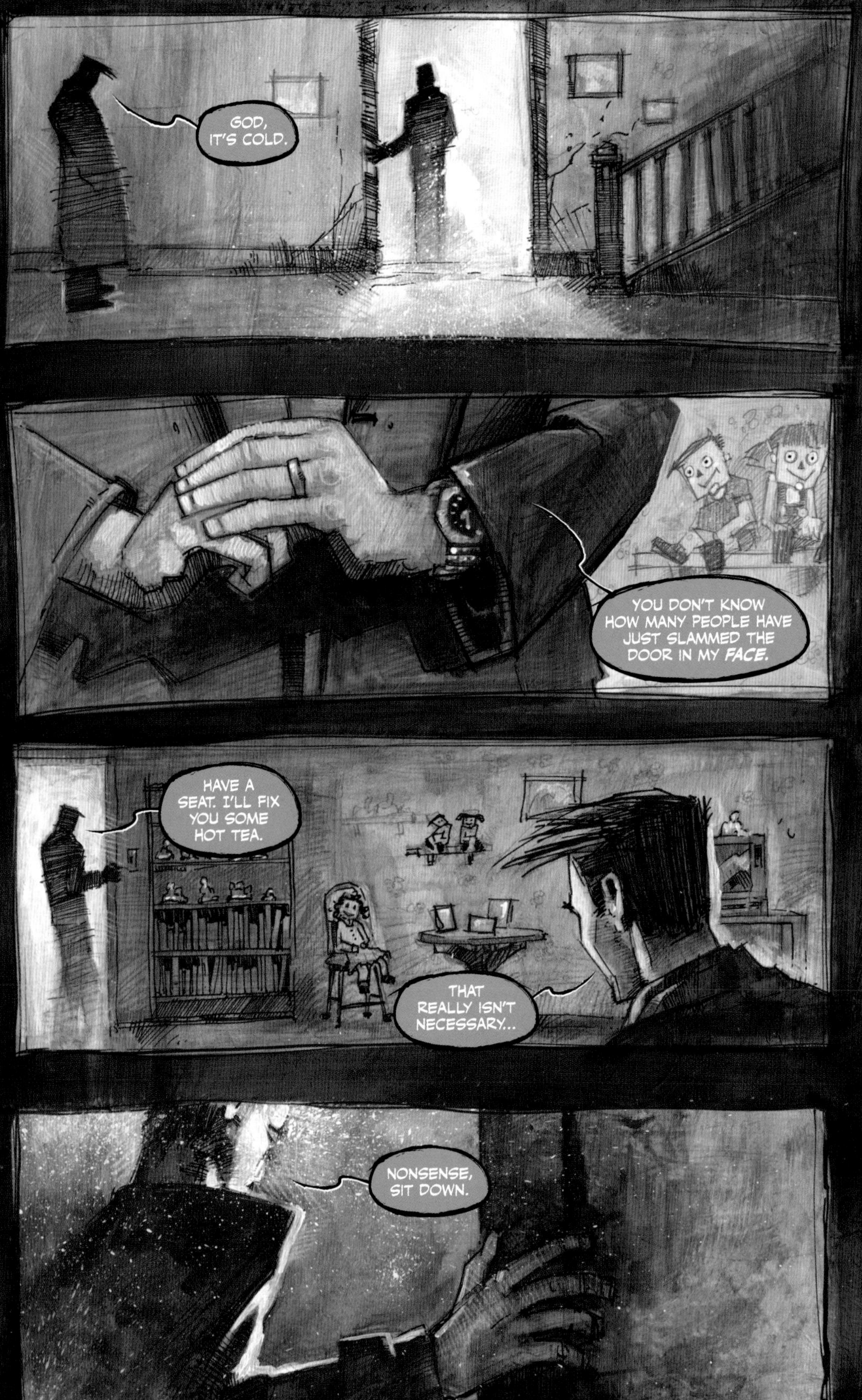
GOD, IT'S COLD.
YOU DON'T KNOW HOW MANY PEOPLE HAVE JUST SLAMMED THE DOOR IN MY *FACE*.
HAVE A SEAT. I'LL FIX YOU SOME HOT TEA.
THAT REALLY ISN'T NECESSARY...
NONSENSE, SIT DOWN.

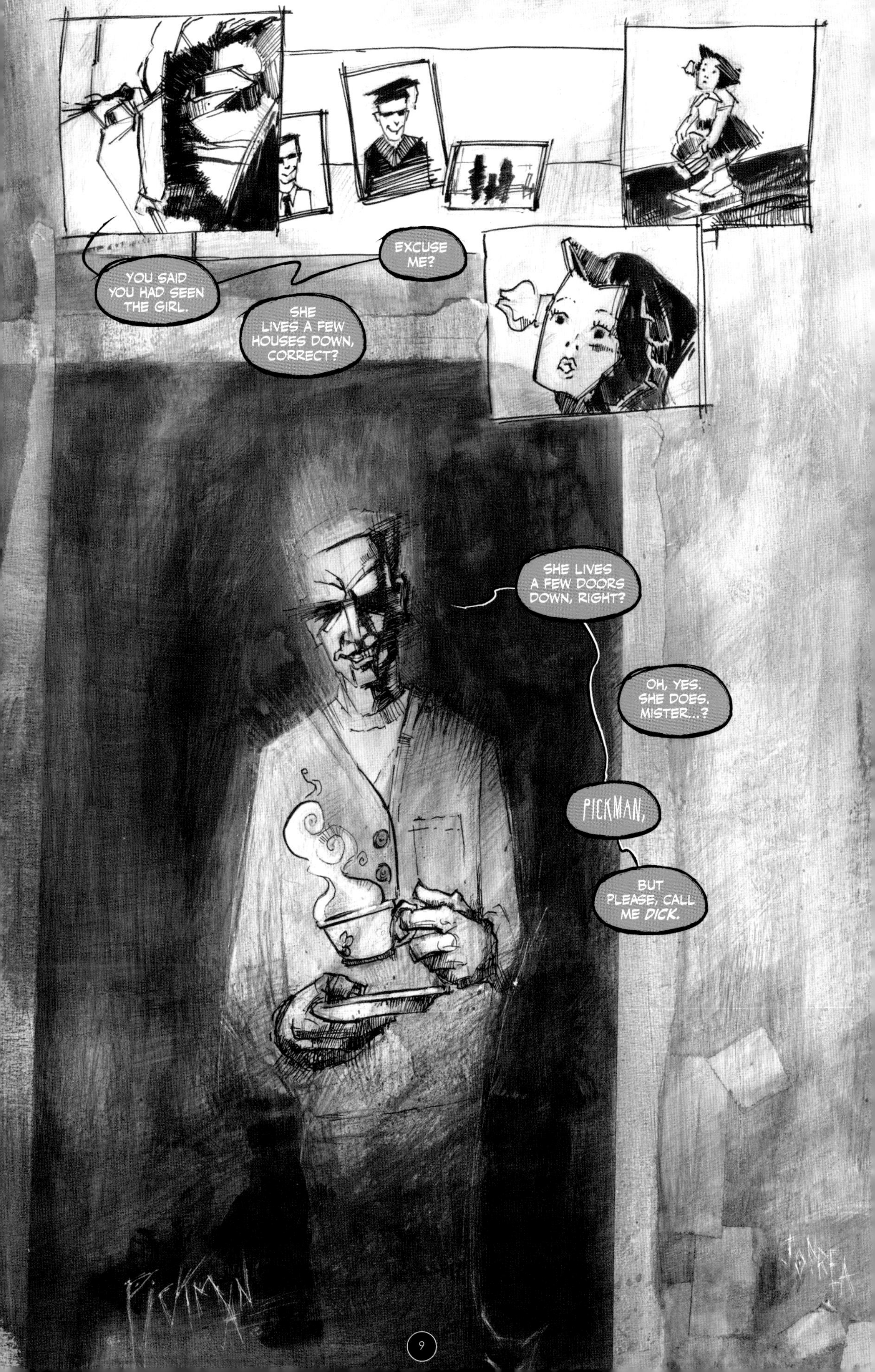
YOU SAID YOU HAD SEEN THE GIRL.
EXCUSE ME?
SHE LIVES A FEW HOUSES DOWN, CORRECT?
SHE LIVES A FEW DOORS DOWN, RIGHT?
OH, YES. SHE DOES. MISTER...?
PICKMAN,
BUT PLEASE, CALL ME *DICK.*
PICKMAN

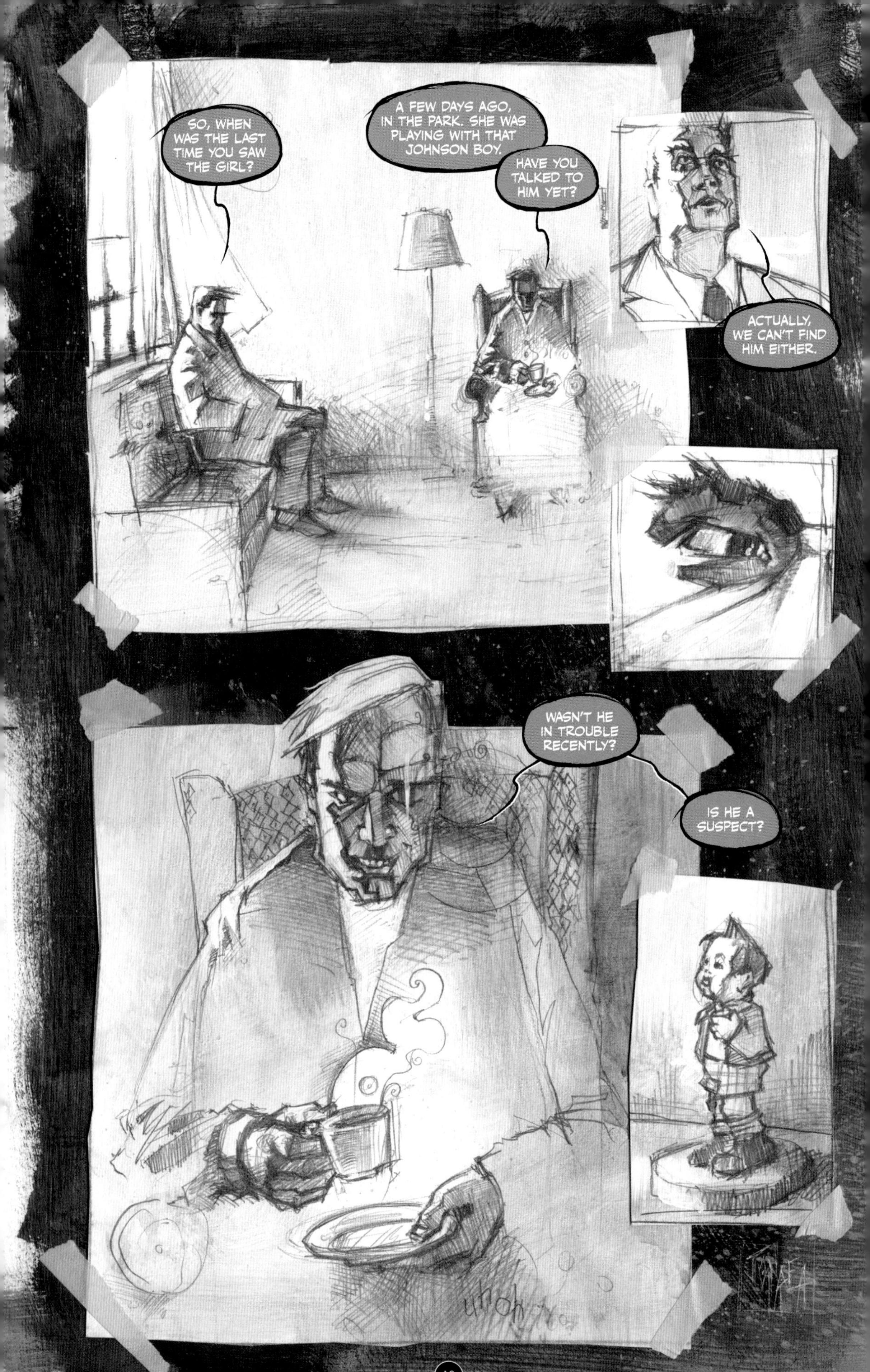
SO, WHEN WAS THE LAST TIME YOU SAW THE GIRL?
A FEW DAYS AGO, IN THE PARK. SHE WAS PLAYING WITH THAT JOHNSON BOY.
HAVE YOU TALKED TO HIM YET?
ACTUALLY, WE CAN'T FIND HIM EITHER.
WASN'T HE IN TROUBLE RECENTLY?
IS HE A SUSPECT?

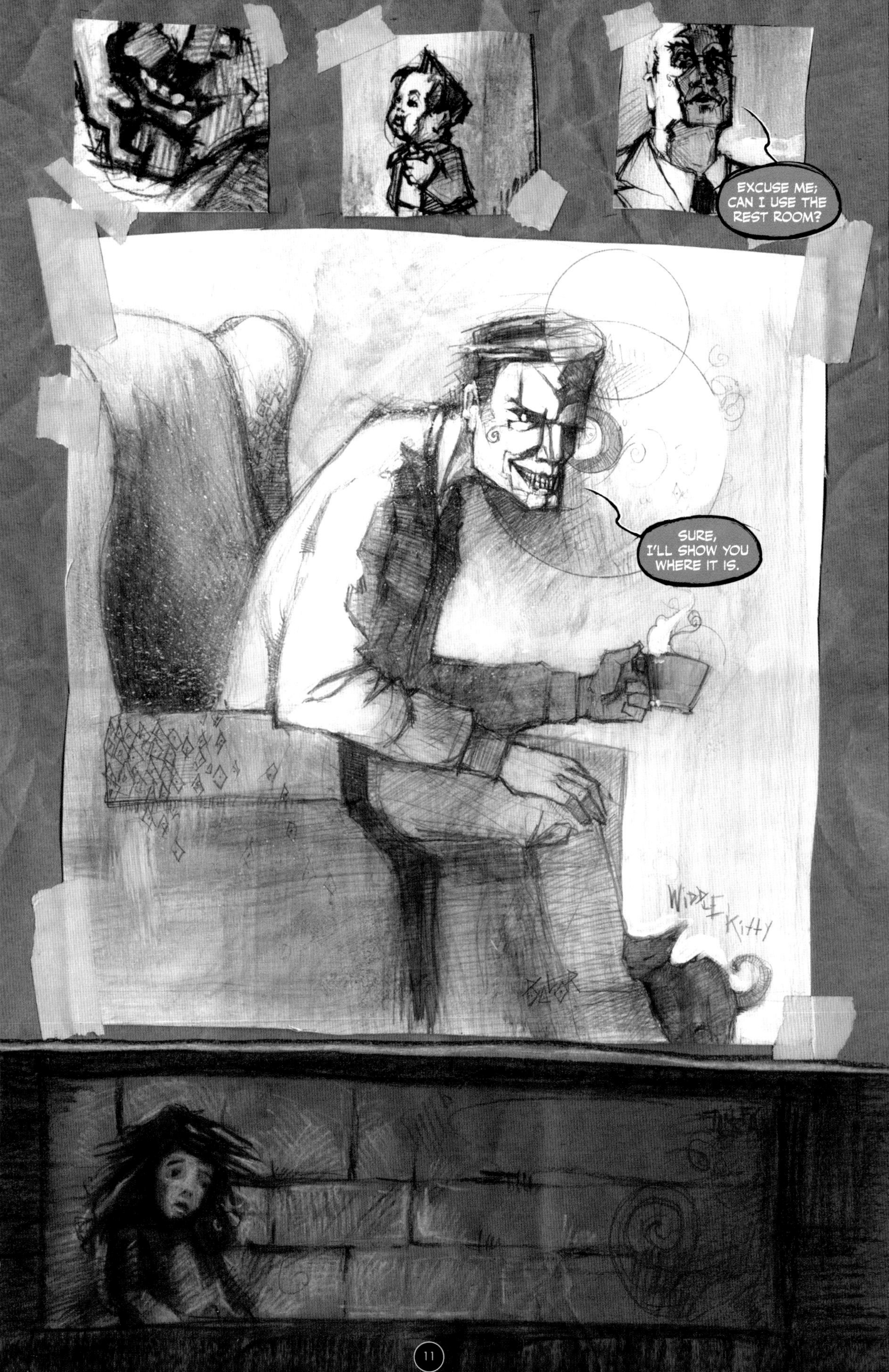
EXCUSE ME; CAN I USE THE REST ROOM?
SURE, I'LL SHOW YOU WHERE IT IS.
WIDDLE KITTY

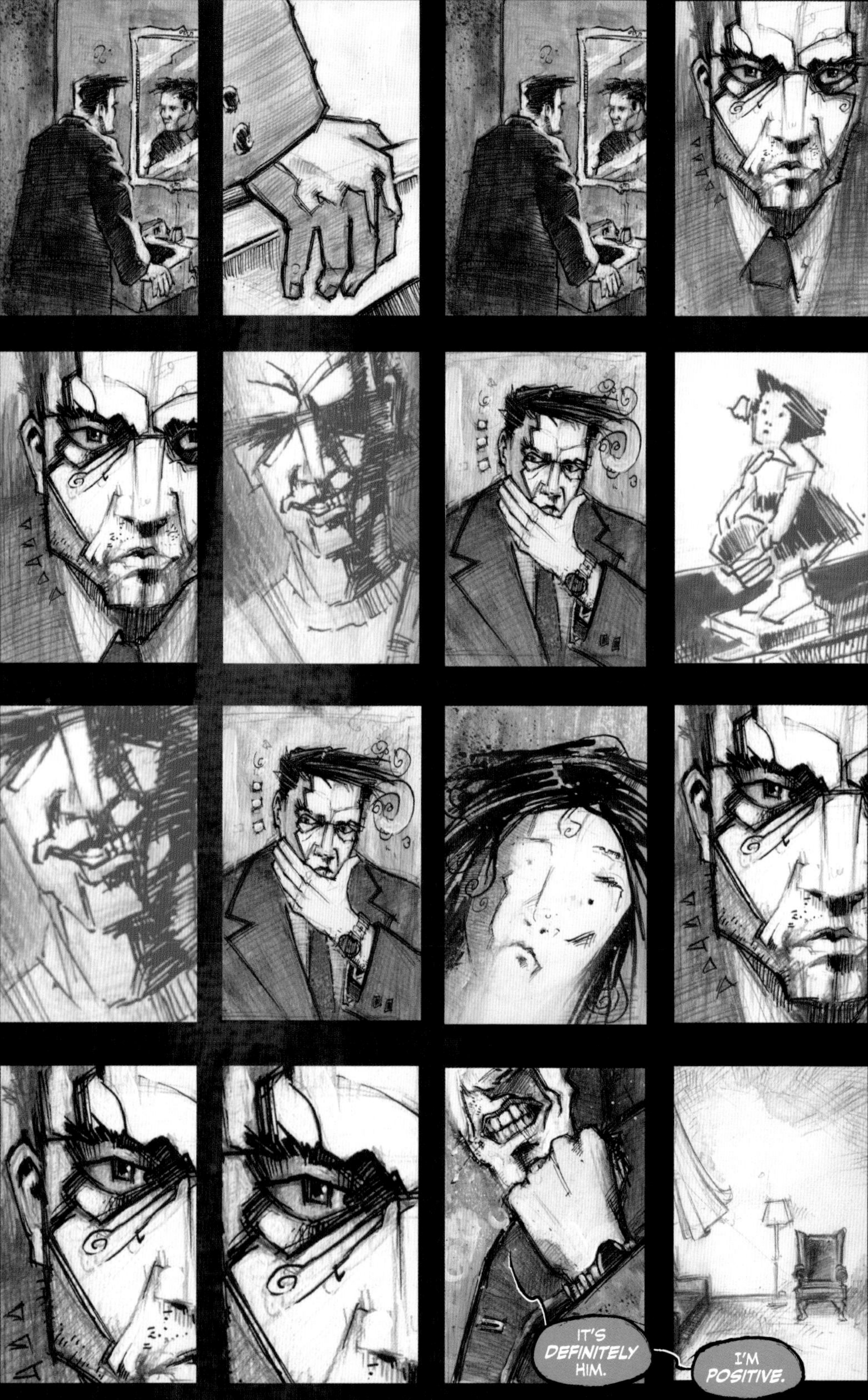
IT'S DEFINITELY HIM.
I'M POSITIVE.

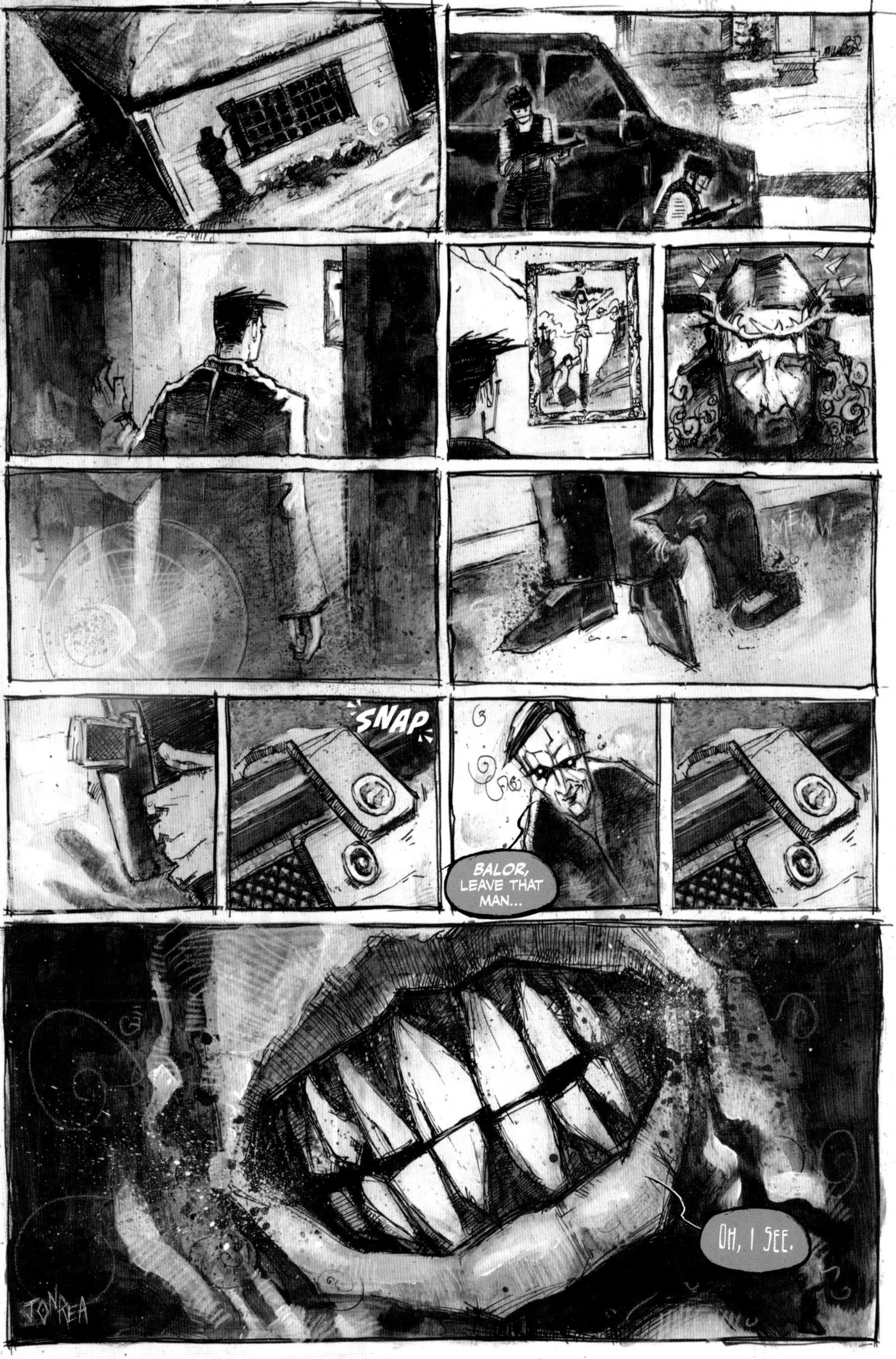
MEOW
SNAP
BALOR, LEAVE THAT MAN...
OH, I SEE.
JON REA

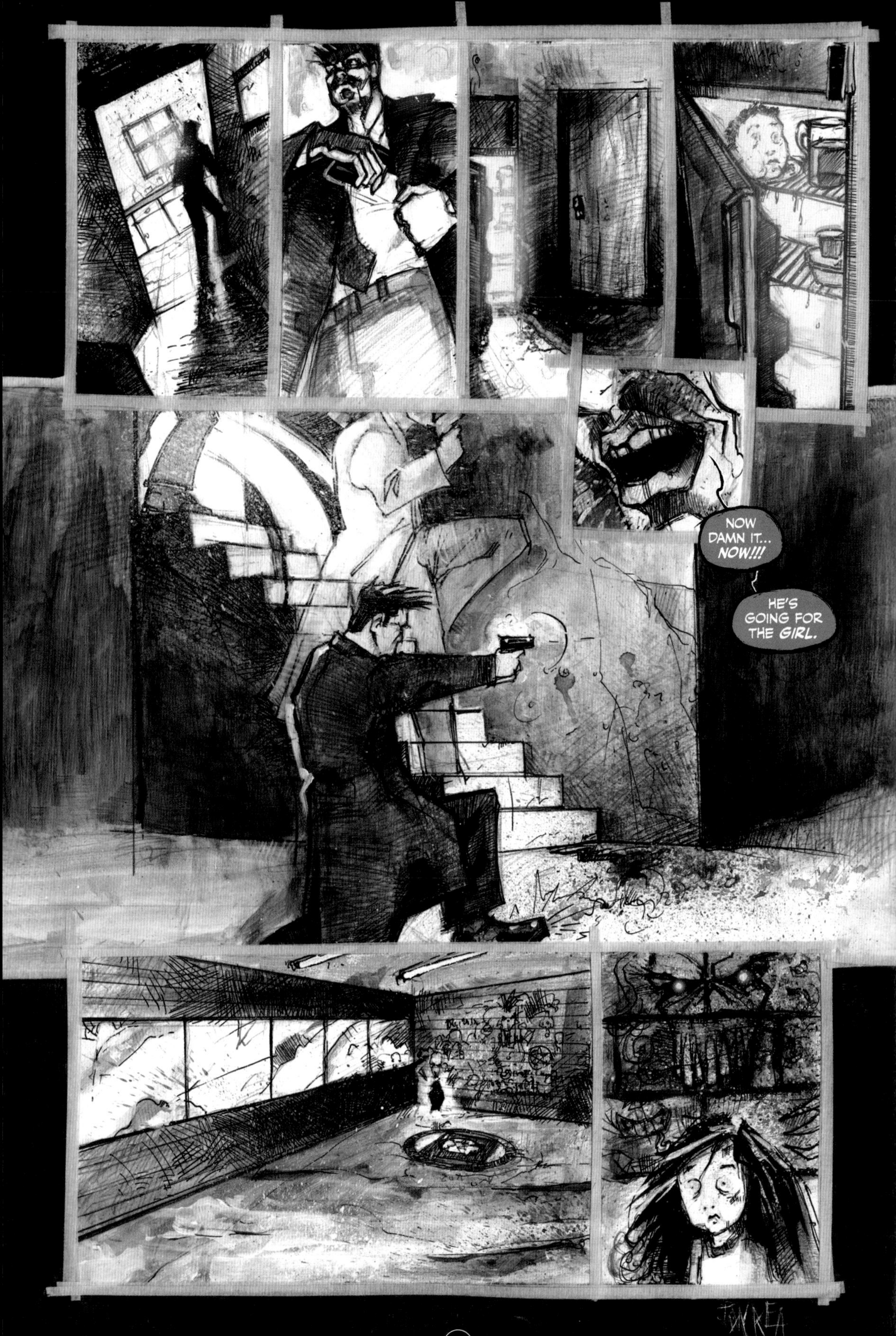
NOW DAMN IT... NOW!!!
HE'S GOING FOR THE GIRL.

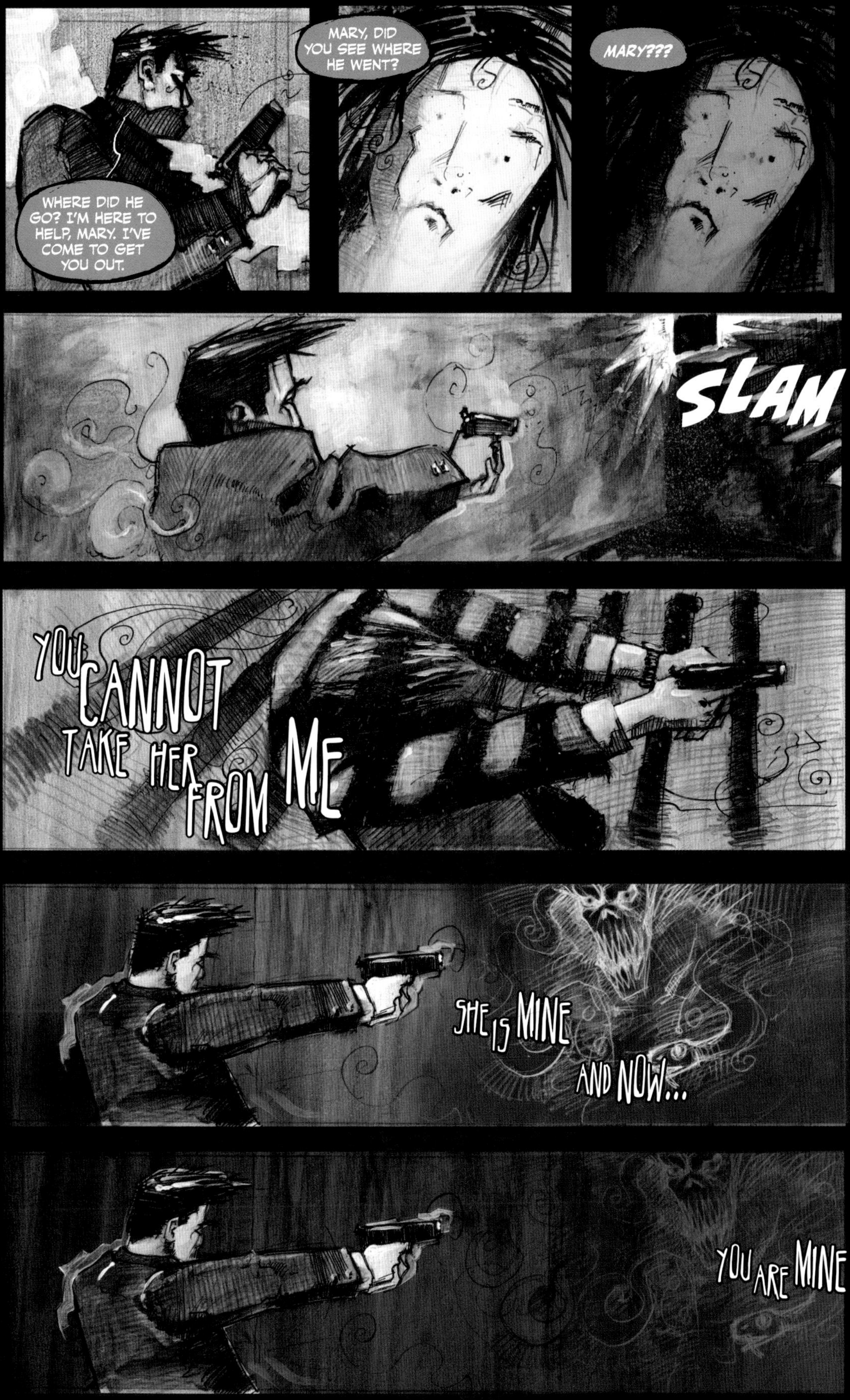
WHERE DID HE GO? I'M HERE TO HELP, MARY. I'VE COME TO GET YOU OUT.
MARY, DID YOU SEE WHERE HE WENT?
MARY???
SLAM
YOU CANNOT TAKE HER FROM ME
SHE IS MINE
AND NOW...
YOU ARE MINE

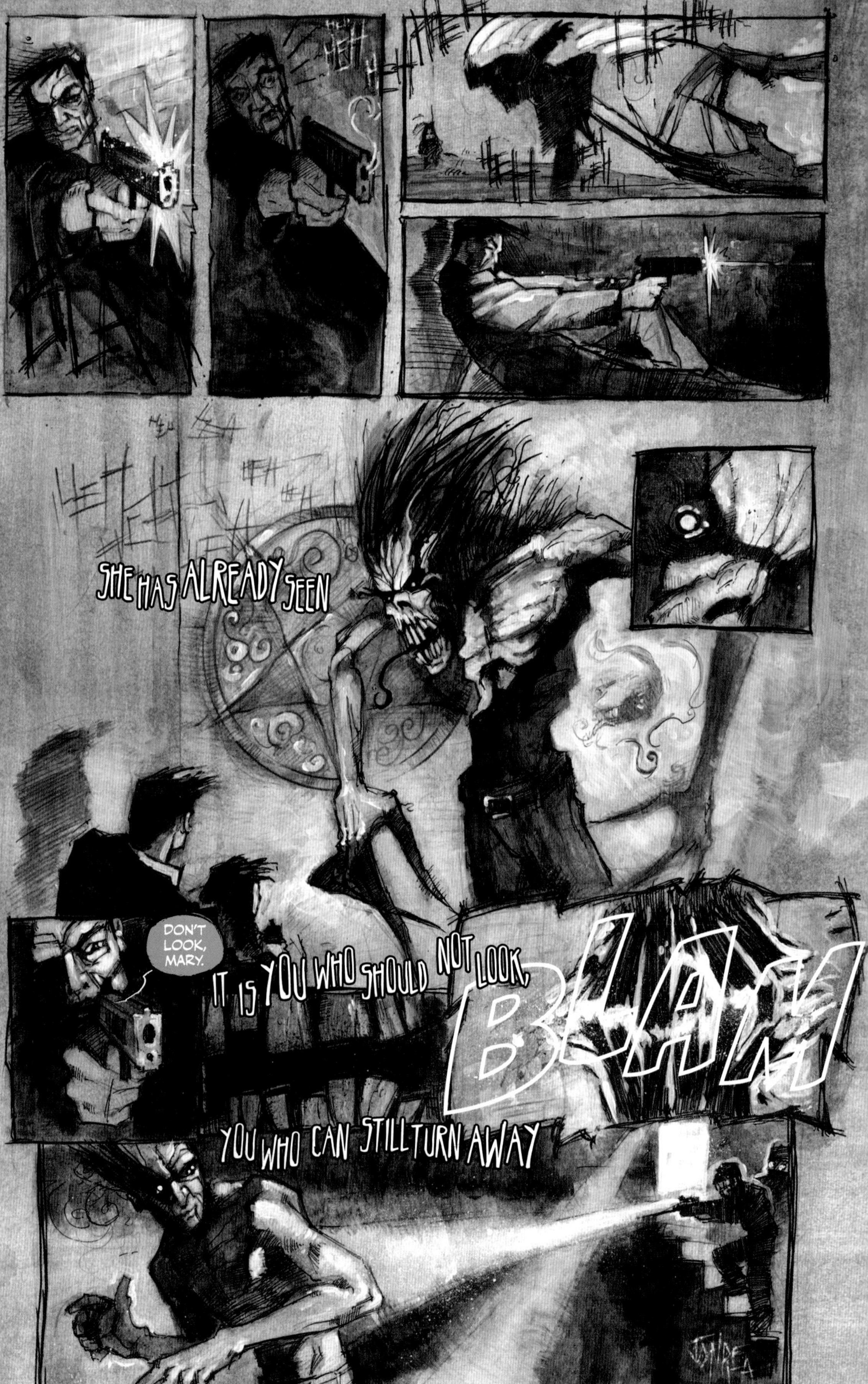
SHE HAS ALREADY SEEN
DON'T LOOK, MARY.
IT IS YOU WHO SHOULD NOT LOOK,
BLAM
YOU WHO CAN STILL TURN AWAY

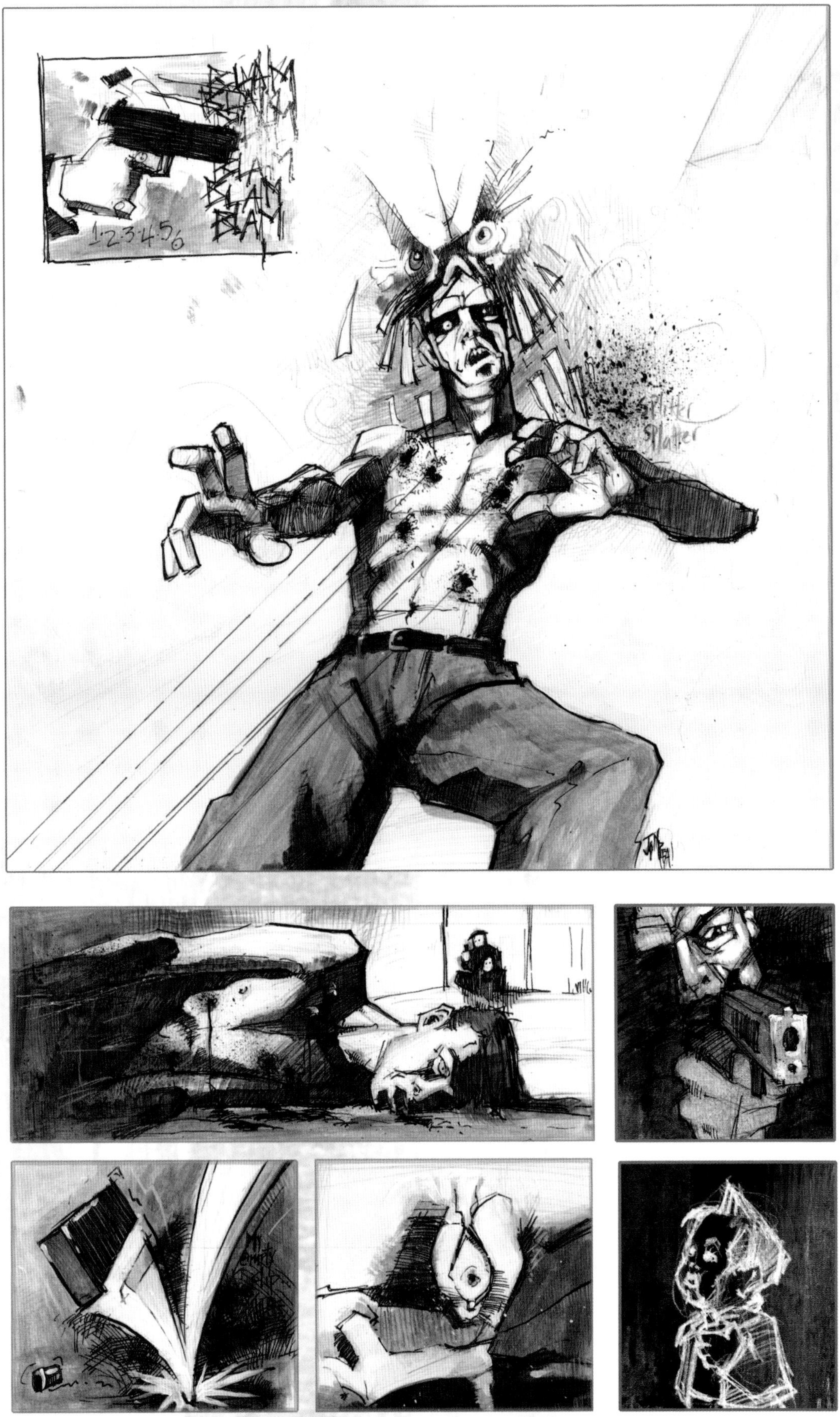
BLAM BLAM BLAM BLAM
1·2·3·4·5 6
splitter splatter

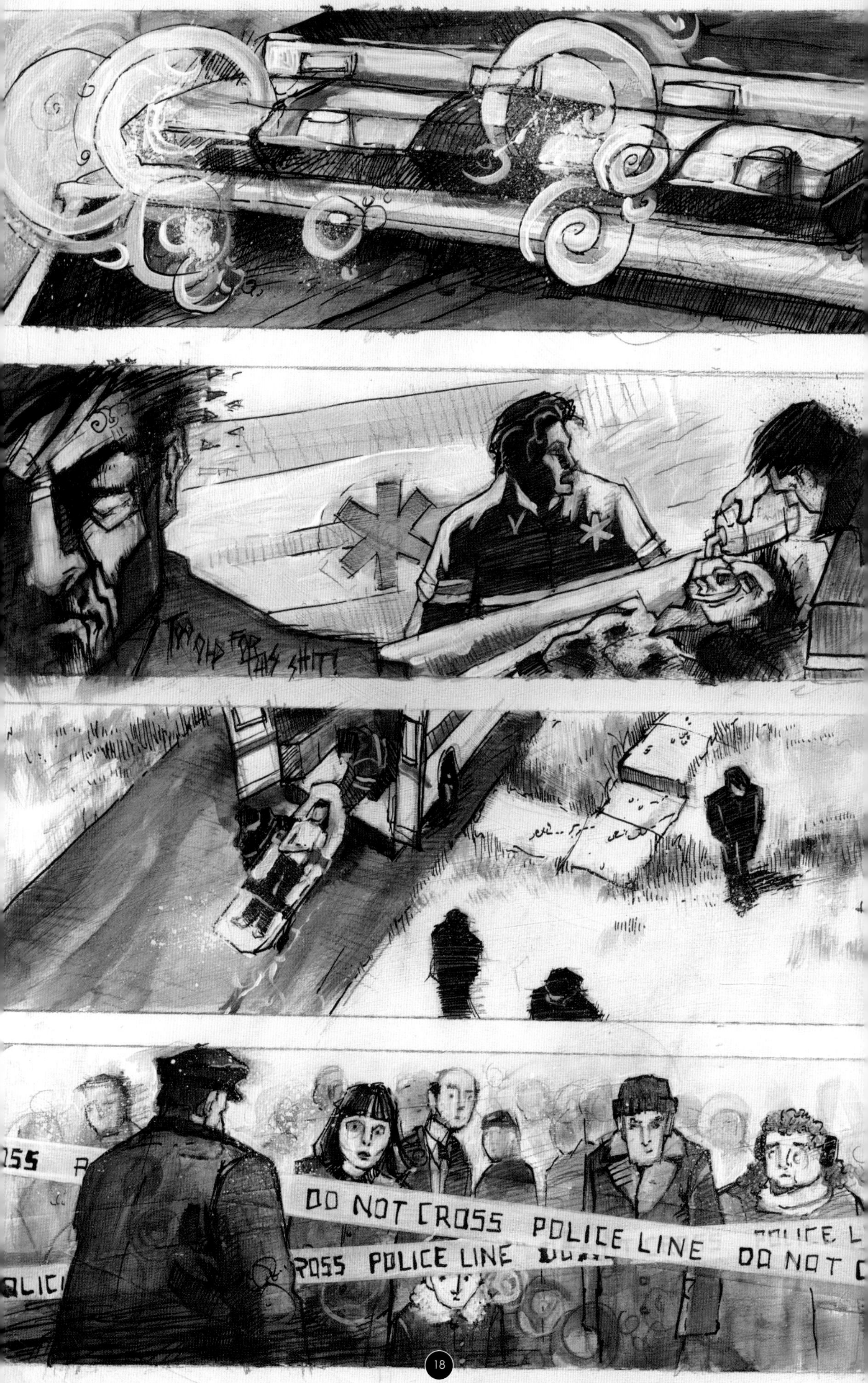
TOO OLD FOR THIS SHIT!
DO NOT CROSS
POLICE LINE
CROSS POLICE LINE
DO NOT

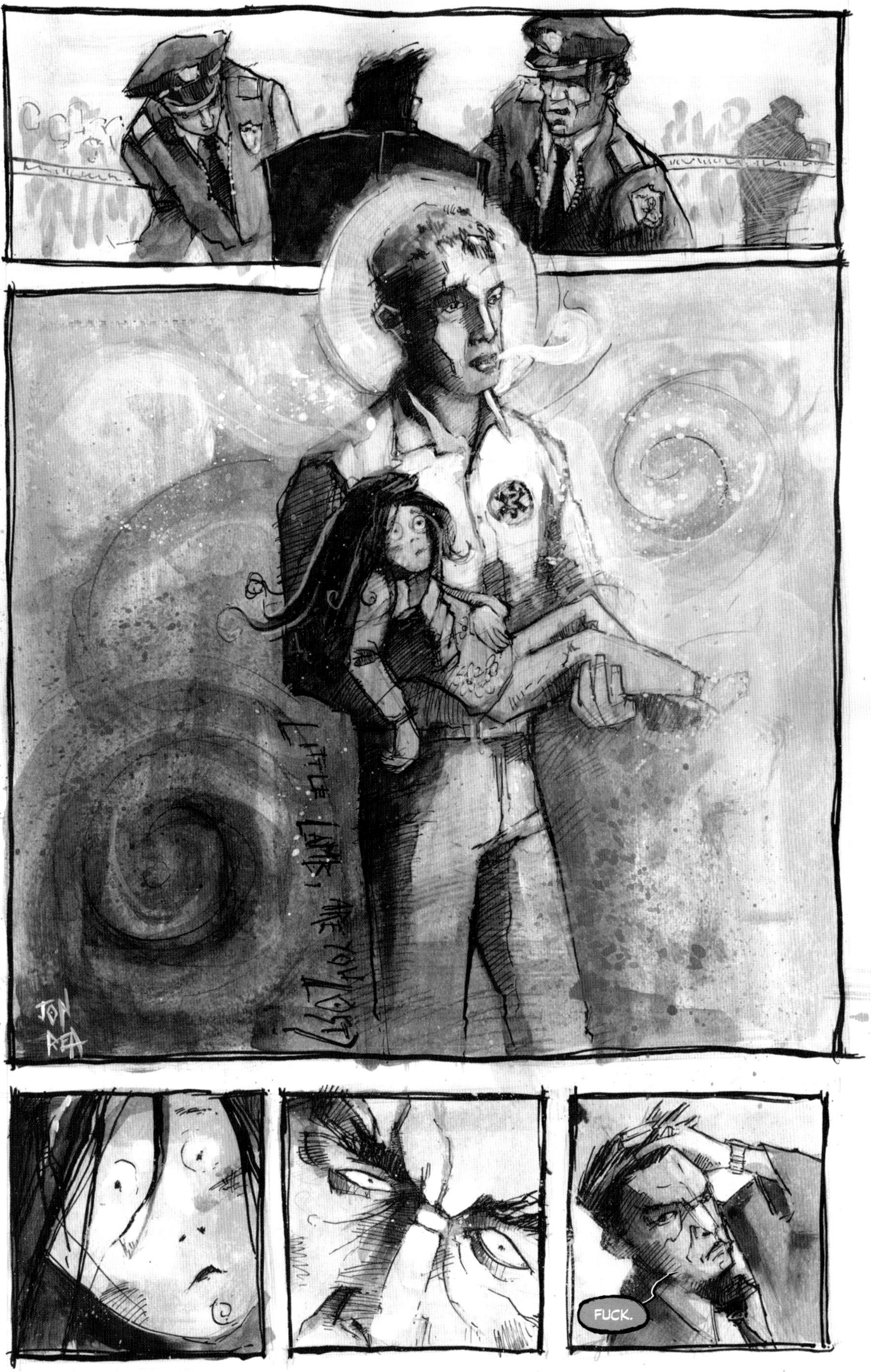
LITTLE LAMB, ARE YOU LOST?
JON REA
FUCK.

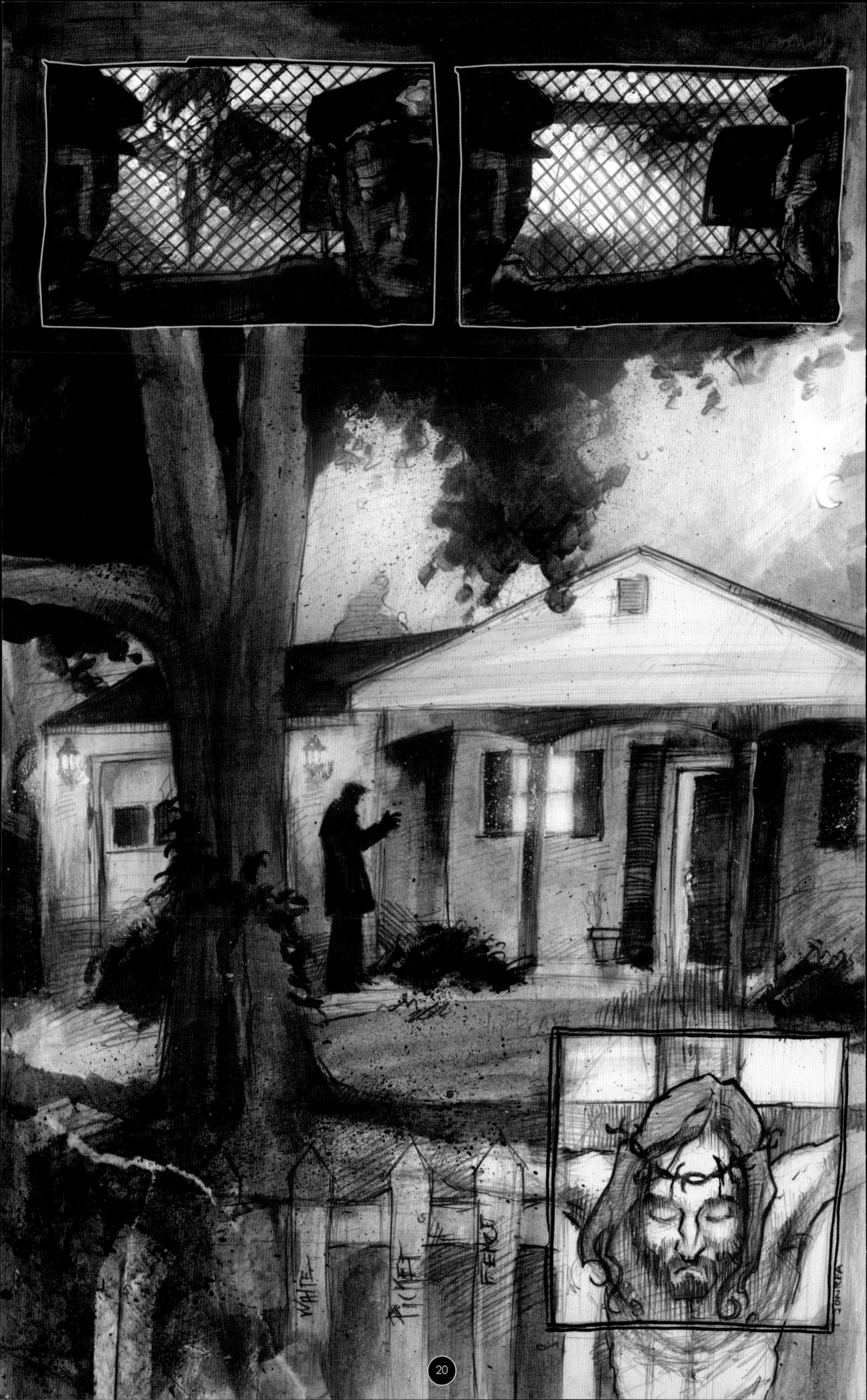
WHITE
PICKET
FENCE
JONREA

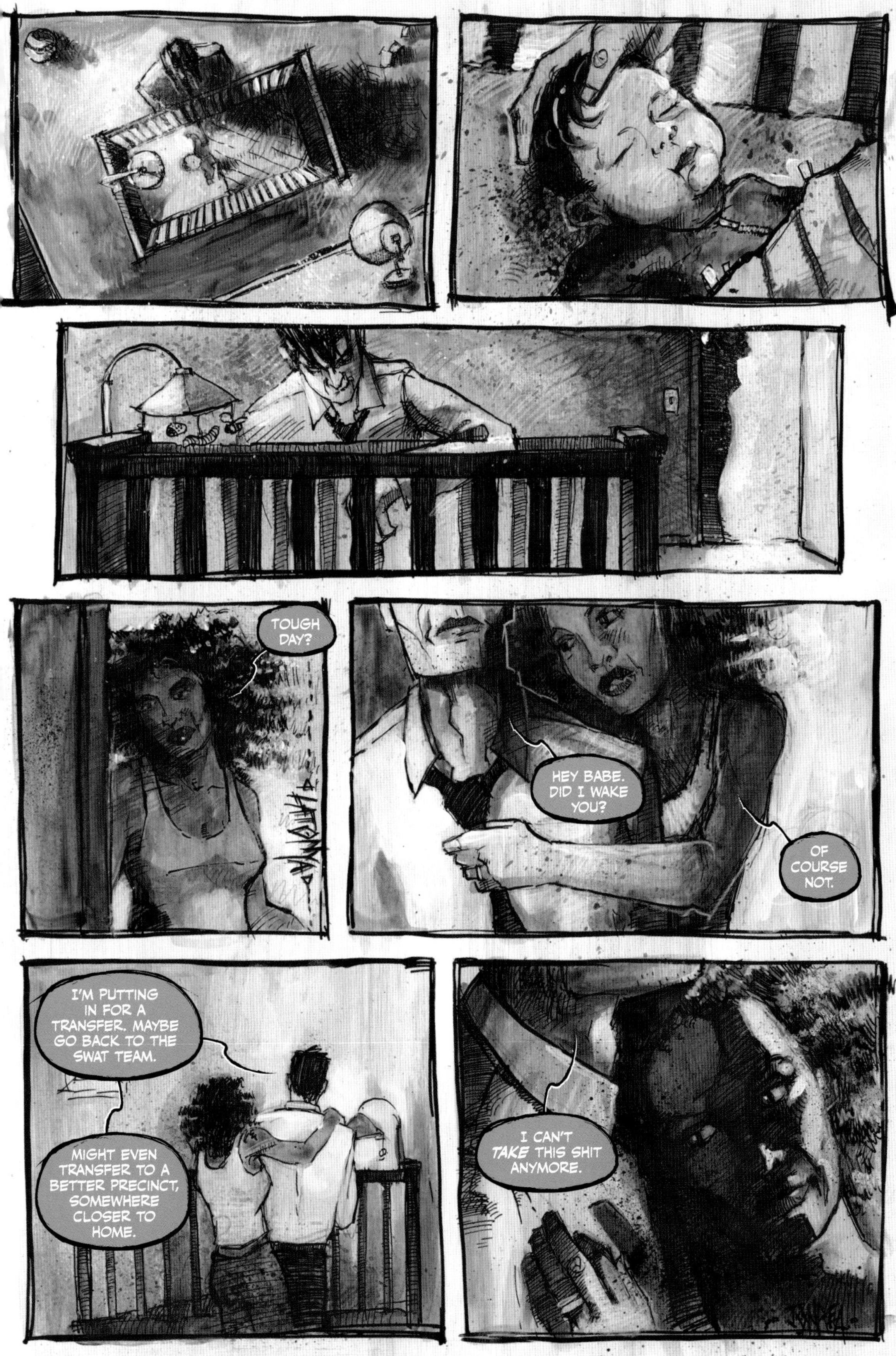
TOUGH DAY?
HEY BABE. DID I WAKE YOU?
OF COURSE NOT.
I'M PUTTING IN FOR A TRANSFER. MAYBE GO BACK TO THE SWAT TEAM.
MIGHT EVEN TRANSFER TO A BETTER PRECINCT, SOMEWHERE CLOSER TO HOME.
I CAN'T *TAKE* THIS SHIT ANYMORE.

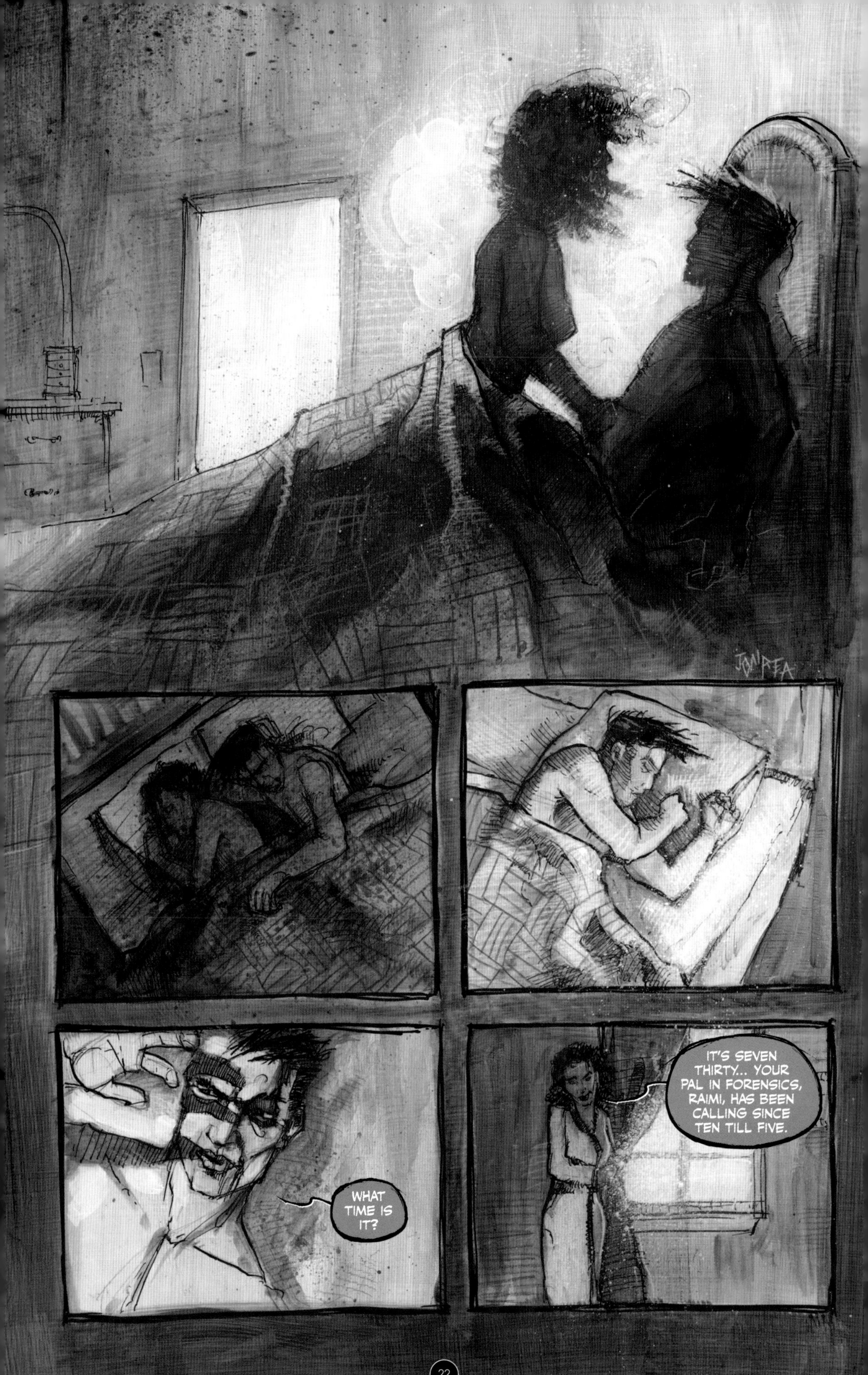
WHAT TIME IS IT?
IT'S SEVEN THIRTY... YOUR PAL IN FORENSICS, RAIMI, HAS BEEN CALLING SINCE TEN TILL FIVE.

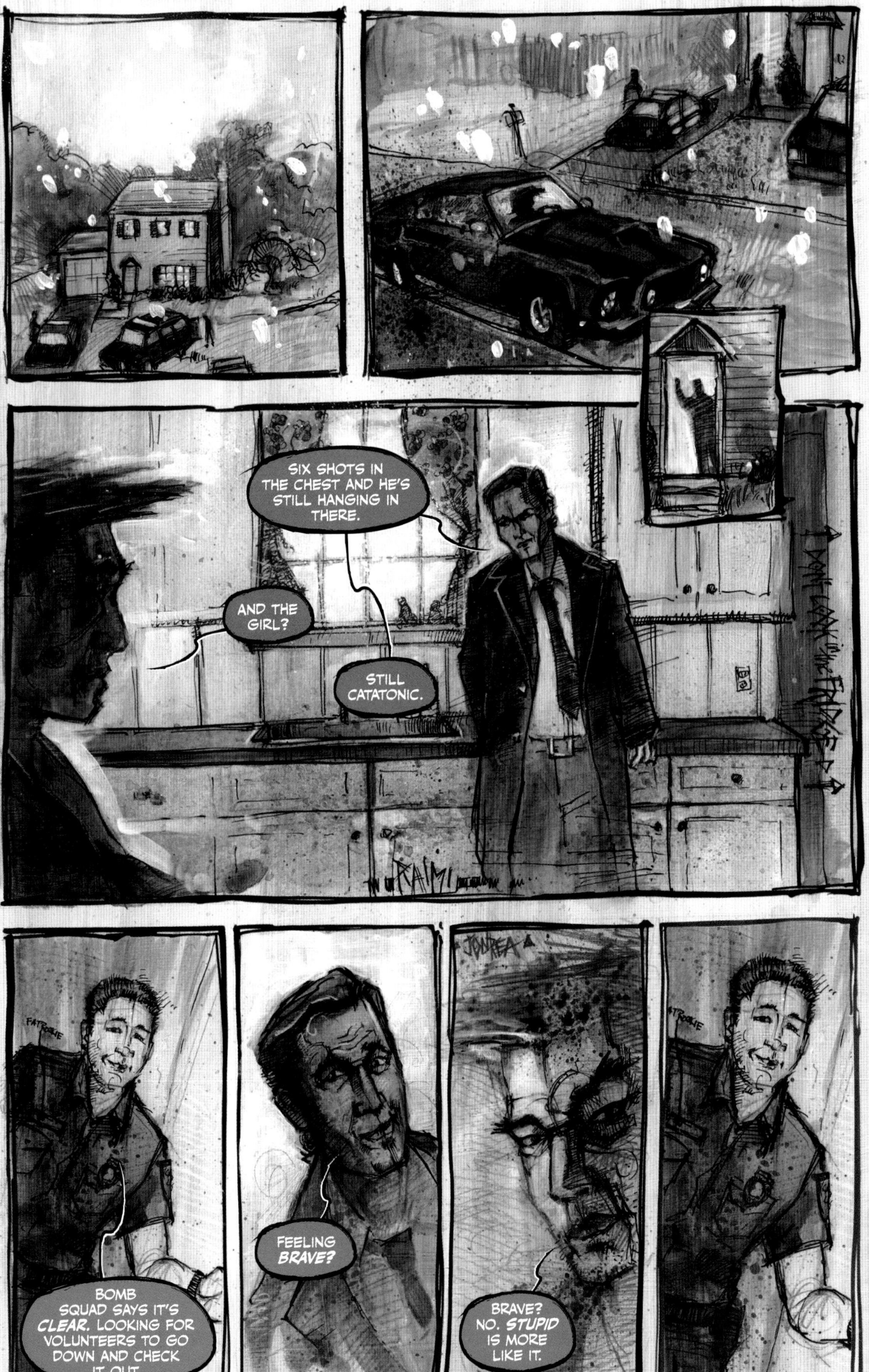
SIX SHOTS IN THE CHEST AND HE'S STILL HANGING IN THERE.
AND THE GIRL?
STILL CATATONIC.
DON'T LOOK IN THE FRIDGE
RAIMI
FAT ROOKIE
BOMB SQUAD SAYS IT'S CLEAR. LOOKING FOR VOLUNTEERS TO GO DOWN AND CHECK IT OUT.
FEELING BRAVE?
JON REA
BRAVE? NO. STUPID IS MORE LIKE IT.
FAT ROOKIE

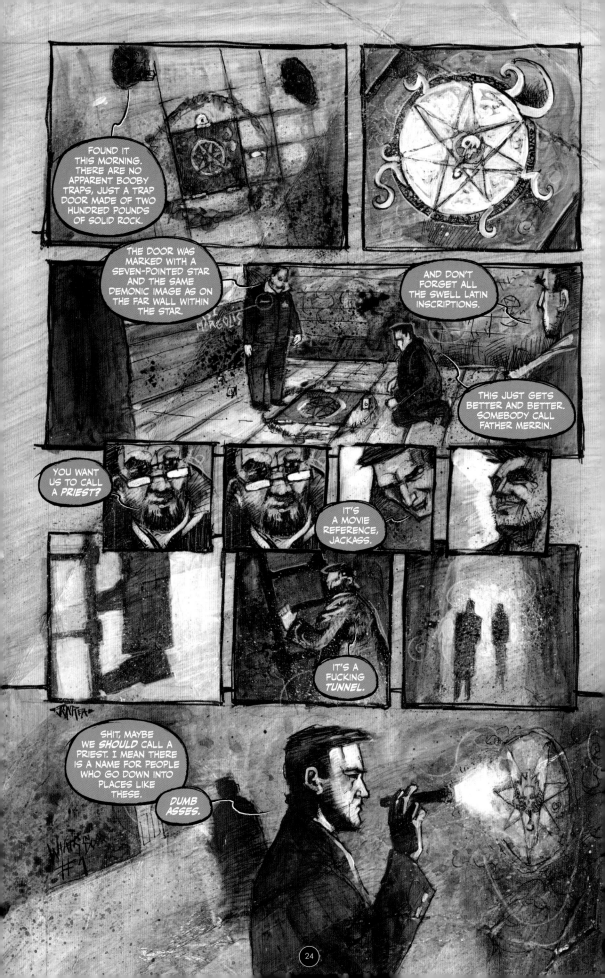

FOUND IT THIS MORNING. THERE ARE NO APPARENT BOOBY TRAPS, JUST A TRAP DOOR MADE OF TWO HUNDRED POUNDS OF SOLID ROCK.

THE DOOR WAS MARKED WITH A SEVEN-POINTED STAR AND THE SAME DEMONIC IMAGE AS ON THE FAR WALL WITHIN THE STAR.

AND DON'T FORGET ALL THE SWELL LATIN INSCRIPTIONS.

THIS JUST GETS BETTER AND BETTER. SOMEBODY CALL FATHER MERRIN.

YOU WANT US TO CALL A *PRIEST?*

IT'S A MOVIE REFERENCE, JACKASS.

IT'S A FUCKING *TUNNEL.*

SHIT, MAYBE WE *SHOULD* CALL A PRIEST. I MEAN THERE IS A NAME FOR PEOPLE WHO GO DOWN INTO PLACES LIKE THESE.

DUMB ASSES.

24

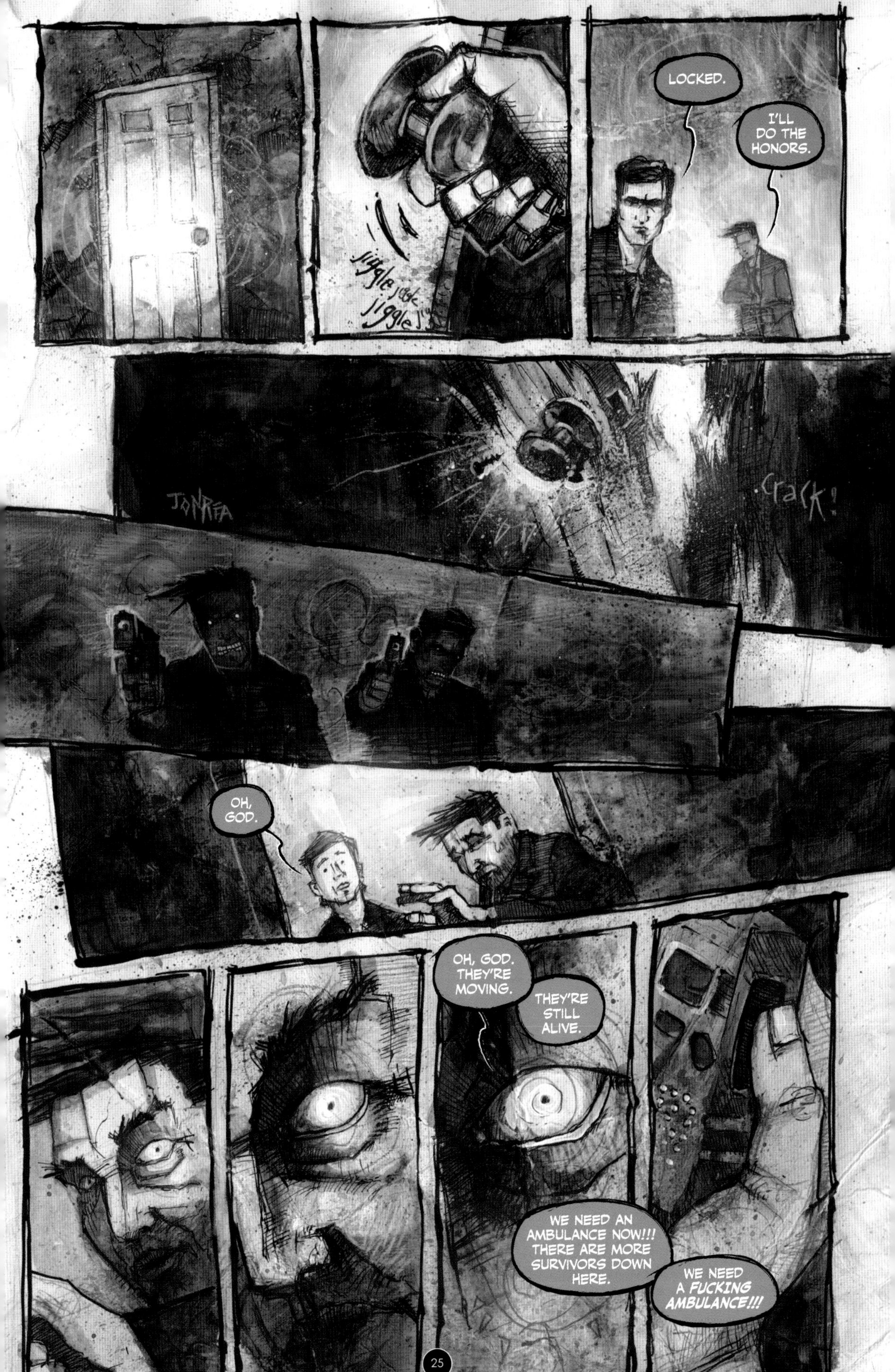
jiggle jiggle jiggle
LOCKED.
I'LL DO THE HONORS.
JONREA
crack!
OH, GOD.
OH, GOD. THEY'RE MOVING.
THEY'RE STILL ALIVE.
WE NEED AN AMBULANCE NOW!!! THERE ARE MORE SURVIVORS DOWN HERE.
WE NEED A *FUCKING AMBULANCE!!!*

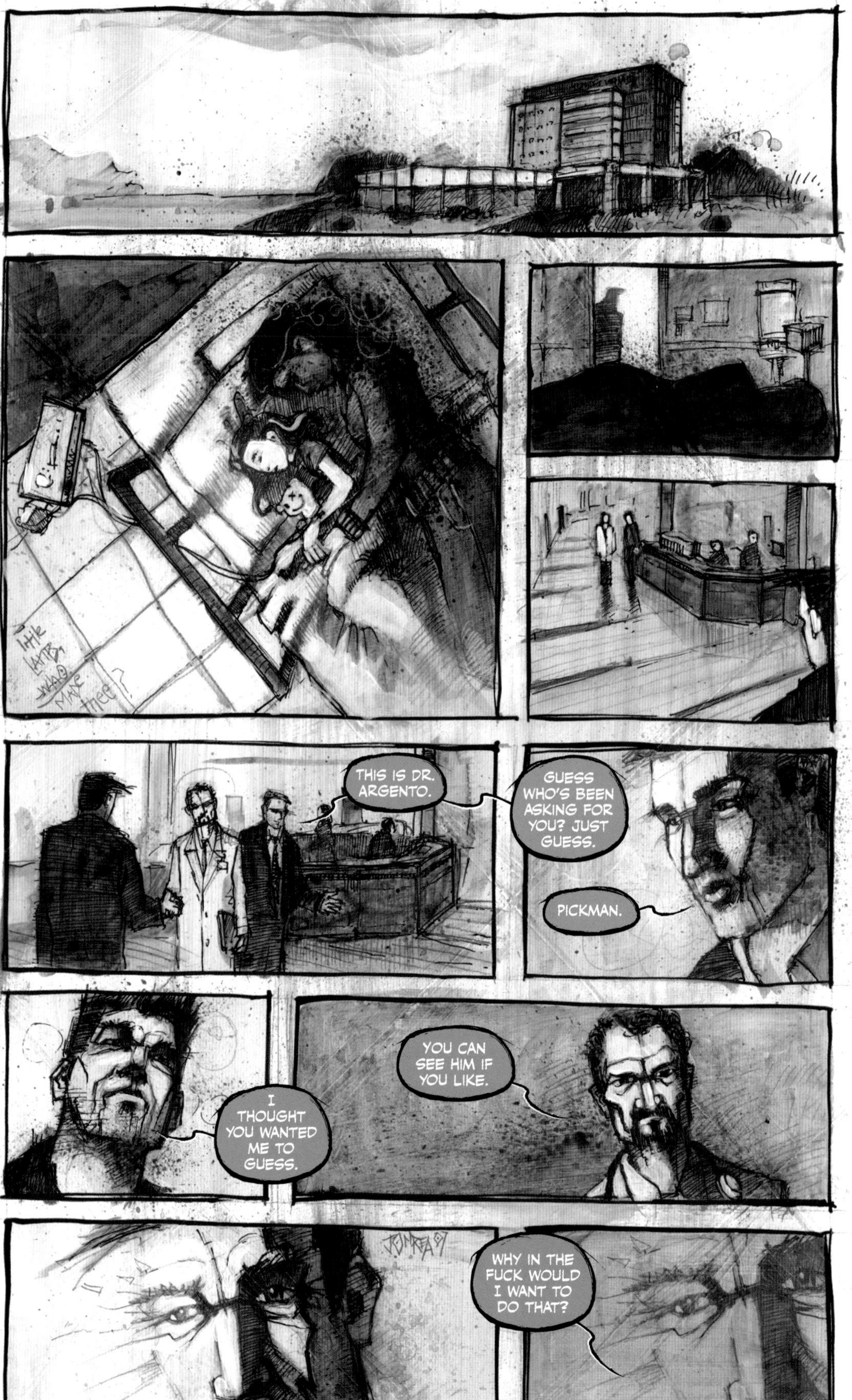

little LAMB, WHO MADE thee?
THIS IS DR. ARGENTO.
GUESS WHO'S BEEN ASKING FOR YOU? JUST GUESS.
PICKMAN.
I THOUGHT YOU WANTED ME TO GUESS.
YOU CAN SEE HIM IF YOU LIKE.
WHY IN THE FUCK WOULD I WANT TO DO THAT?

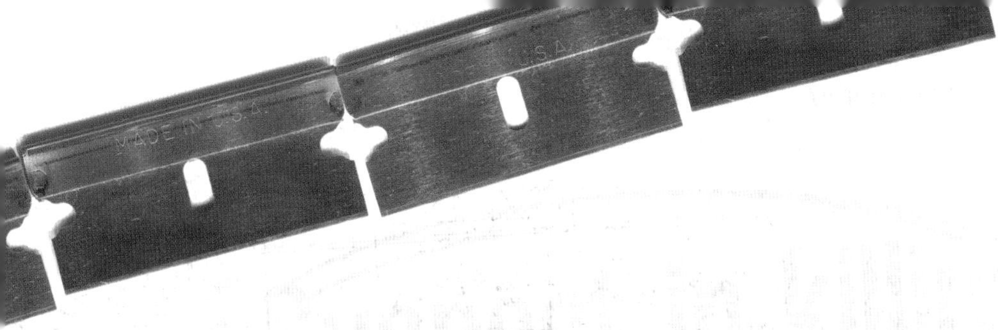
MADE IN U.S.A.

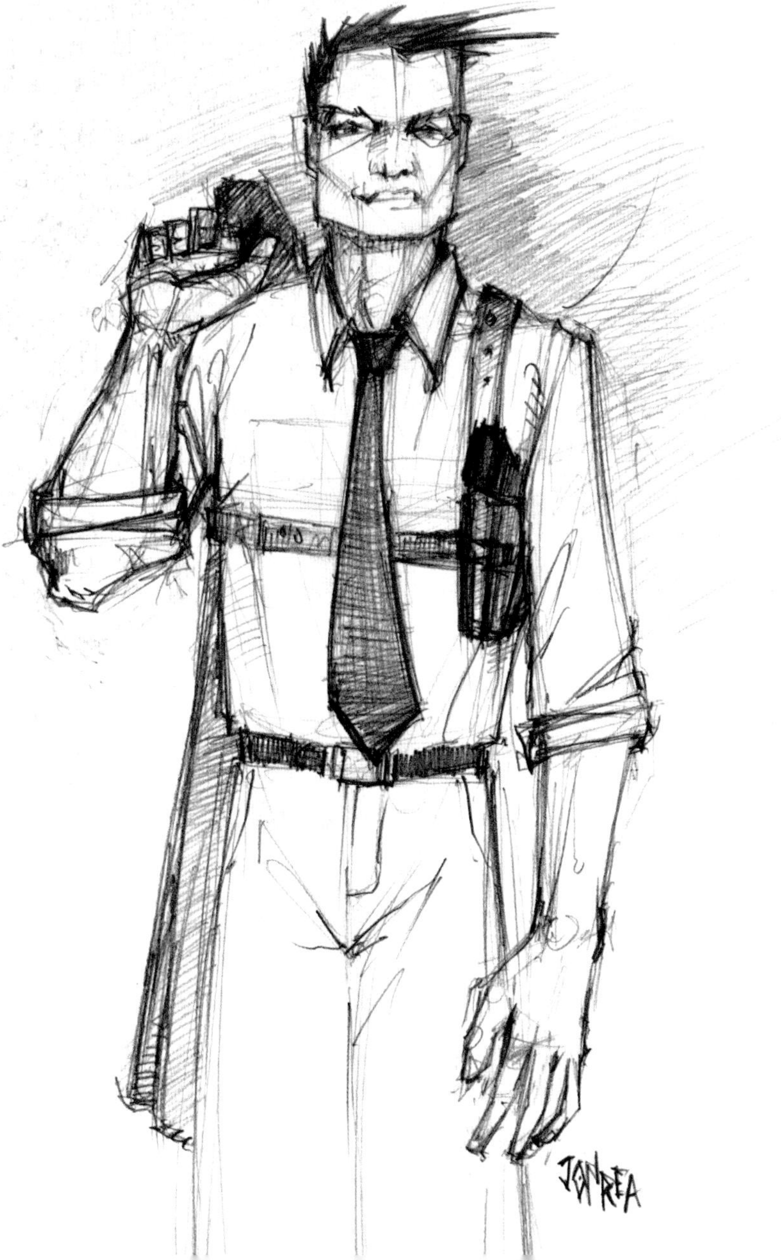

chapter two
WITH ENVY + ANGER

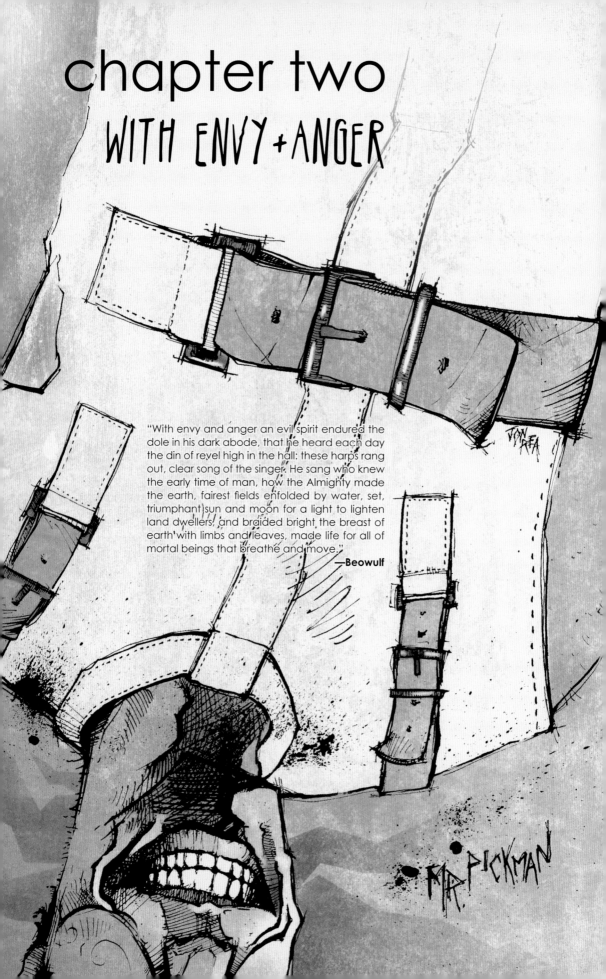

"With envy and anger an evil spirit endured the dole in his dark abode, that he heard each day the din of revel high in the hall: these harps rang out, clear song of the singer. He sang who knew the early time of man, how the Almighty made the earth, fairest fields enfolded by water, set, triumphant sun and moon for a light to lighten land dwellers, and braided bright the breast of earth with limbs and leaves, made life for all of mortal beings that breathe and move."
—Beowulf

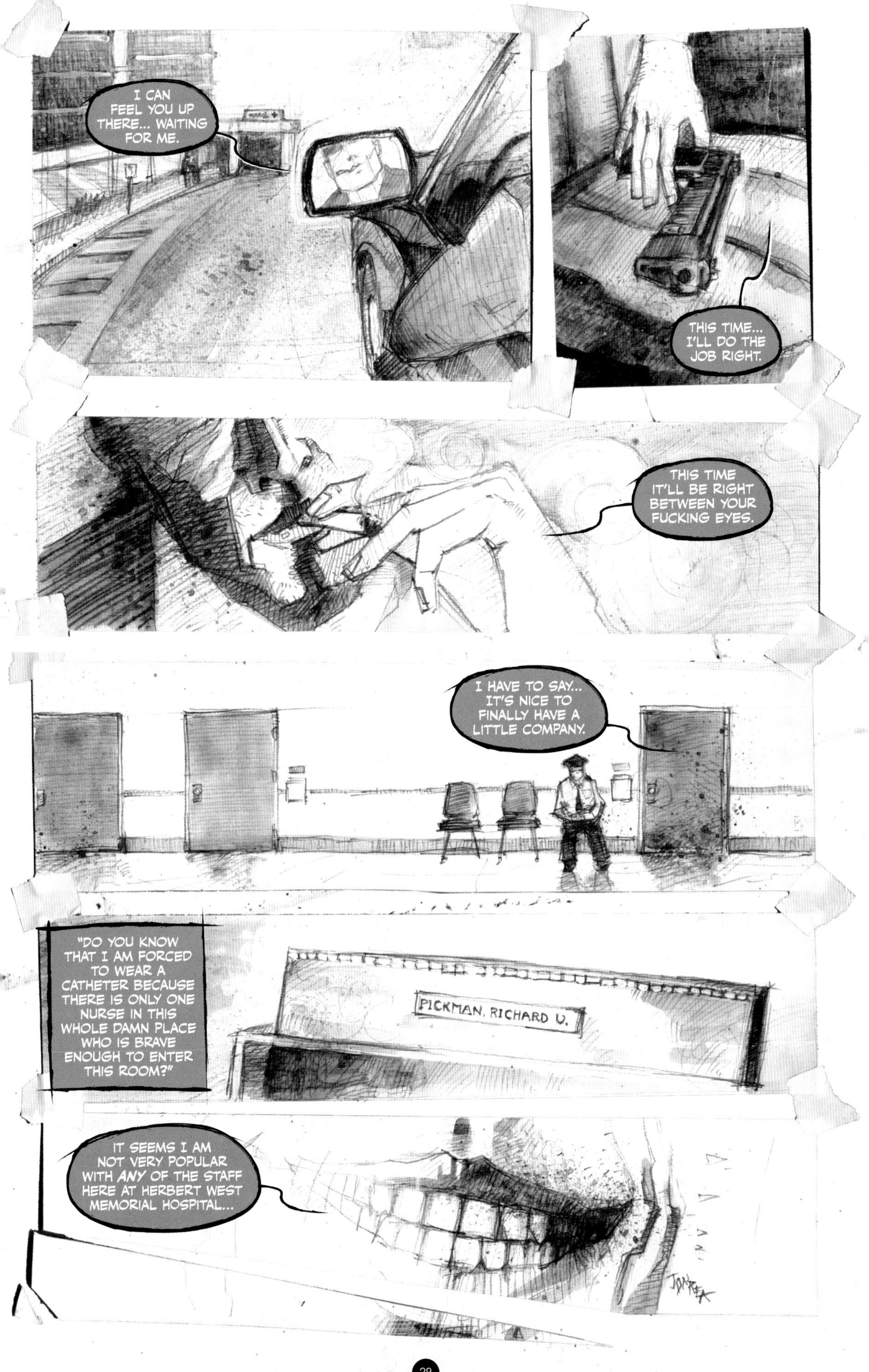
I CAN FEEL YOU UP THERE... WAITING FOR ME.
THIS TIME... I'LL DO THE JOB RIGHT.
THIS TIME IT'LL BE RIGHT BETWEEN YOUR FUCKING EYES.
I HAVE TO SAY... IT'S NICE TO FINALLY HAVE A LITTLE COMPANY.
"DO YOU KNOW THAT I AM FORCED TO WEAR A CATHETER BECAUSE THERE IS ONLY ONE NURSE IN THIS WHOLE DAMN PLACE WHO IS BRAVE ENOUGH TO ENTER THIS ROOM?"
PICKMAN, RICHARD U.
IT SEEMS I AM NOT VERY POPULAR WITH *ANY* OF THE STAFF HERE AT HERBERT WEST MEMORIAL HOSPITAL...
JONREX

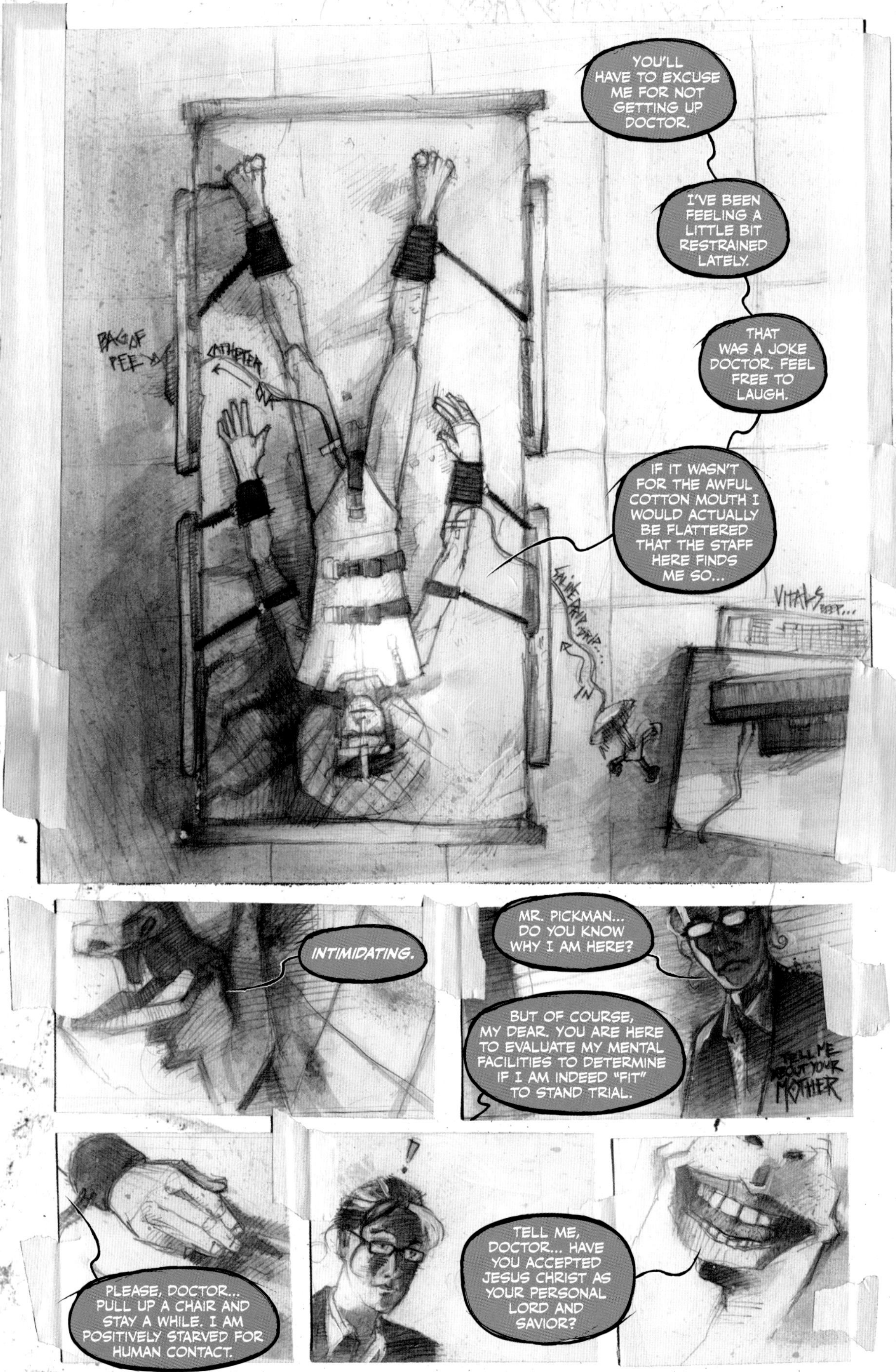
YOU'LL HAVE TO EXCUSE ME FOR NOT GETTING UP DOCTOR.
I'VE BEEN FEELING A LITTLE BIT RESTRAINED LATELY.
THAT WAS A JOKE DOCTOR. FEEL FREE TO LAUGH.
IF IT WASN'T FOR THE AWFUL COTTON MOUTH I WOULD ACTUALLY BE FLATTERED THAT THE STAFF HERE FINDS ME SO...
BAG OF PEE
CATHETER
VITALS BEEP...
INTIMIDATING.
MR. PICKMAN... DO YOU KNOW WHY I AM HERE?
BUT OF COURSE, MY DEAR. YOU ARE HERE TO EVALUATE MY MENTAL FACILITIES TO DETERMINE IF I AM INDEED "FIT" TO STAND TRIAL.
TELL ME ABOUT YOUR MOTHER
PLEASE, DOCTOR... PULL UP A CHAIR AND STAY A WHILE. I AM POSITIVELY STARVED FOR HUMAN CONTACT.
!
TELL ME, DOCTOR... HAVE YOU ACCEPTED JESUS CHRIST AS YOUR PERSONAL LORD AND SAVIOR?

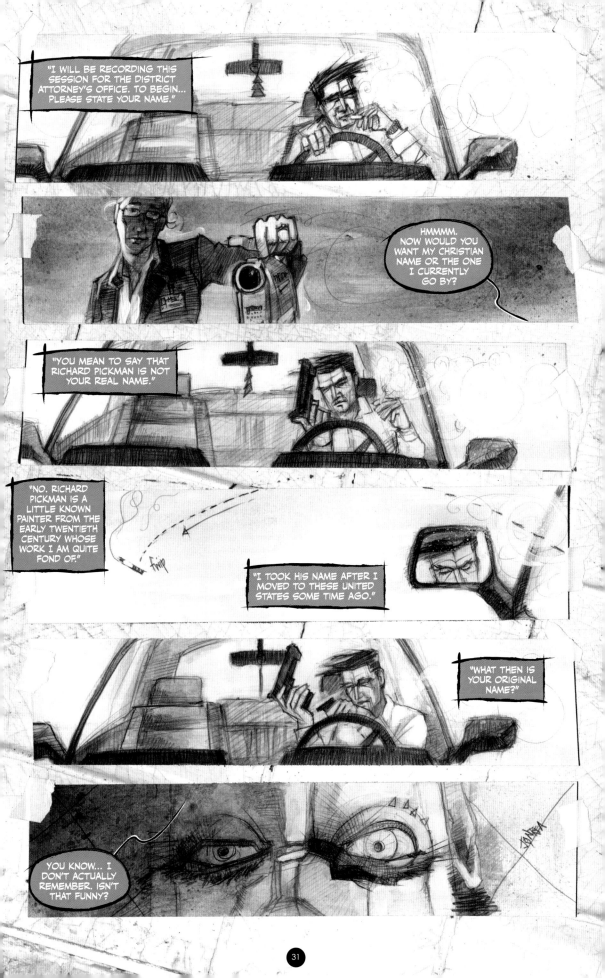

"I WILL BE RECORDING THIS SESSION FOR THE DISTRICT ATTORNEY'S OFFICE. TO BEGIN... PLEASE STATE YOUR NAME."

HMMMM. NOW WOULD YOU WANT MY CHRISTIAN NAME OR THE ONE I CURRENTLY GO BY?

"YOU MEAN TO SAY THAT RICHARD PICKMAN IS NOT YOUR REAL NAME."

"NO. RICHARD PICKMAN IS A LITTLE KNOWN PAINTER FROM THE EARLY TWENTIETH CENTURY WHOSE WORK I AM QUITE FOND OF."

"I TOOK HIS NAME AFTER I MOVED TO THESE UNITED STATES SOME TIME AGO."

"WHAT THEN IS YOUR ORIGINAL NAME?"

YOU KNOW... I DON'T ACTUALLY REMEMBER. ISN'T THAT FUNNY?

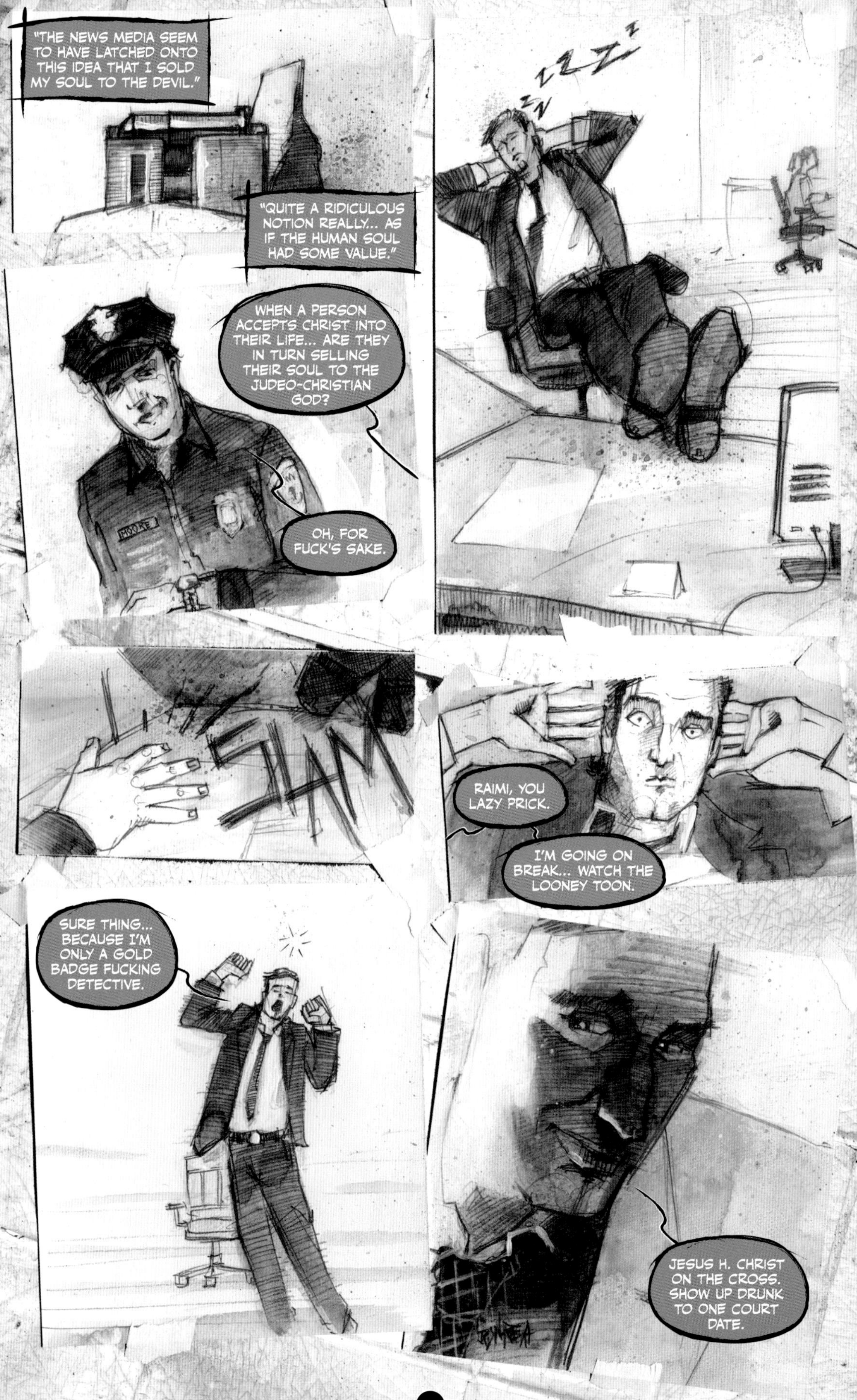
"THE NEWS MEDIA SEEM TO HAVE LATCHED ONTO THIS IDEA THAT I SOLD MY SOUL TO THE DEVIL."
"QUITE A RIDICULOUS NOTION REALLY... AS IF THE HUMAN SOUL HAD SOME VALUE."
ZZZZZ
WHEN A PERSON ACCEPTS CHRIST INTO THEIR LIFE... ARE THEY IN TURN SELLING THEIR SOUL TO THE JUDEO-CHRISTIAN GOD?
OH, FOR FUCK'S SAKE.
SLAM
RAIMI, YOU LAZY PRICK.
I'M GOING ON BREAK... WATCH THE LOONEY TOON.
SURE THING... BECAUSE I'M ONLY A GOLD BADGE FUCKING DETECTIVE.
JESUS H. CHRIST ON THE CROSS. SHOW UP DRUNK TO ONE COURT DATE.

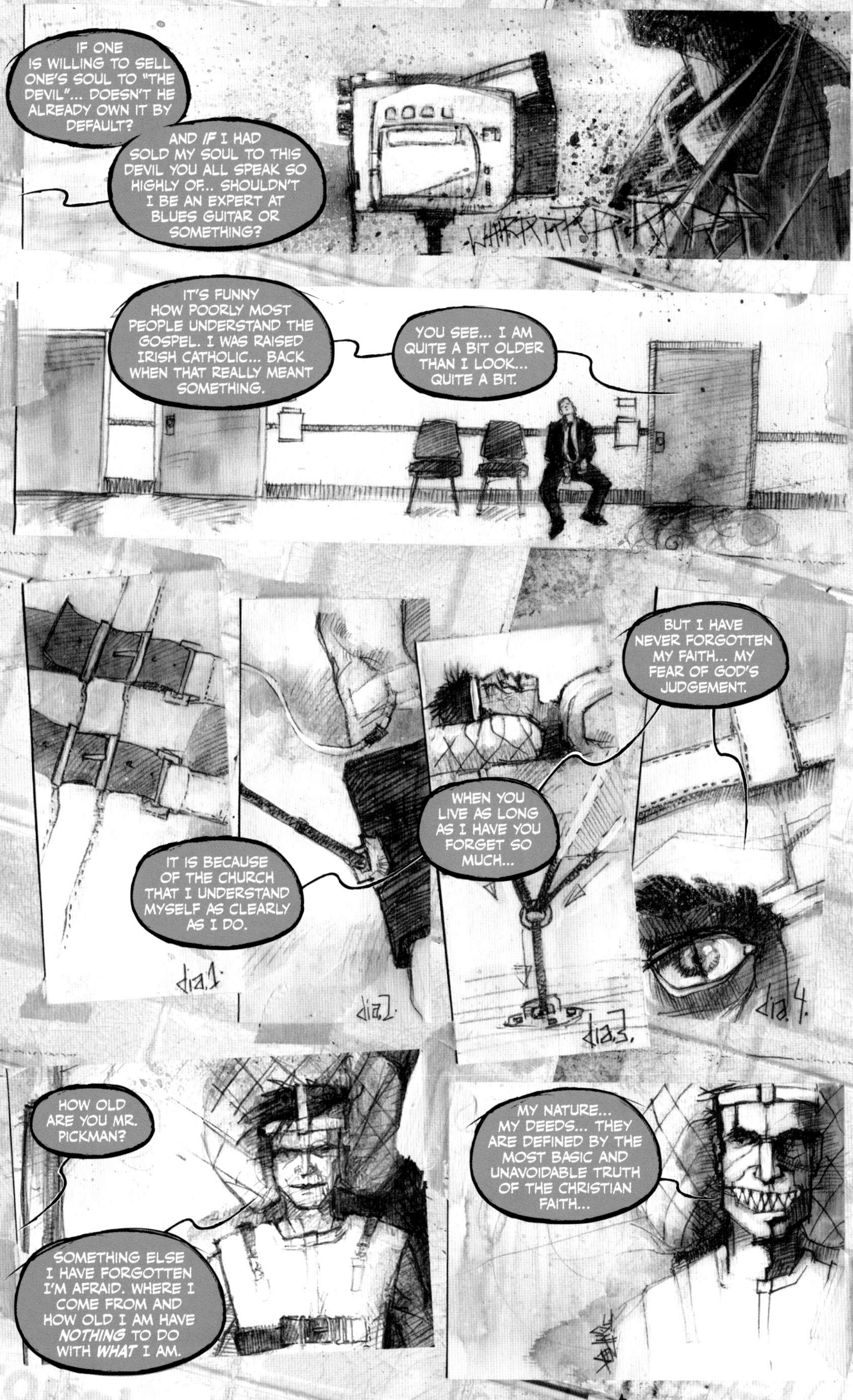
IF ONE IS WILLING TO SELL ONE'S SOUL TO "THE DEVIL"... DOESN'T HE ALREADY OWN IT BY DEFAULT?
AND *IF* I HAD SOLD MY SOUL TO THIS DEVIL YOU ALL SPEAK SO HIGHLY OF.. SHOULDN'T I BE AN EXPERT AT BLUES GUITAR OR SOMETHING?
WHIRRRR
IT'S FUNNY HOW POORLY MOST PEOPLE UNDERSTAND THE GOSPEL. I WAS RAISED IRISH CATHOLIC... BACK WHEN THAT REALLY MEANT SOMETHING.
YOU SEE... I AM QUITE A BIT OLDER THAN I LOOK... QUITE A BIT.
IT IS BECAUSE OF THE CHURCH THAT I UNDERSTAND MYSELF AS CLEARLY AS I DO.
WHEN YOU LIVE AS LONG AS I HAVE YOU FORGET SO MUCH...
BUT I HAVE NEVER FORGOTTEN MY FAITH... MY FEAR OF GOD'S JUDGEMENT.
dia.1
dia.2
dia.3
dia.4
HOW OLD ARE YOU MR. PICKMAN?
SOMETHING ELSE I HAVE FORGOTTEN I'M AFRAID. WHERE I COME FROM AND HOW OLD I AM HAVE *NOTHING* TO DO WITH *WHAT* I AM.
MY NATURE... MY DEEDS... THEY ARE DEFINED BY THE MOST BASIC AND UNAVOIDABLE TRUTH OF THE CHRISTIAN FAITH...

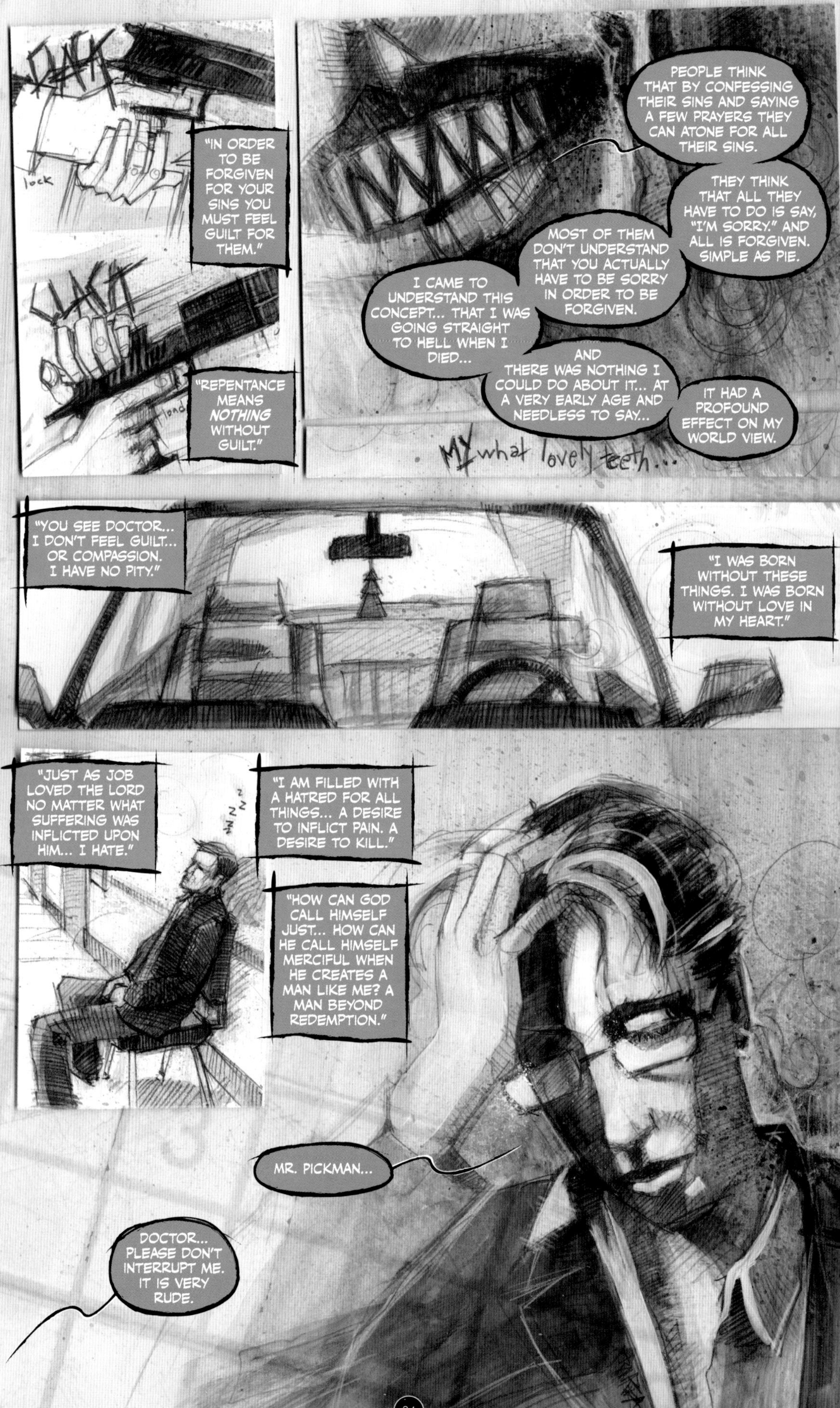

lock
"IN ORDER TO BE FORGIVEN FOR YOUR SINS YOU MUST FEEL GUILT FOR THEM."
"REPENTANCE MEANS *NOTHING* WITHOUT GUILT."
PEOPLE THINK THAT BY CONFESSING THEIR SINS AND SAYING A FEW PRAYERS THEY CAN ATONE FOR ALL THEIR SINS.
THEY THINK THAT ALL THEY HAVE TO DO IS SAY, "I'M SORRY." AND ALL IS FORGIVEN. SIMPLE AS PIE.
MOST OF THEM DON'T UNDERSTAND THAT YOU ACTUALLY HAVE TO BE SORRY IN ORDER TO BE FORGIVEN.
I CAME TO UNDERSTAND THIS CONCEPT... THAT I WAS GOING STRAIGHT TO HELL WHEN I DIED...
AND THERE WAS NOTHING I COULD DO ABOUT IT... AT A VERY EARLY AGE AND NEEDLESS TO SAY...
IT HAD A PROFOUND EFFECT ON MY WORLD VIEW.
MY what lovely teeth...
"YOU SEE DOCTOR... I DON'T FEEL GUILT... OR COMPASSION. I HAVE NO PITY."
"I WAS BORN WITHOUT THESE THINGS. I WAS BORN WITHOUT LOVE IN MY HEART."
"JUST AS JOB LOVED THE LORD NO MATTER WHAT SUFFERING WAS INFLICTED UPON HIM... I HATE."
Z Z Z
"I AM FILLED WITH A HATRED FOR ALL THINGS... A DESIRE TO INFLICT PAIN. A DESIRE TO KILL."
"HOW CAN GOD CALL HIMSELF JUST... HOW CAN HE CALL HIMSELF MERCIFUL WHEN HE CREATES A MAN LIKE ME? A MAN BEYOND REDEMPTION."
MR. PICKMAN...
DOCTOR... PLEASE DON'T INTERRUPT ME. IT IS VERY RUDE.

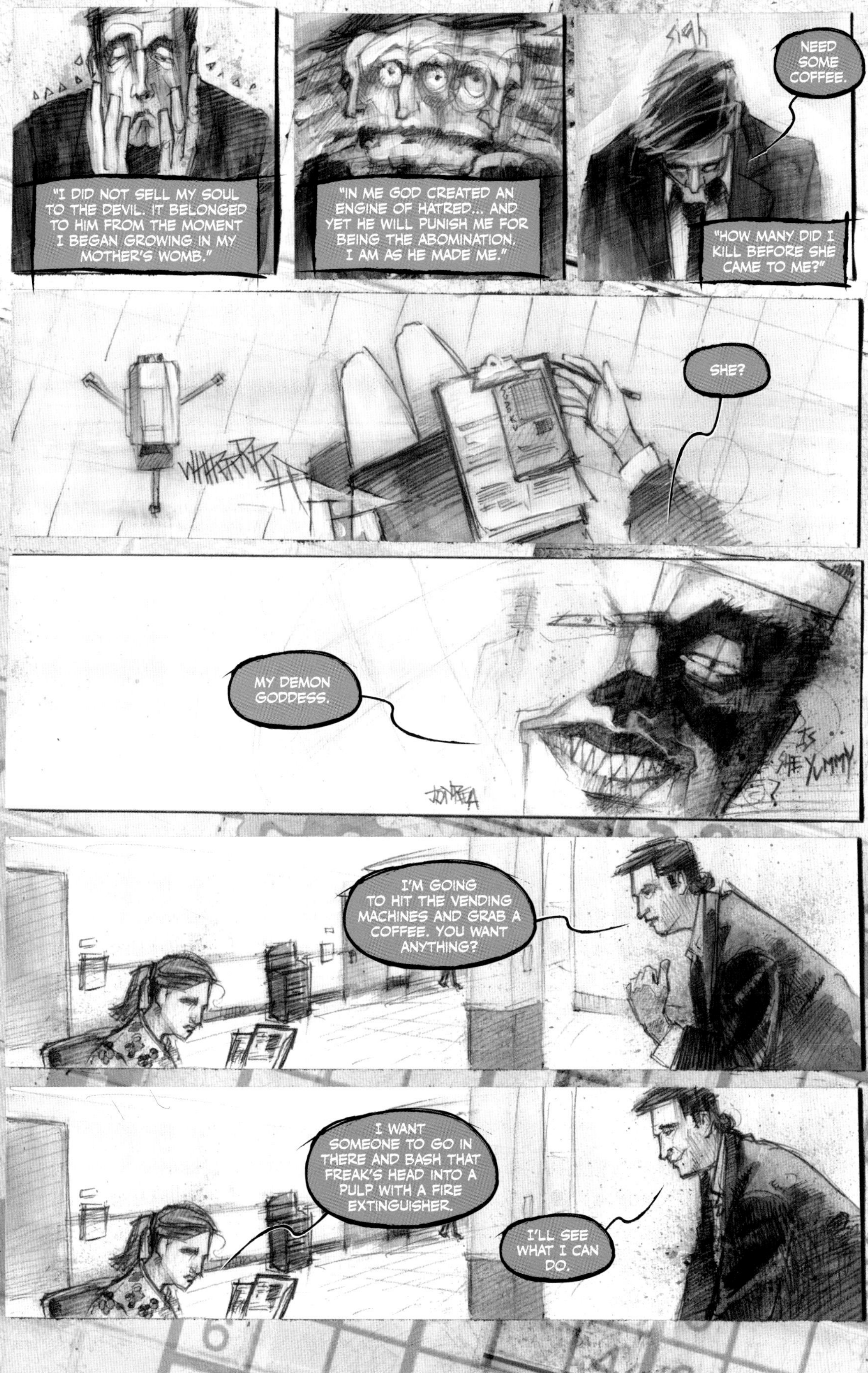
"I DID NOT SELL MY SOUL TO THE DEVIL. IT BELONGED TO HIM FROM THE MOMENT I BEGAN GROWING IN MY MOTHER'S WOMB."
"IN ME GOD CREATED AN ENGINE OF HATRED... AND YET HE WILL PUNISH ME FOR BEING THE ABOMINATION. I AM AS HE MADE ME."
sigh
NEED SOME COFFEE.
"HOW MANY DID I KILL BEFORE SHE CAME TO ME?"
SHE?
MY DEMON GODDESS.
IS SHE YUMMY
I'M GOING TO HIT THE VENDING MACHINES AND GRAB A COFFEE. YOU WANT ANYTHING?
I WANT SOMEONE TO GO IN THERE AND BASH THAT FREAK'S HEAD INTO A PULP WITH A FIRE EXTINGUISHER.
I'LL SEE WHAT I CAN DO.

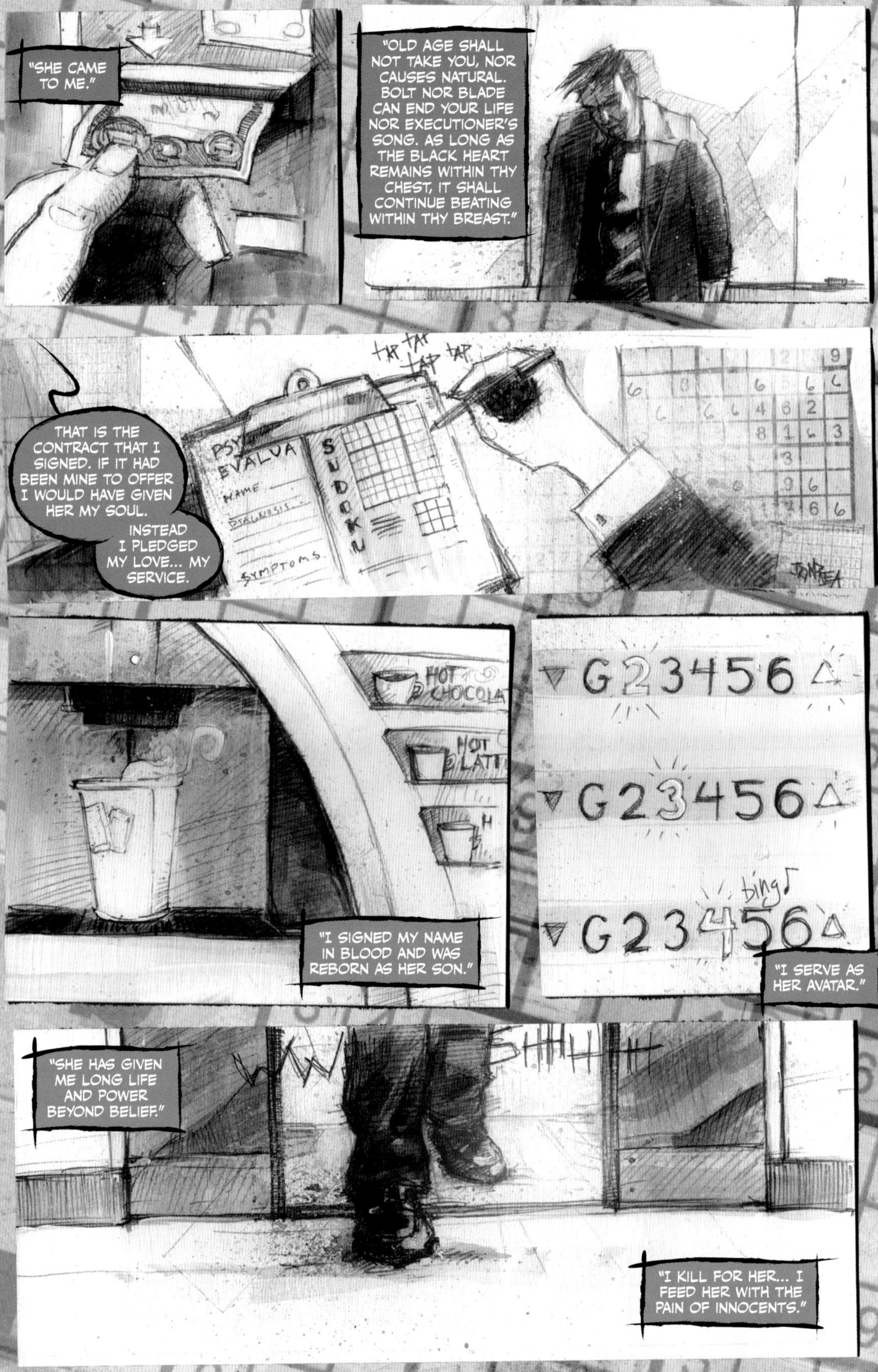
"SHE CAME TO ME."
"OLD AGE SHALL NOT TAKE YOU, NOR CAUSES NATURAL. BOLT NOR BLADE CAN END YOUR LIFE NOR EXECUTIONER'S SONG. AS LONG AS THE BLACK HEART REMAINS WITHIN THY CHEST, IT SHALL CONTINUE BEATING WITHIN THY BREAST."
TAP TAP TAP TAP
THAT IS THE CONTRACT THAT I SIGNED. IF IT HAD BEEN MINE TO OFFER I WOULD HAVE GIVEN HER MY SOUL.
INSTEAD I PLEDGED MY LOVE... MY SERVICE.
PSY EVALUA
NAME
DIAGNOSIS
SYMPTOMS
SUDOKU
HOT CHOCOLAT
HOT LATT
"I SIGNED MY NAME IN BLOOD AND WAS REBORN AS HER SON."
G23456
G23456
bing
G23456
"I SERVE AS HER AVATAR."
"SHE HAS GIVEN ME LONG LIFE AND POWER BEYOND BELIEF."
"I KILL FOR HER... I FEED HER WITH THE PAIN OF INNOCENTS."

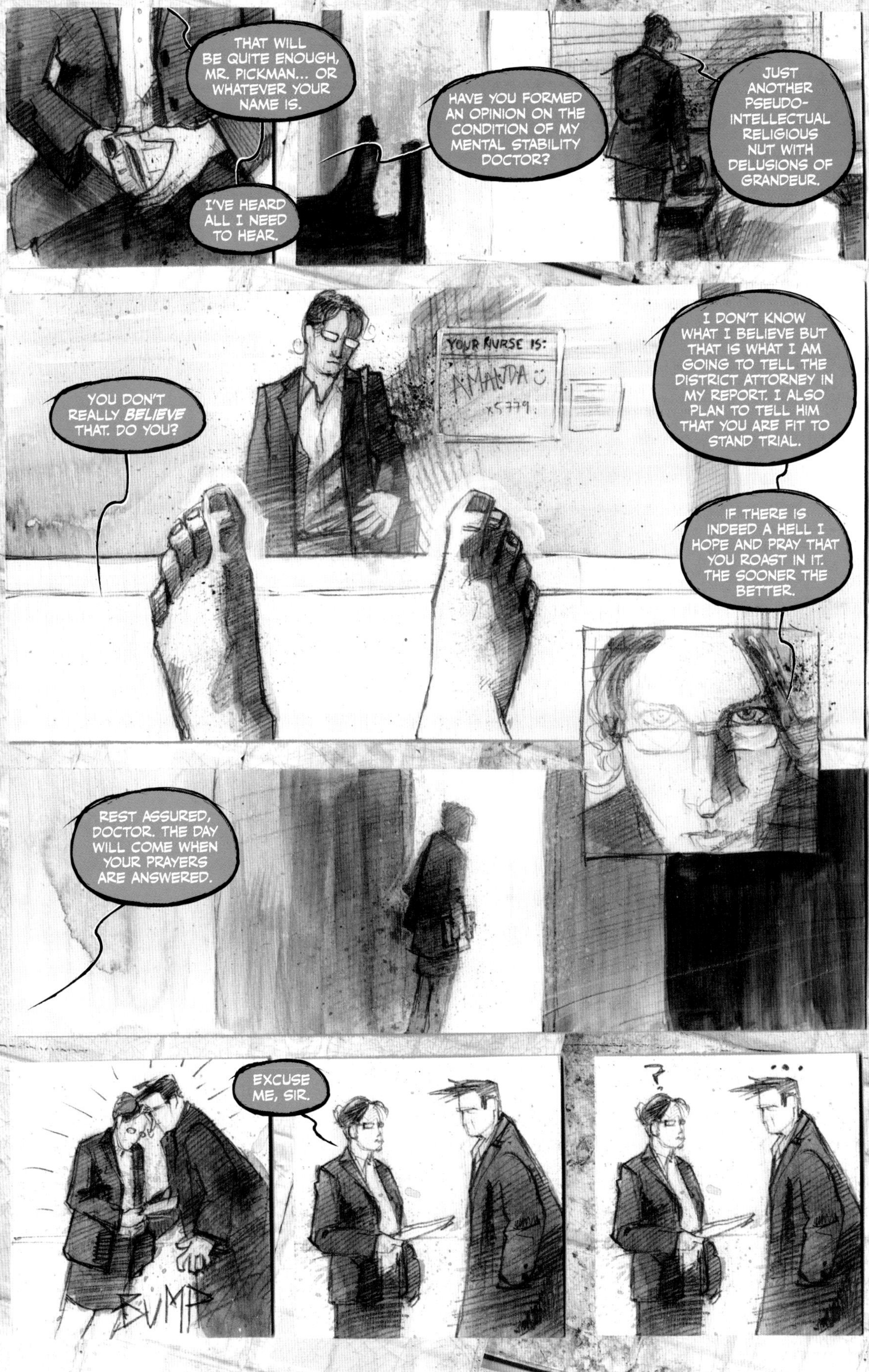
THAT WILL BE QUITE ENOUGH, MR. PICKMAN... OR WHATEVER YOUR NAME IS.
I'VE HEARD ALL I NEED TO HEAR.
HAVE YOU FORMED AN OPINION ON THE CONDITION OF MY MENTAL STABILITY DOCTOR?
JUST ANOTHER PSEUDO-INTELLECTUAL RELIGIOUS NUT WITH DELUSIONS OF GRANDEUR.
YOUR NURSE IS:
AMANDA
x5779
YOU DON'T REALLY *BELIEVE* THAT. DO YOU?
I DON'T KNOW WHAT I BELIEVE BUT THAT IS WHAT I AM GOING TO TELL THE DISTRICT ATTORNEY IN MY REPORT. I ALSO PLAN TO TELL HIM THAT YOU ARE FIT TO STAND TRIAL.
IF THERE IS INDEED A HELL I HOPE AND PRAY THAT YOU ROAST IN IT. THE SOONER THE BETTER.
REST ASSURED, DOCTOR. THE DAY WILL COME WHEN YOUR PRAYERS ARE ANSWERED.
BUMP
EXCUSE ME, SIR.
?

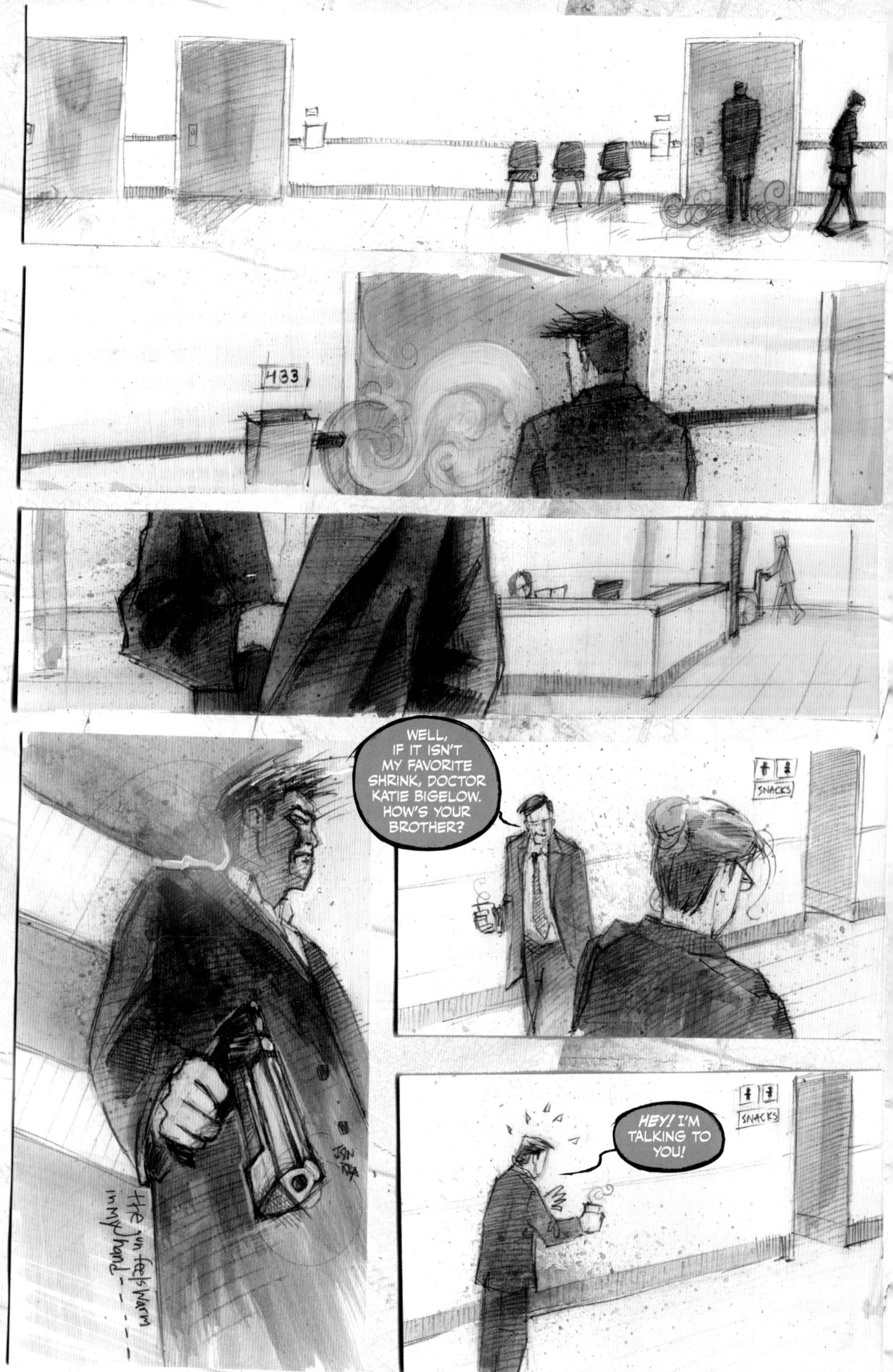
433
the gun feels warm in my hand - - -
WELL, IF IT ISN'T MY FAVORITE SHRINK, DOCTOR KATIE BIGELOW. HOW'S YOUR BROTHER?
SNACKS
HEY! I'M TALKING TO YOU!
SNACKS

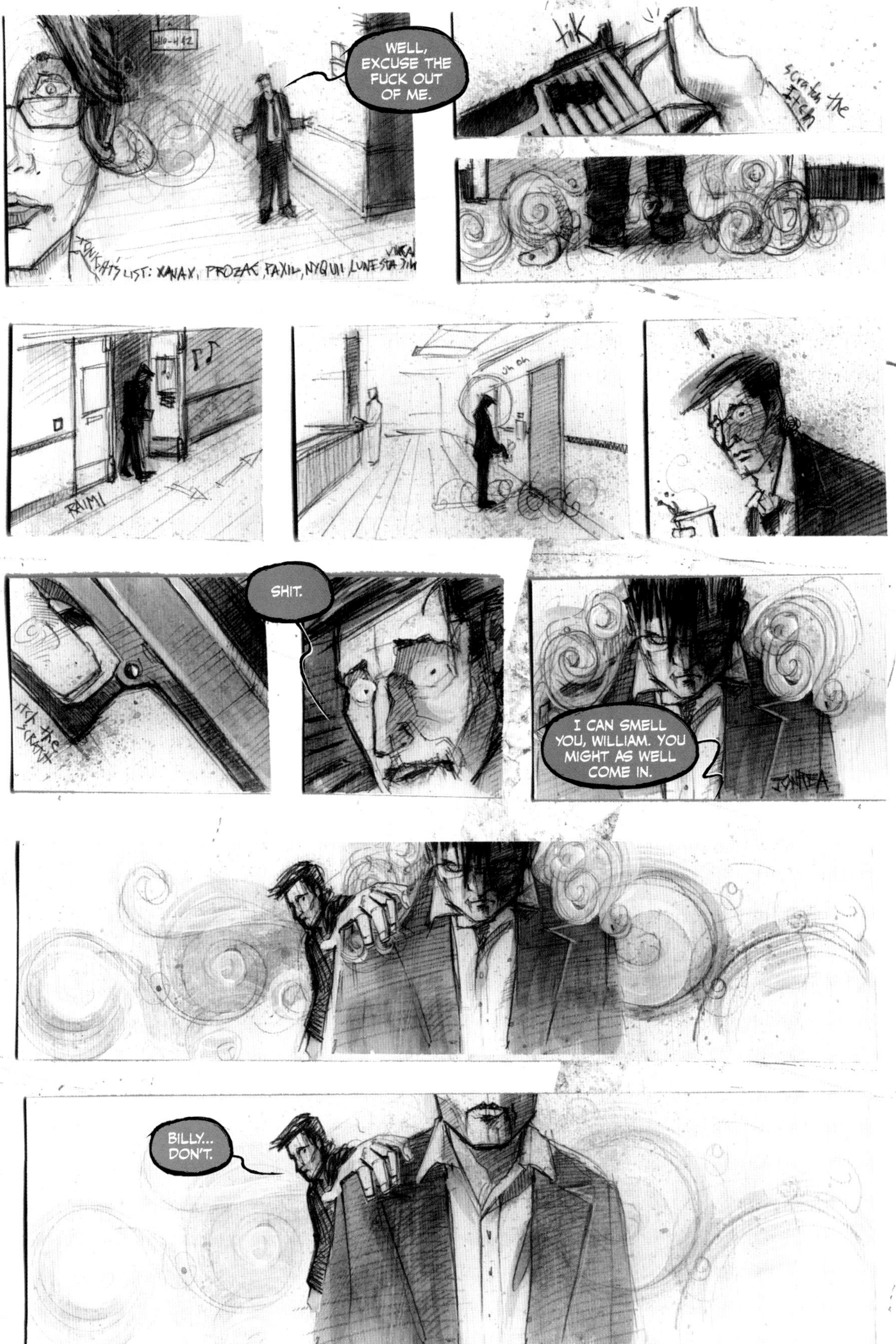
WELL, EXCUSE THE FUCK OUT OF ME.
tik
Scratch the Itch
RAIMI
SHIT.
I CAN SMELL YOU, WILLIAM. YOU MIGHT AS WELL COME IN.
BILLY... DON'T.

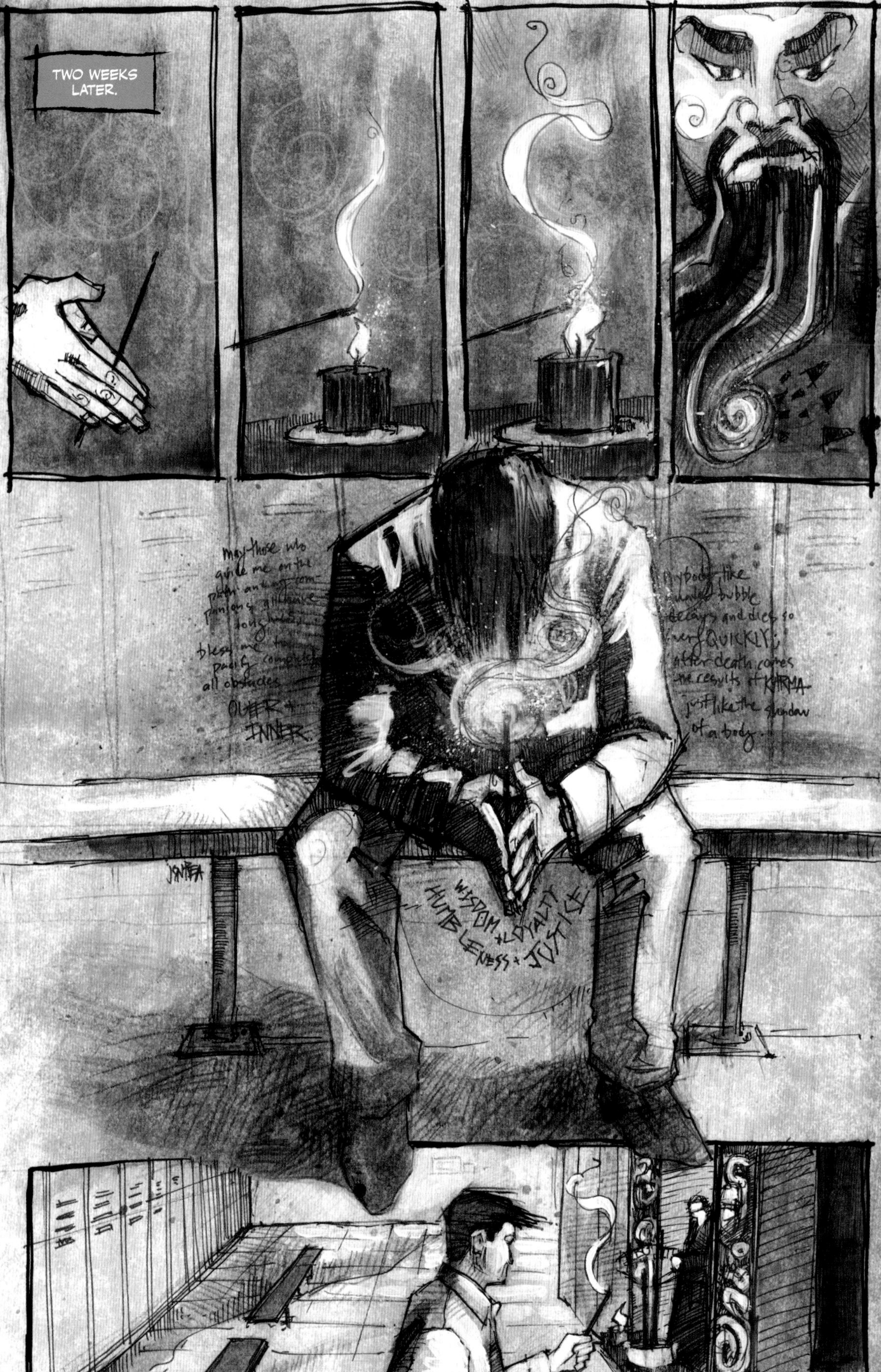
TWO WEEKS LATER.
may those who
guide me on the
blessed me
all obstacles
OUTER +
INNER.
my body like
bubble
decays and dies so
QUICKLY;
after death comes
the results of KARMA
just like the
of a body.
WISDOM + LOYALTY
HUMBLENESS + JUSTICE

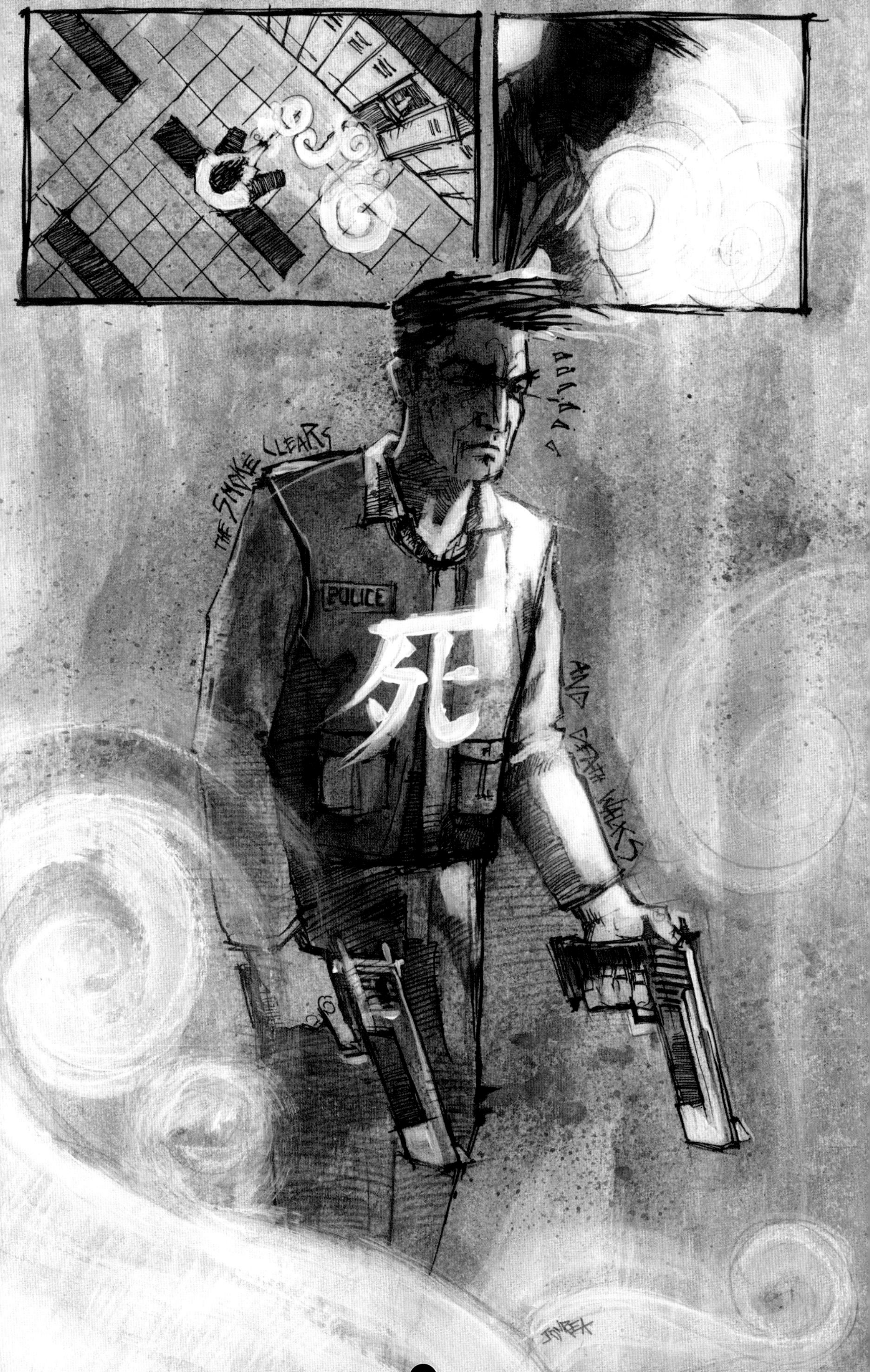
THE SMOKE CLEARS
POLICE
死
AND DEATH WALKS

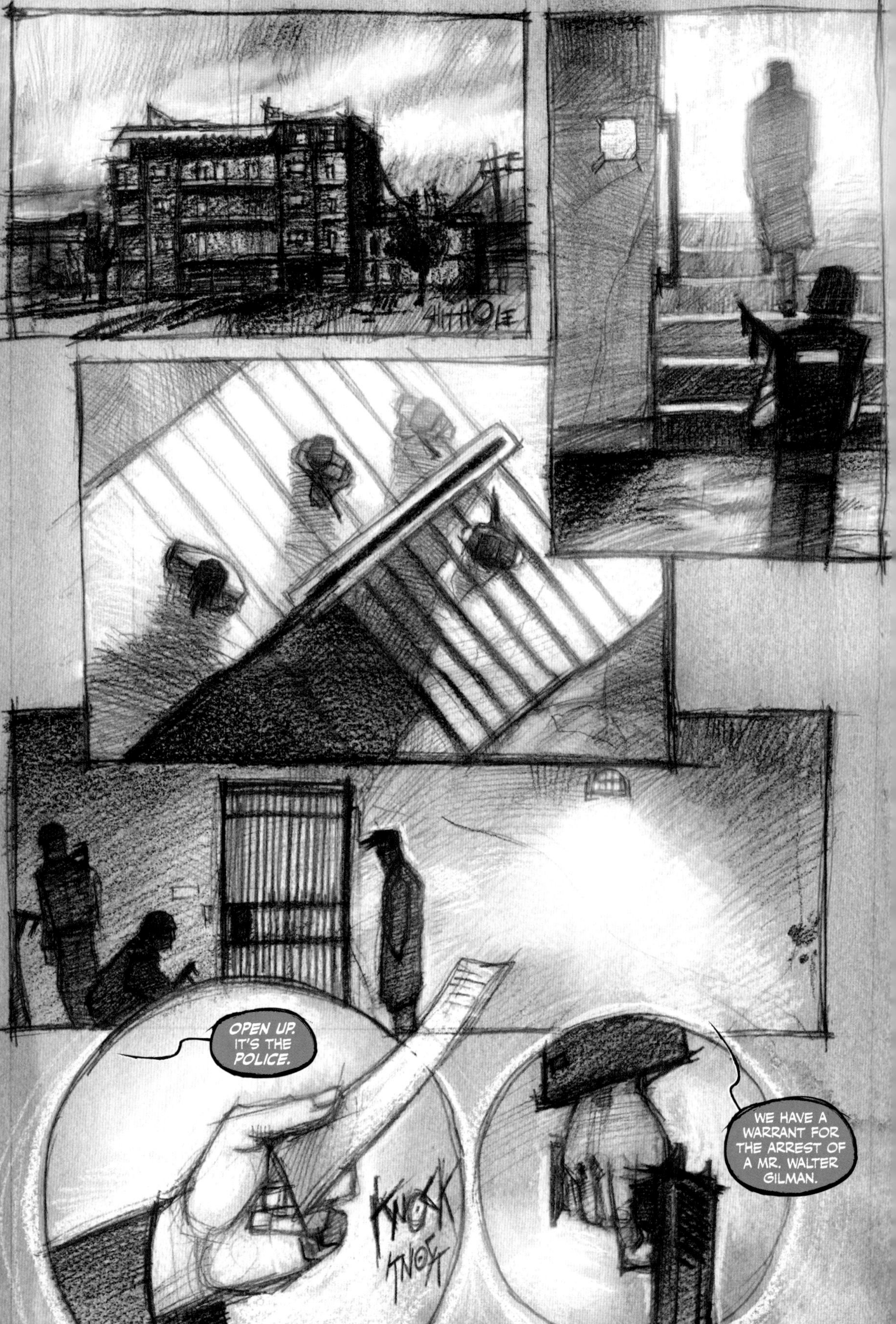
OPEN UP. IT'S THE POLICE.
KNOCK
KNOCK
WE HAVE A WARRANT FOR THE ARREST OF A MR. WALTER GILMAN.

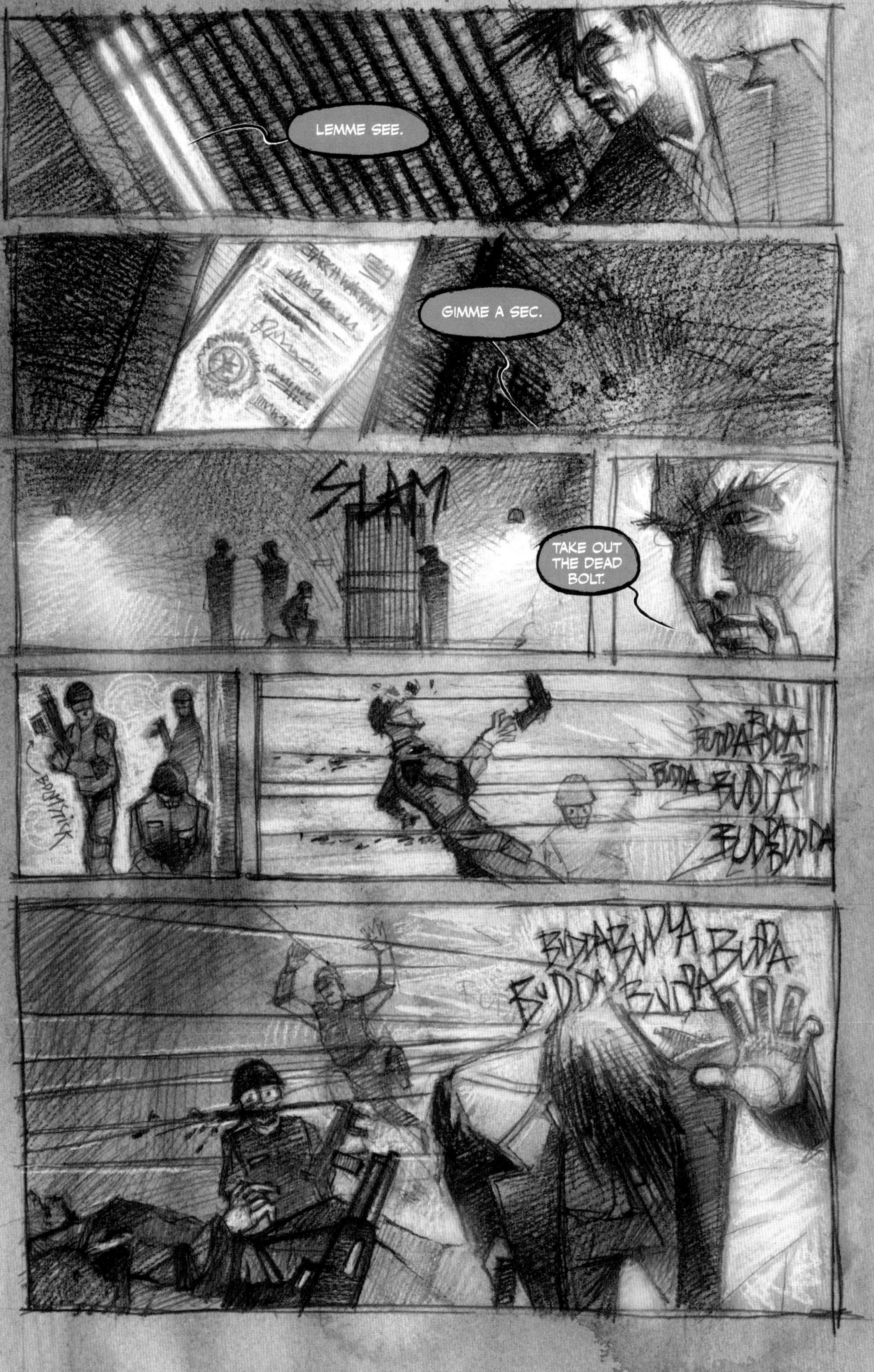
LEMME SEE.
GIMME A SEC.
SLAM
TAKE OUT THE DEAD BOLT.

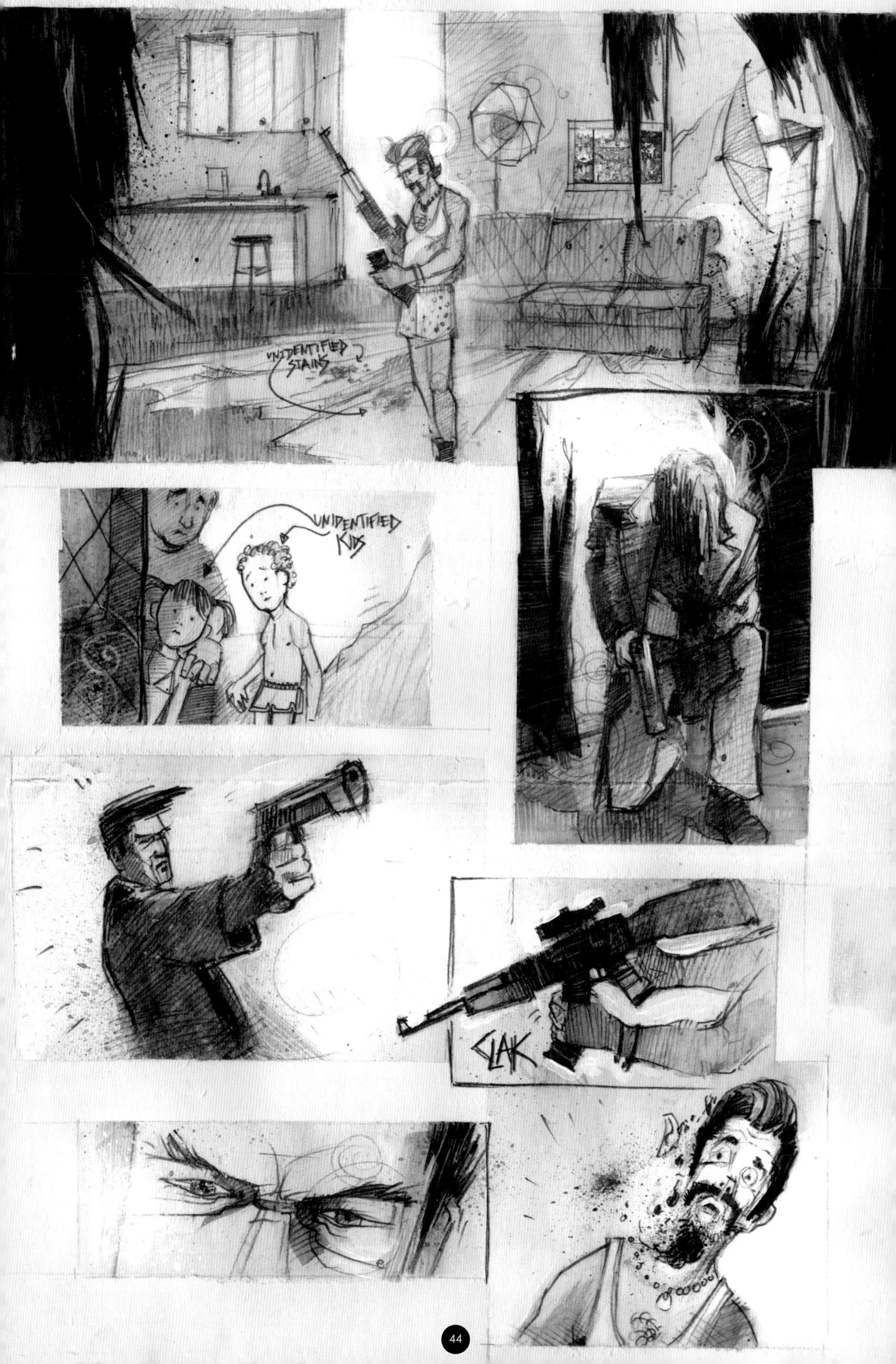
UNIDENTIFIED STAINS
UNIDENTIFIED KIDS
CLAK

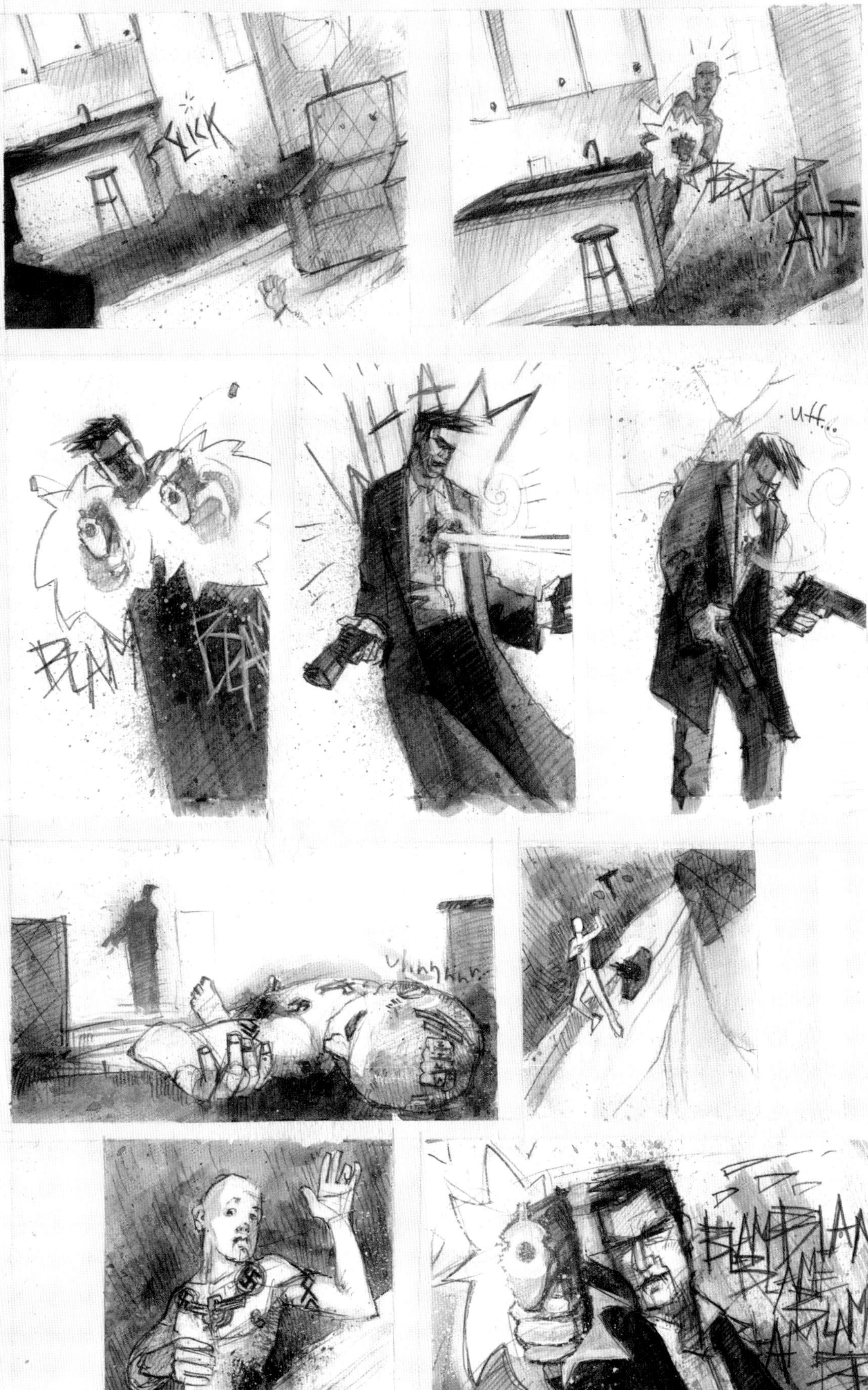
CLICK
BBRRAT
BLAM
BLAM
uff...
Uhnnhnn...
BLAM BLAM
BLAM

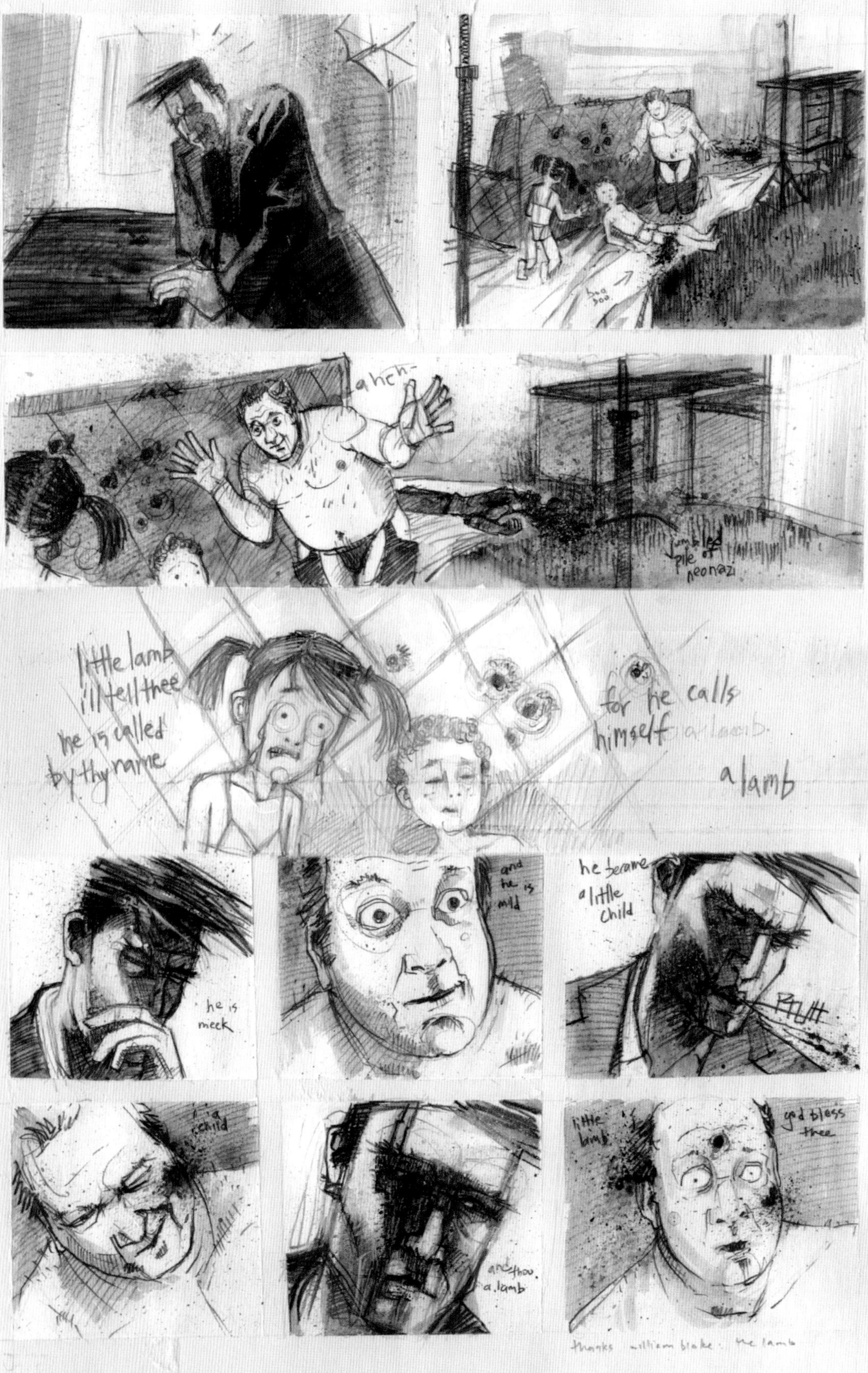
ahch-
jumbled pile of neonazi
little lamb i'll tell thee
he is called by thy name
for he calls himself
a lamb
he is meek
and he is mild
he became a little child
PTUH
a child
and thou a lamb
little lamb
god bless thee
thanks william blake : the lamb

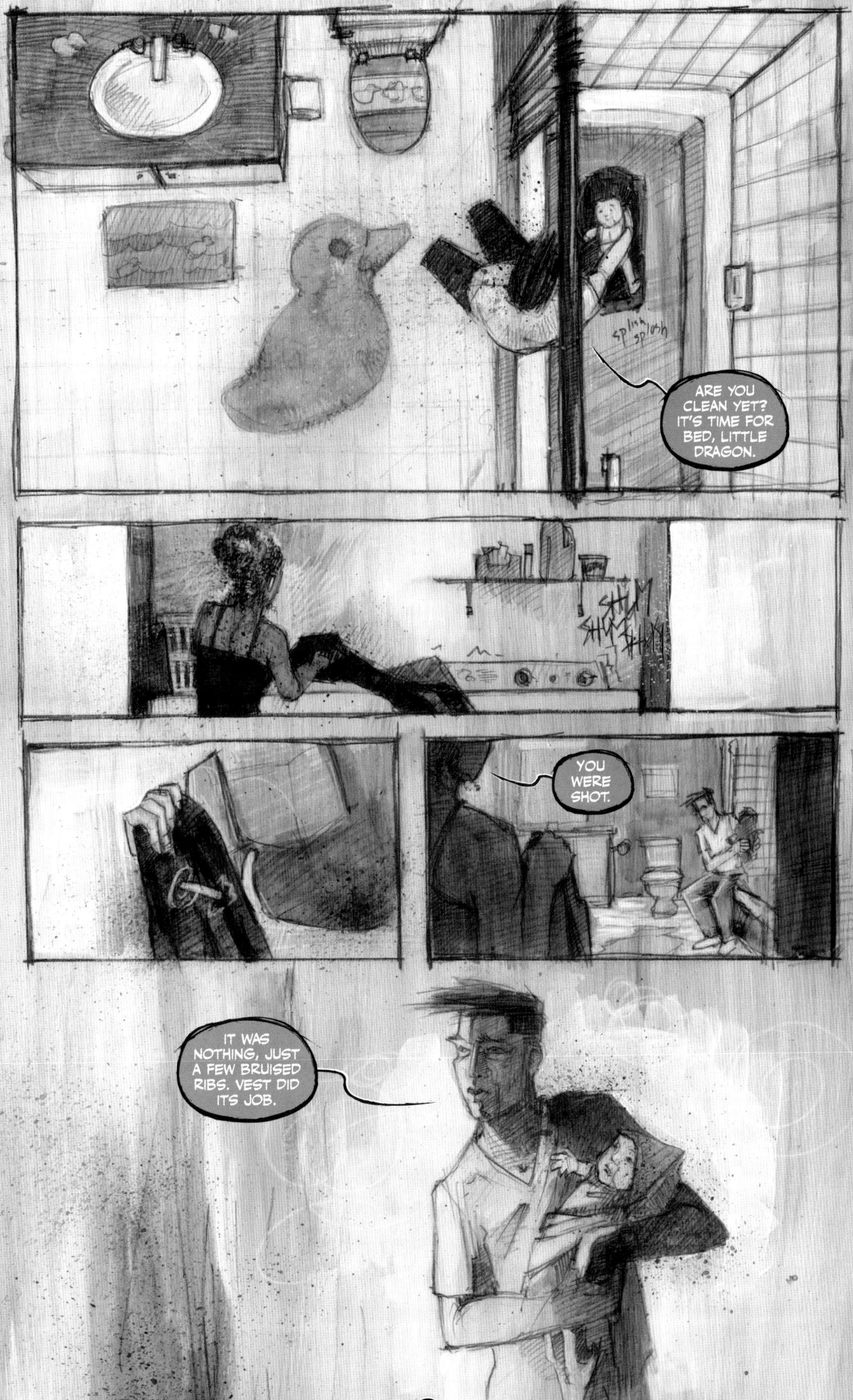
splish splosh
ARE YOU CLEAN YET? IT'S TIME FOR BED, LITTLE DRAGON.
YOU WERE SHOT.
IT WAS NOTHING, JUST A FEW BRUISED RIBS. VEST DID ITS JOB.

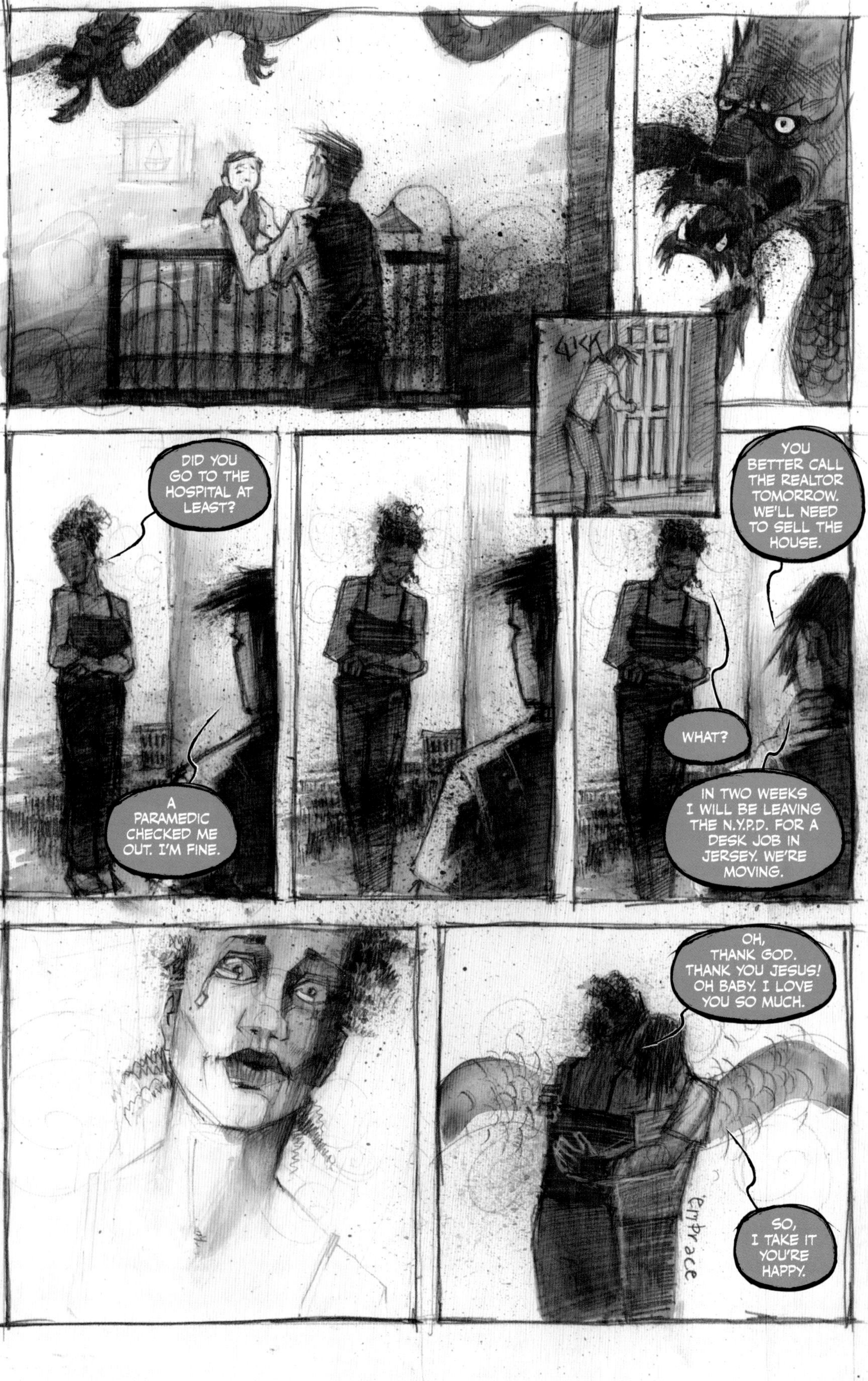
CLICK
DID YOU GO TO THE HOSPITAL AT LEAST?
A PARAMEDIC CHECKED ME OUT. I'M FINE.
YOU BETTER CALL THE REALTOR TOMORROW. WE'LL NEED TO SELL THE HOUSE.
WHAT?
IN TWO WEEKS I WILL BE LEAVING THE N.Y.P.D. FOR A DESK JOB IN JERSEY. WE'RE MOVING.
OH, THANK GOD. THANK YOU JESUS! OH BABY. I LOVE YOU SO MUCH.
embrace
SO, I TAKE IT YOU'RE HAPPY.

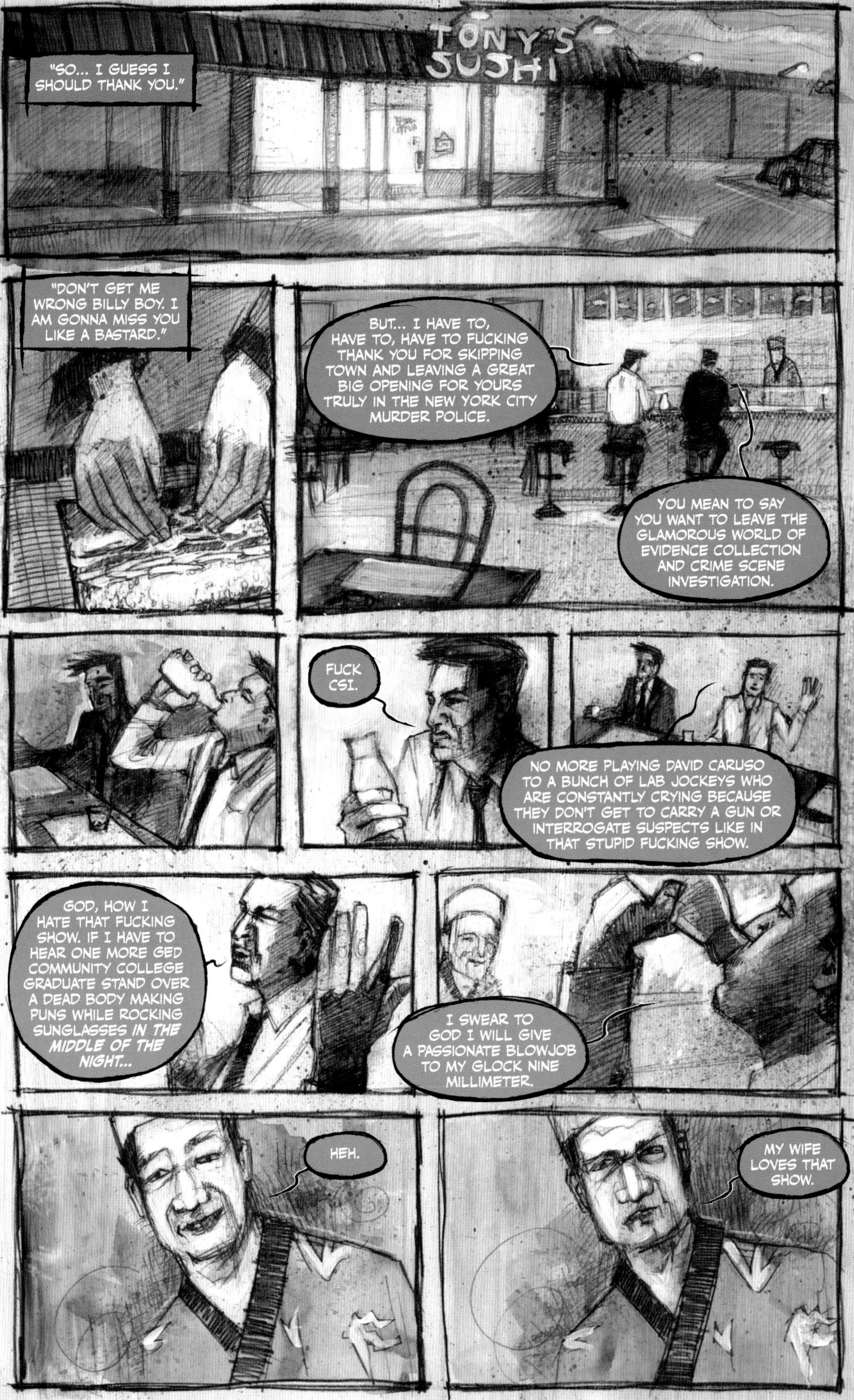
TONY'S SUSHI
"SO... I GUESS I SHOULD THANK YOU."
"DON'T GET ME WRONG BILLY BOY. I AM GONNA MISS YOU LIKE A BASTARD."
BUT... I HAVE TO, HAVE TO, HAVE TO FUCKING THANK YOU FOR SKIPPING TOWN AND LEAVING A GREAT BIG OPENING FOR YOURS TRULY IN THE NEW YORK CITY MURDER POLICE.
YOU MEAN TO SAY YOU WANT TO LEAVE THE GLAMOROUS WORLD OF EVIDENCE COLLECTION AND CRIME SCENE INVESTIGATION.
FUCK CSI.
NO MORE PLAYING DAVID CARUSO TO A BUNCH OF LAB JOCKEYS WHO ARE CONSTANTLY CRYING BECAUSE THEY DON'T GET TO CARRY A GUN OR INTERROGATE SUSPECTS LIKE IN THAT STUPID FUCKING SHOW.
GOD, HOW I HATE THAT FUCKING SHOW. IF I HAVE TO HEAR ONE MORE GED COMMUNITY COLLEGE GRADUATE STAND OVER A DEAD BODY MAKING PUNS WHILE ROCKING SUNGLASSES *IN THE MIDDLE OF THE NIGHT...*
I SWEAR TO GOD I WILL GIVE A PASSIONATE BLOWJOB TO MY GLOCK NINE MILLIMETER.
HEH.
MY WIFE LOVES THAT SHOW.

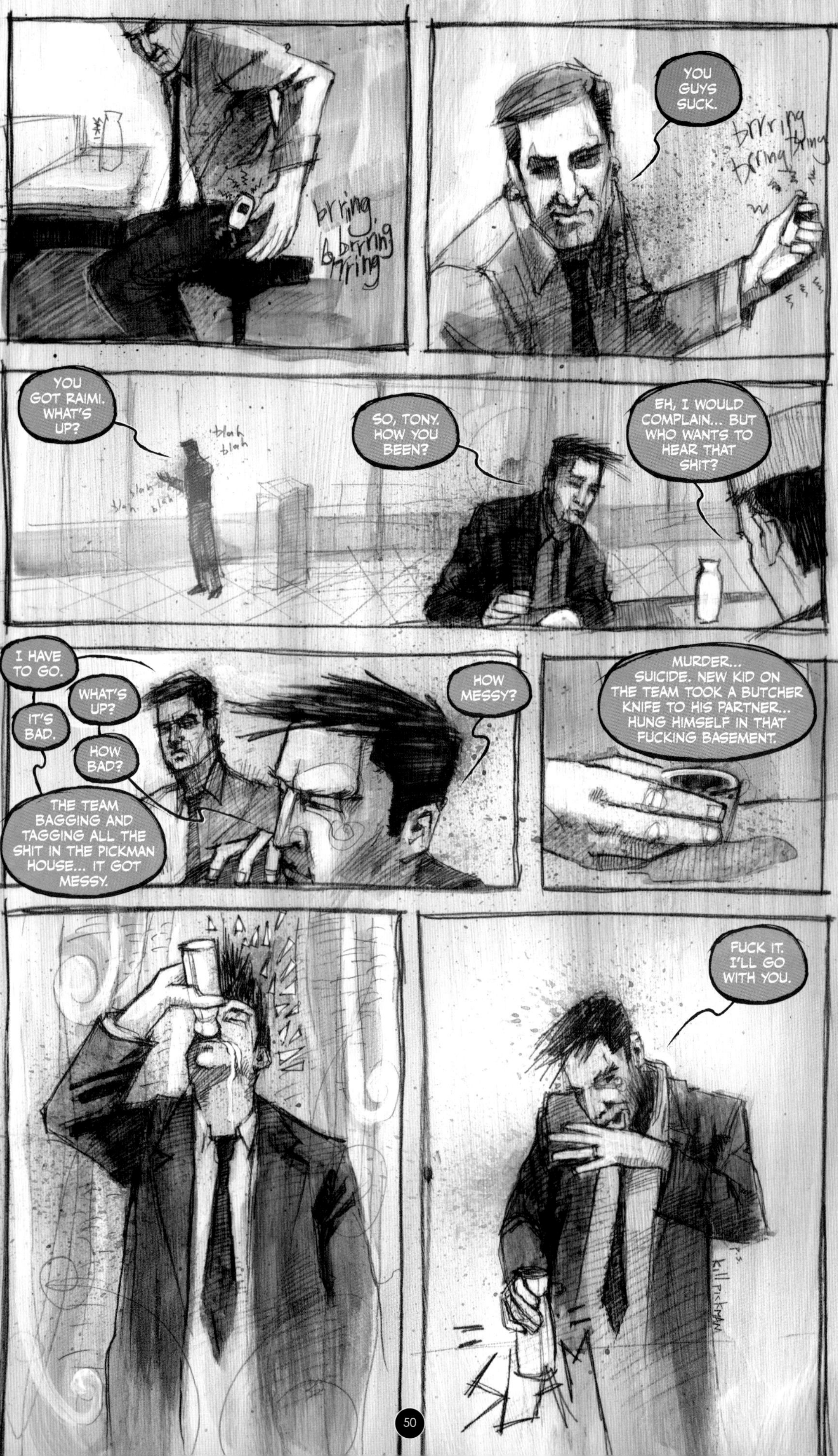
YOU GUYS SUCK.
YOU GOT RAIMI. WHAT'S UP?
SO, TONY. HOW YOU BEEN?
EH, I WOULD COMPLAIN... BUT WHO WANTS TO HEAR THAT SHIT?
I HAVE TO GO.
WHAT'S UP?
IT'S BAD.
HOW BAD?
THE TEAM BAGGING AND TAGGING ALL THE SHIT IN THE PICKMAN HOUSE... IT GOT MESSY.
HOW MESSY?
MURDER... SUICIDE. NEW KID ON THE TEAM TOOK A BUTCHER KNIFE TO HIS PARTNER... HUNG HIMSELF IN THAT FUCKING BASEMENT.
FUCK IT. I'LL GO WITH YOU.

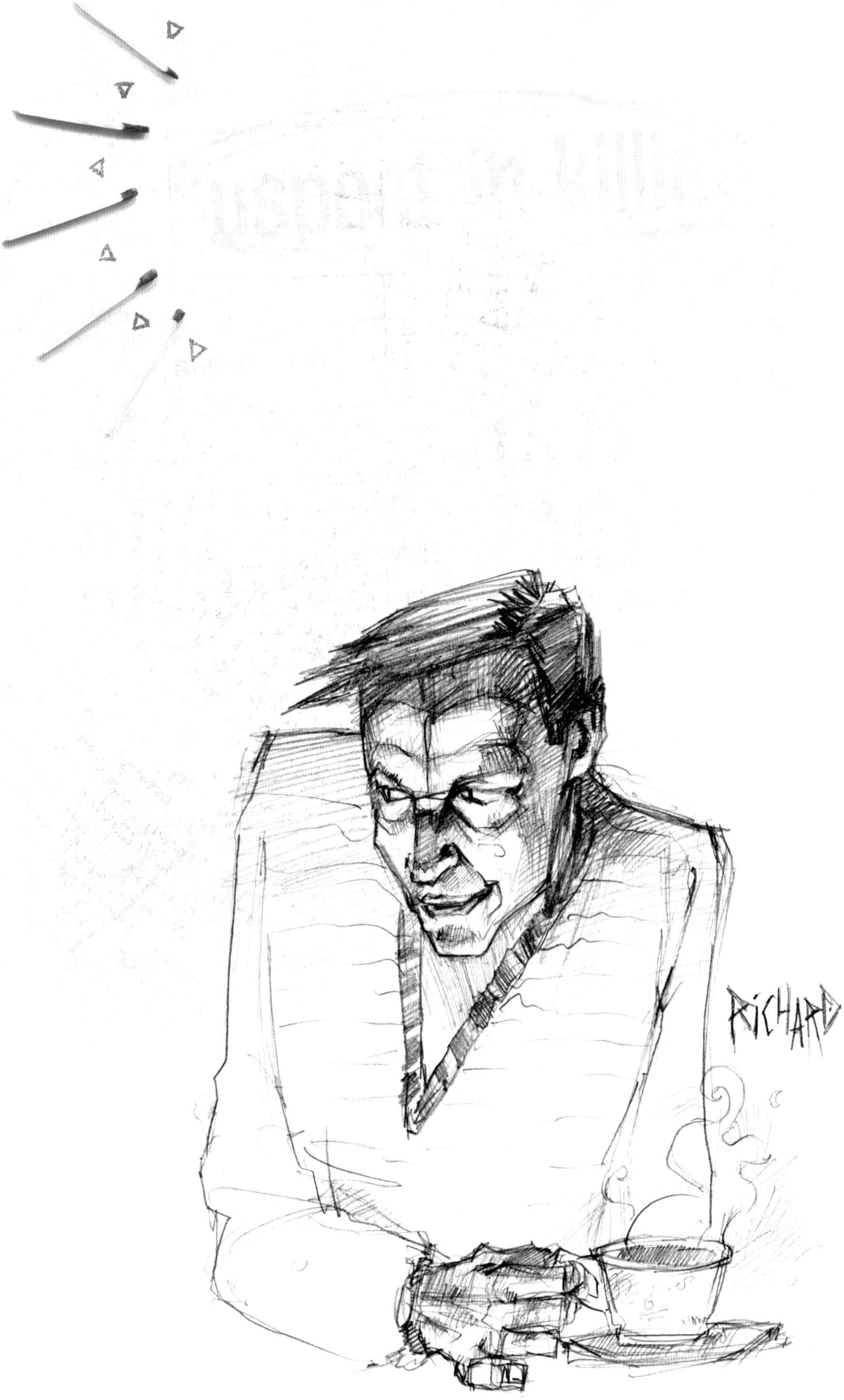
RICHARD

chapter three

HATER OF MEN

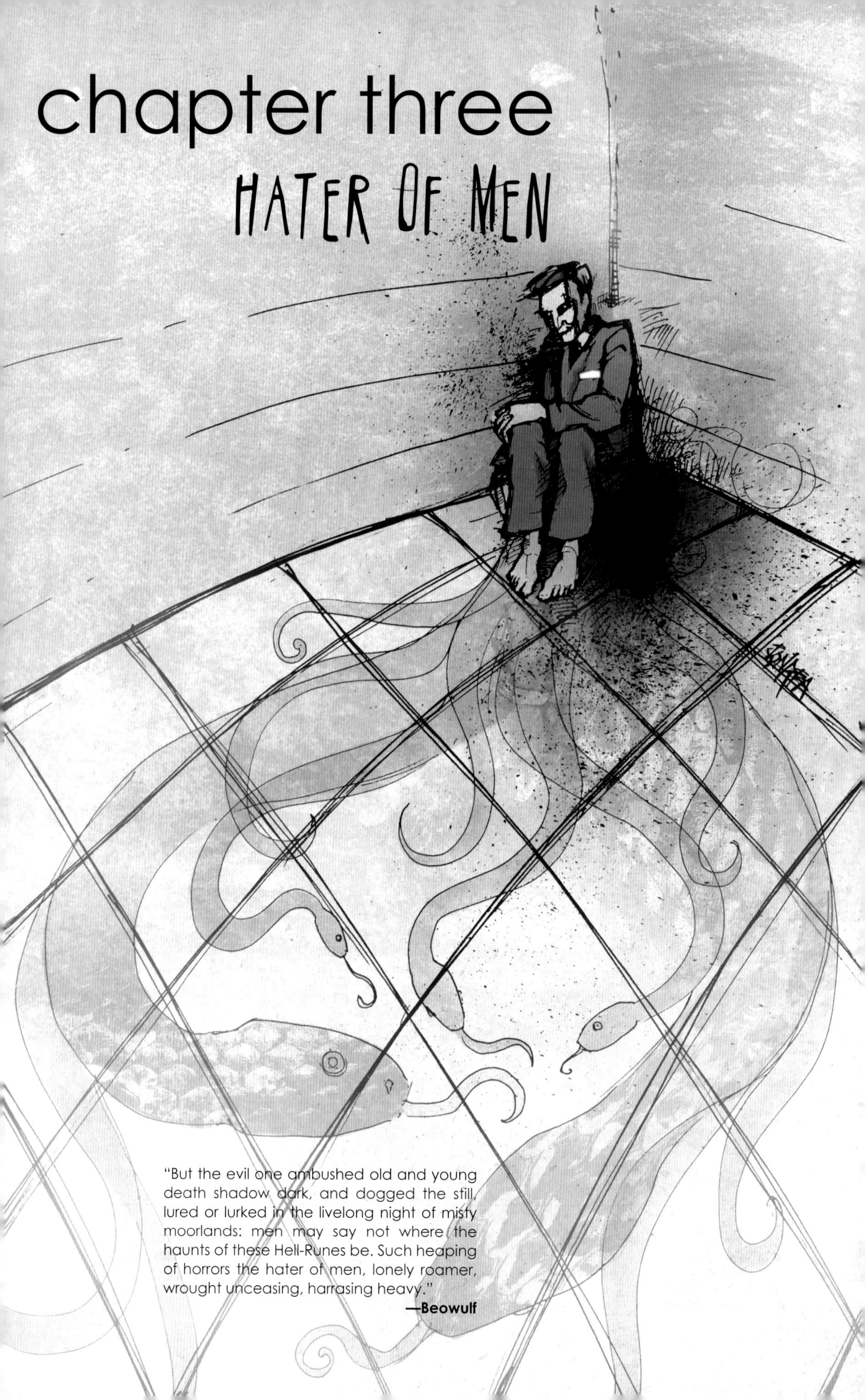

"But the evil one ambushed old and young death shadow dark, and dogged the still, lured or lurked in the livelong night of misty moorlands: men may say not where the haunts of these Hell-Runes be. Such heaping of horrors the hater of men, lonely roamer, wrought unceasing, harrasing heavy."

—Beowulf

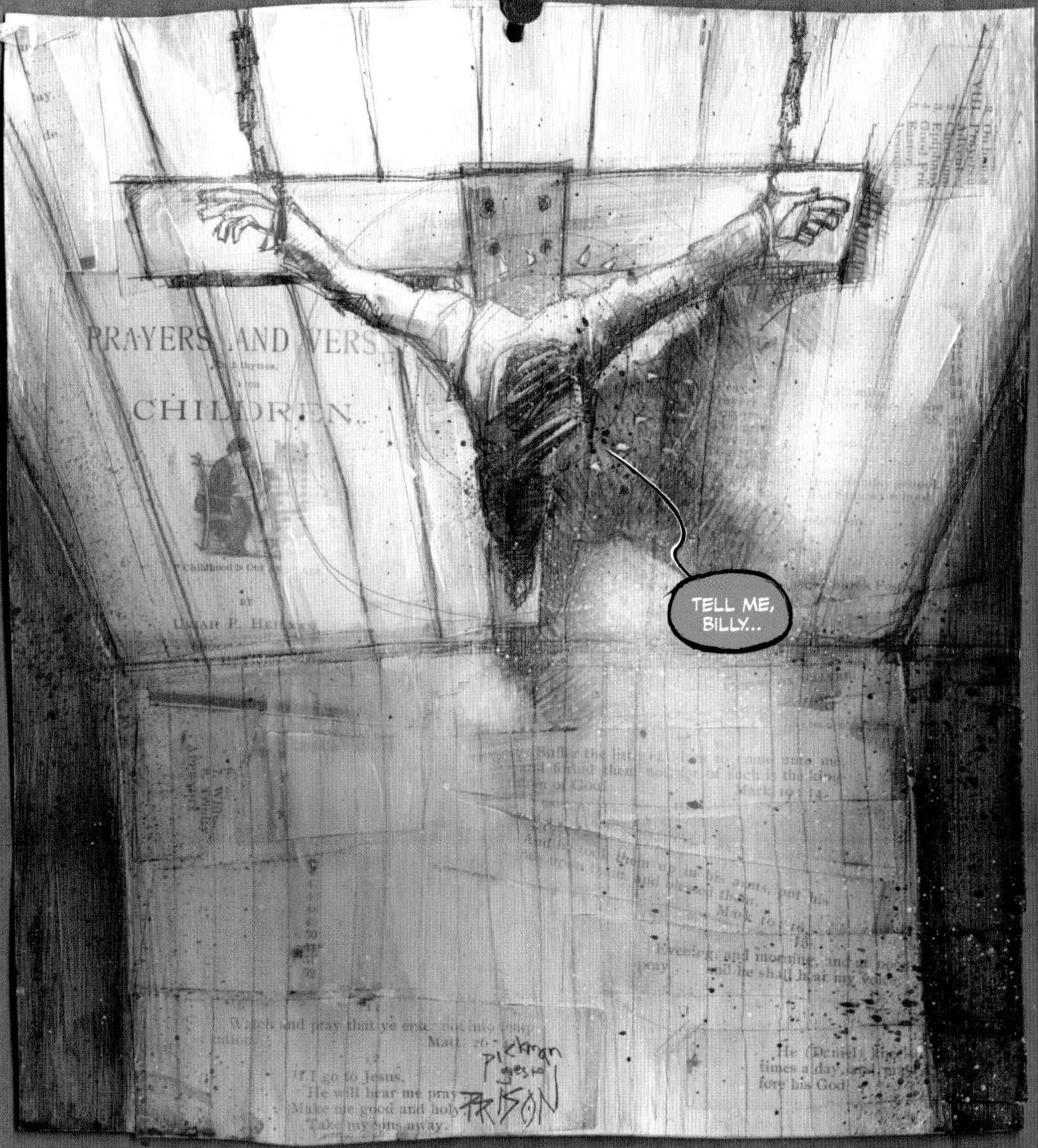
TELL ME, BILLY...
pickman goes to PRISON

pickman's eyes open... bill's eyes... open.

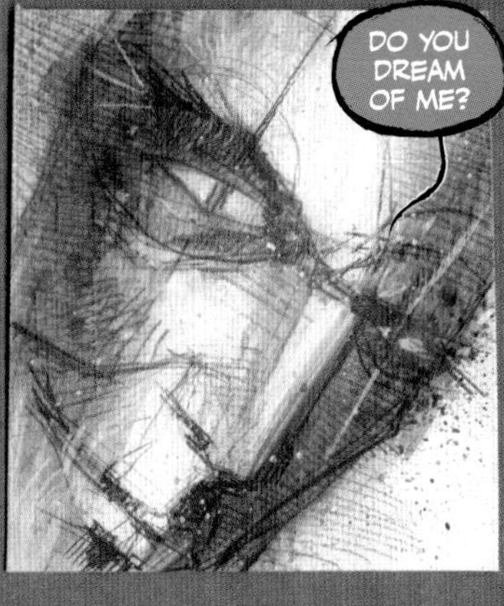
DO YOU DREAM OF ME?

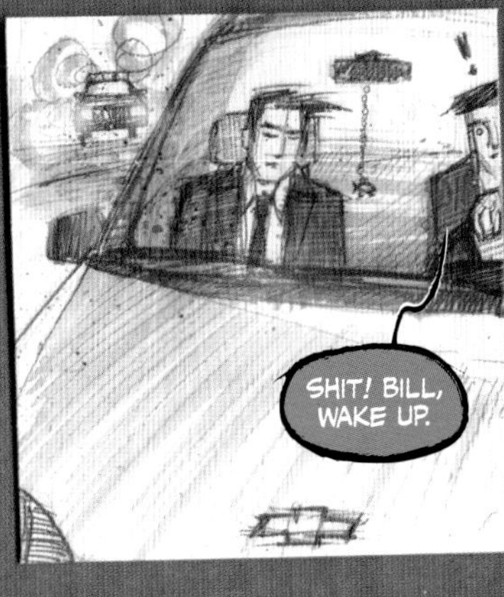
!
SHIT! BILL, WAKE UP.

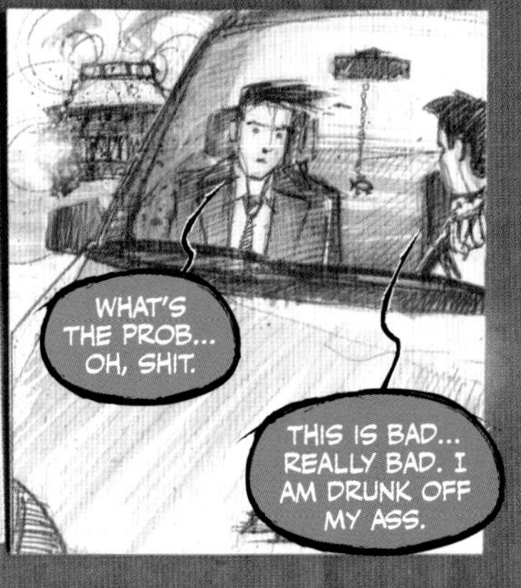
WHAT'S THE PROB... OH, SHIT.
THIS IS BAD... REALLY BAD. I AM DRUNK OFF MY ASS.

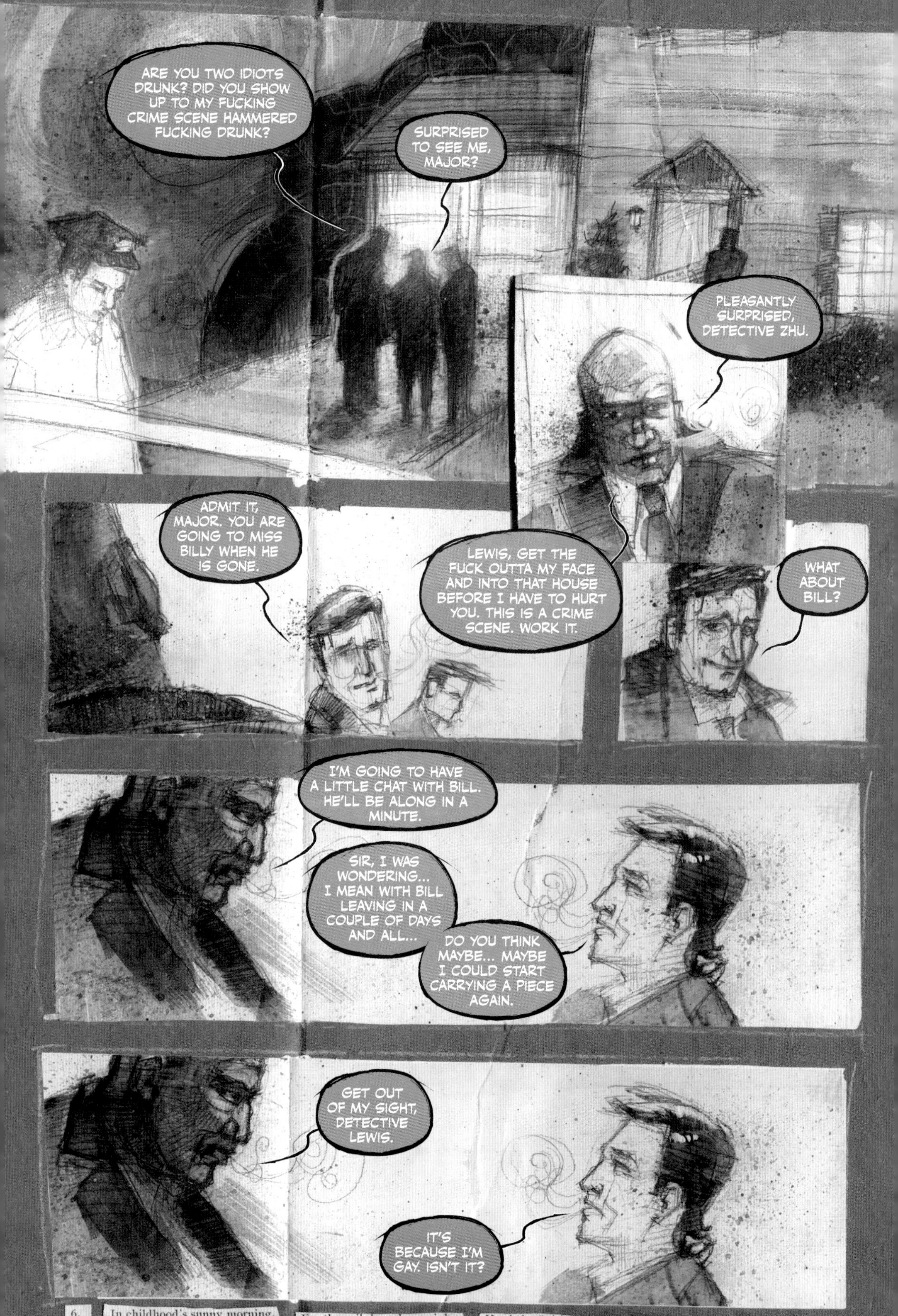
ARE YOU TWO IDIOTS DRUNK? DID YOU SHOW UP TO MY FUCKING CRIME SCENE HAMMERED FUCKING DRUNK?
SURPRISED TO SEE ME, MAJOR?
PLEASANTLY SURPRISED, DETECTIVE ZHU.
ADMIT IT, MAJOR. YOU ARE GOING TO MISS BILLY WHEN HE IS GONE.
LEWIS, GET THE FUCK OUTTA MY FACE AND INTO THAT HOUSE BEFORE I HAVE TO HURT YOU. THIS IS A CRIME SCENE. WORK IT.
WHAT ABOUT BILL?
I'M GOING TO HAVE A LITTLE CHAT WITH BILL. HE'LL BE ALONG IN A MINUTE.
SIR, I WAS WONDERING... I MEAN WITH BILL LEAVING IN A COUPLE OF DAYS AND ALL...
DO YOU THINK MAYBE... MAYBE I COULD START CARRYING A PIECE AGAIN.
GET OUT OF MY SIGHT, DETECTIVE LEWIS.
IT'S BECAUSE I'M GAY. ISN'T IT?

6. In childhood's sunny morning, Ere the evil days draw nigh. Heed the Spirit's tender warning. To the arms of Jesus fly.

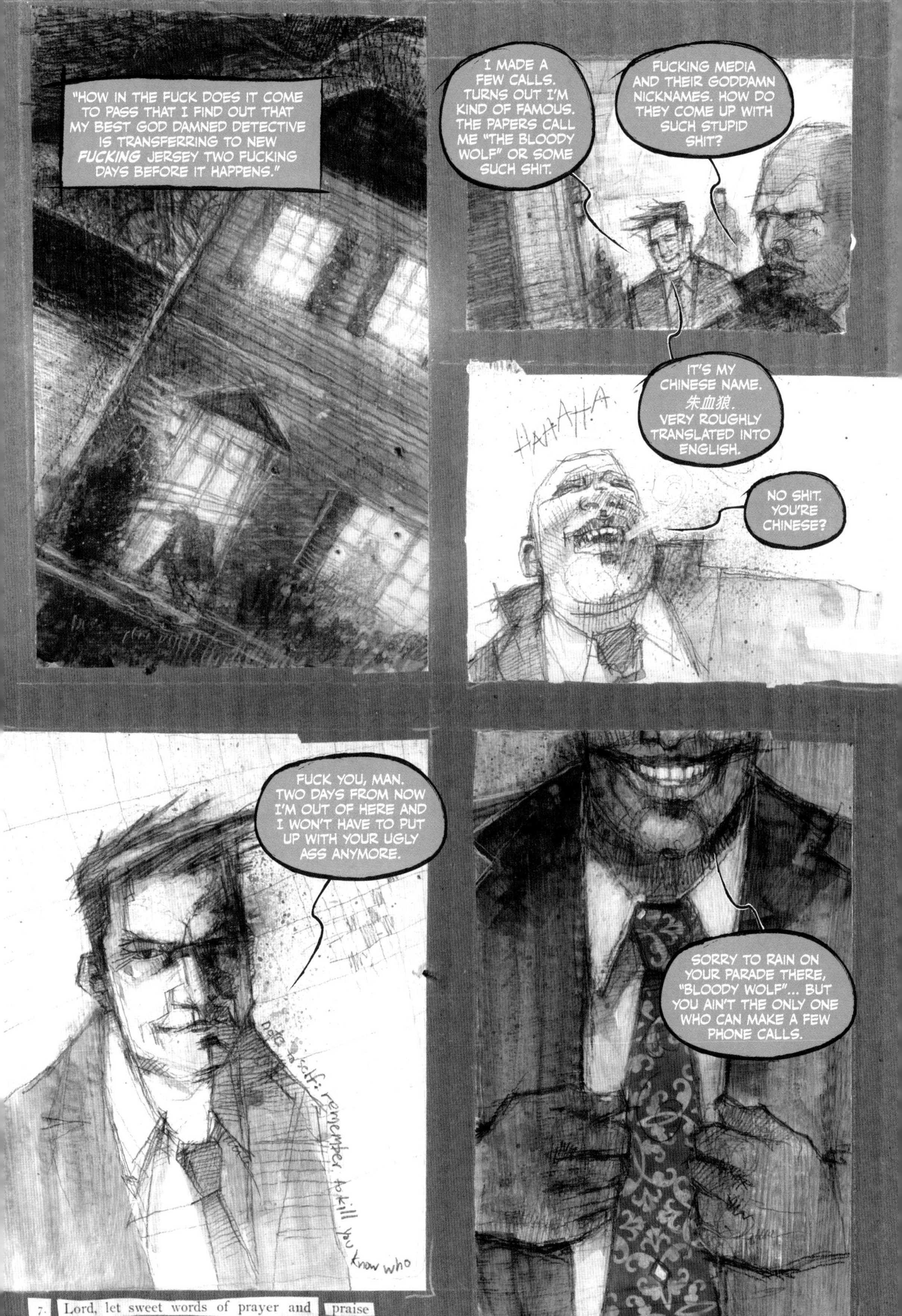
"HOW IN THE FUCK DOES IT COME TO PASS THAT I FIND OUT THAT MY BEST GOD DAMNED DETECTIVE IS TRANSFERRING TO NEW *FUCKING* JERSEY TWO FUCKING DAYS BEFORE IT HAPPENS."
I MADE A FEW CALLS. TURNS OUT I'M KIND OF FAMOUS. THE PAPERS CALL ME "THE BLOODY WOLF" OR SOME SUCH SHIT.
FUCKING MEDIA AND THEIR GODDAMN NICKNAMES. HOW DO THEY COME UP WITH SUCH STUPID SHIT?
IT'S MY CHINESE NAME. 朱血狼. VERY ROUGHLY TRANSLATED INTO ENGLISH.
HAHAHA
NO SHIT. YOU'RE CHINESE?
FUCK YOU, MAN. TWO DAYS FROM NOW I'M OUT OF HERE AND I WON'T HAVE TO PUT UP WITH YOUR UGLY ASS ANYMORE.
Note to self: remember to kill you know who
SORRY TO RAIN ON YOUR PARADE THERE, "BLOODY WOLF"... BUT YOU AIN'T THE ONLY ONE WHO CAN MAKE A FEW PHONE CALLS.

7. Lord, let sweet words of prayer and praise
Employ my youngest breath; Thus I'm prepared for longer days,
Or fit for early death. Amen.

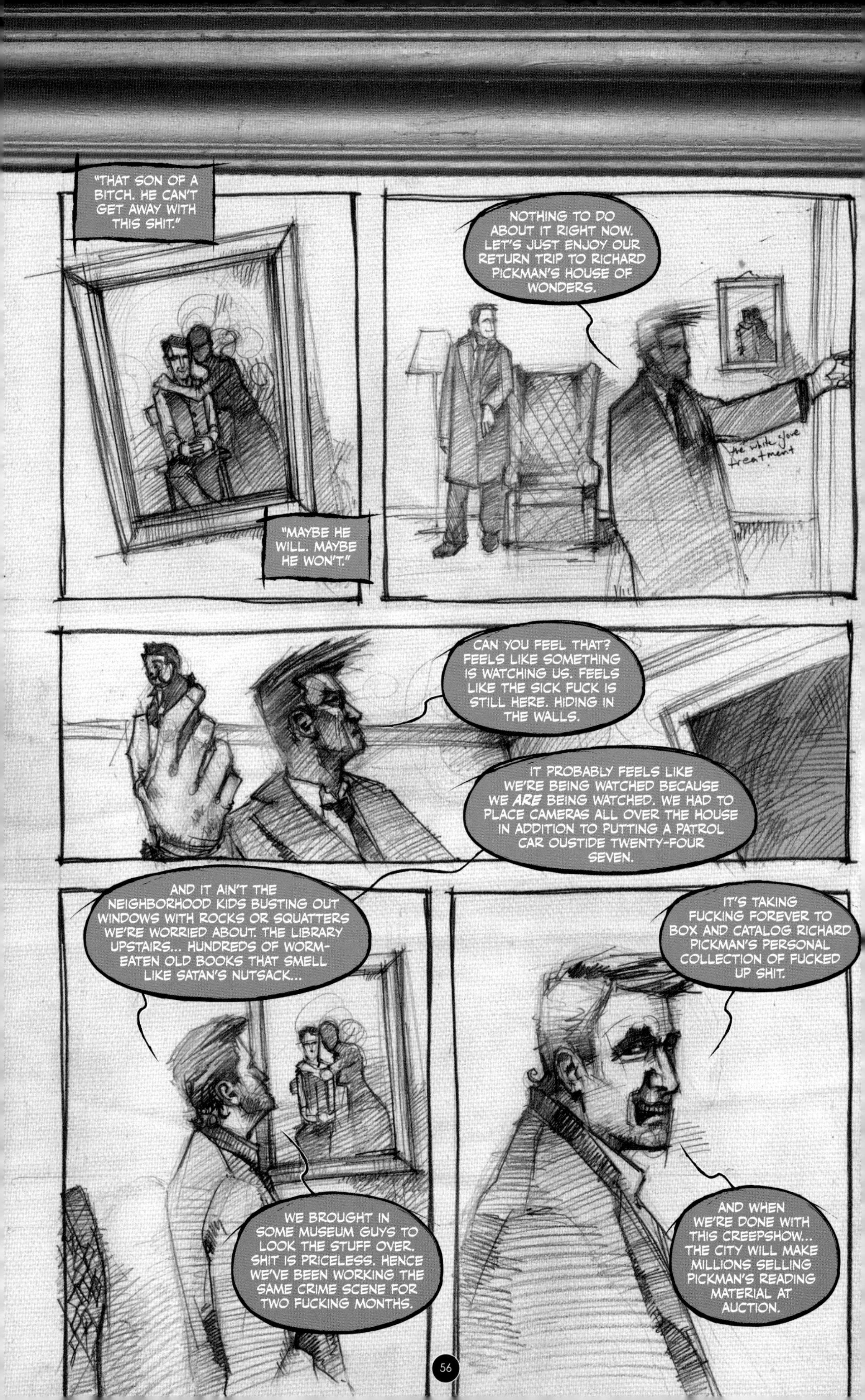

"THAT SON OF A BITCH. HE CAN'T GET AWAY WITH THIS SHIT."
"MAYBE HE WILL. MAYBE HE WON'T."
NOTHING TO DO ABOUT IT RIGHT NOW. LET'S JUST ENJOY OUR RETURN TRIP TO RICHARD PICKMAN'S HOUSE OF WONDERS.
the white glove treatment
CAN YOU FEEL THAT? FEELS LIKE SOMETHING IS WATCHING US. FEELS LIKE THE SICK FUCK IS STILL HERE. HIDING IN THE WALLS.
IT PROBABLY FEELS LIKE WE'RE BEING WATCHED BECAUSE WE *ARE* BEING WATCHED. WE HAD TO PLACE CAMERAS ALL OVER THE HOUSE IN ADDITION TO PUTTING A PATROL CAR OUSTIDE TWENTY-FOUR SEVEN.
AND IT AIN'T THE NEIGHBORHOOD KIDS BUSTING OUT WINDOWS WITH ROCKS OR SQUATTERS WE'RE WORRIED ABOUT. THE LIBRARY UPSTAIRS... HUNDREDS OF WORM-EATEN OLD BOOKS THAT SMELL LIKE SATAN'S NUTSACK...
WE BROUGHT IN SOME MUSEUM GUYS TO LOOK THE STUFF OVER. SHIT IS PRICELESS. HENCE WE'VE BEEN WORKING THE SAME CRIME SCENE FOR TWO FUCKING MONTHS.
IT'S TAKING FUCKING FOREVER TO BOX AND CATALOG RICHARD PICKMAN'S PERSONAL COLLECTION OF FUCKED UP SHIT.
AND WHEN WE'RE DONE WITH THIS CREEPSHOW... THE CITY WILL MAKE MILLIONS SELLING PICKMAN'S READING MATERIAL AT AUCTION.

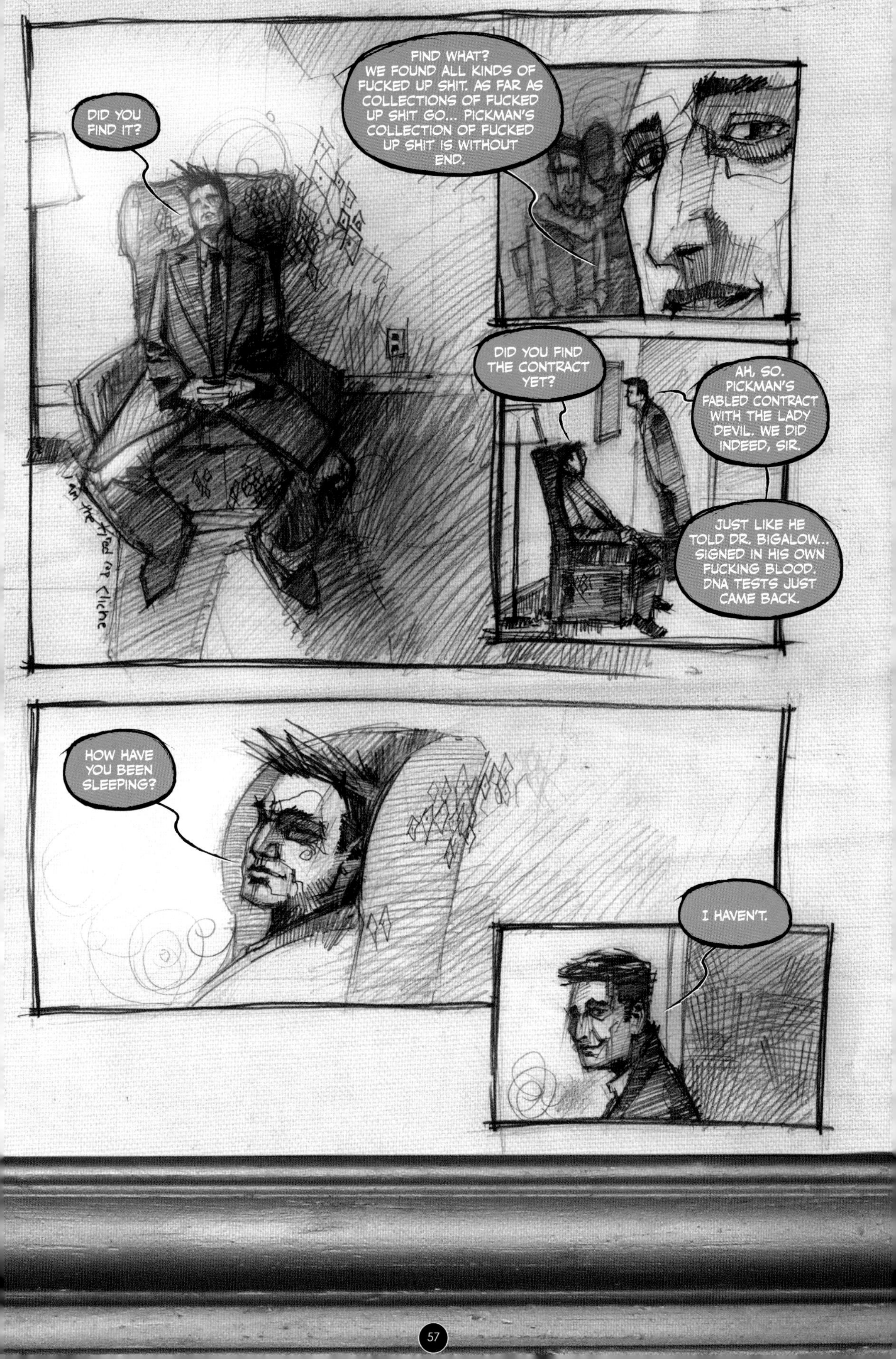
DID YOU FIND IT?
FIND WHAT? WE FOUND ALL KINDS OF FUCKED UP SHIT. AS FAR AS COLLECTIONS OF FUCKED UP SHIT GO... PICKMAN'S COLLECTION OF FUCKED UP SHIT IS WITHOUT END.
I am the tired cop cliche
DID YOU FIND THE CONTRACT YET?
AH, SO. PICKMAN'S FABLED CONTRACT WITH THE LADY DEVIL. WE DID INDEED, SIR.
JUST LIKE HE TOLD DR. BIGALOW... SIGNED IN HIS OWN FUCKING BLOOD. DNA TESTS JUST CAME BACK.
HOW HAVE YOU BEEN SLEEPING?
I HAVEN'T.

This little book contains short prayers— mostly in rhymes—for the use of children. It also contains little verses, which have a tendency to form correct habits in the young, and to build them up in holiness.

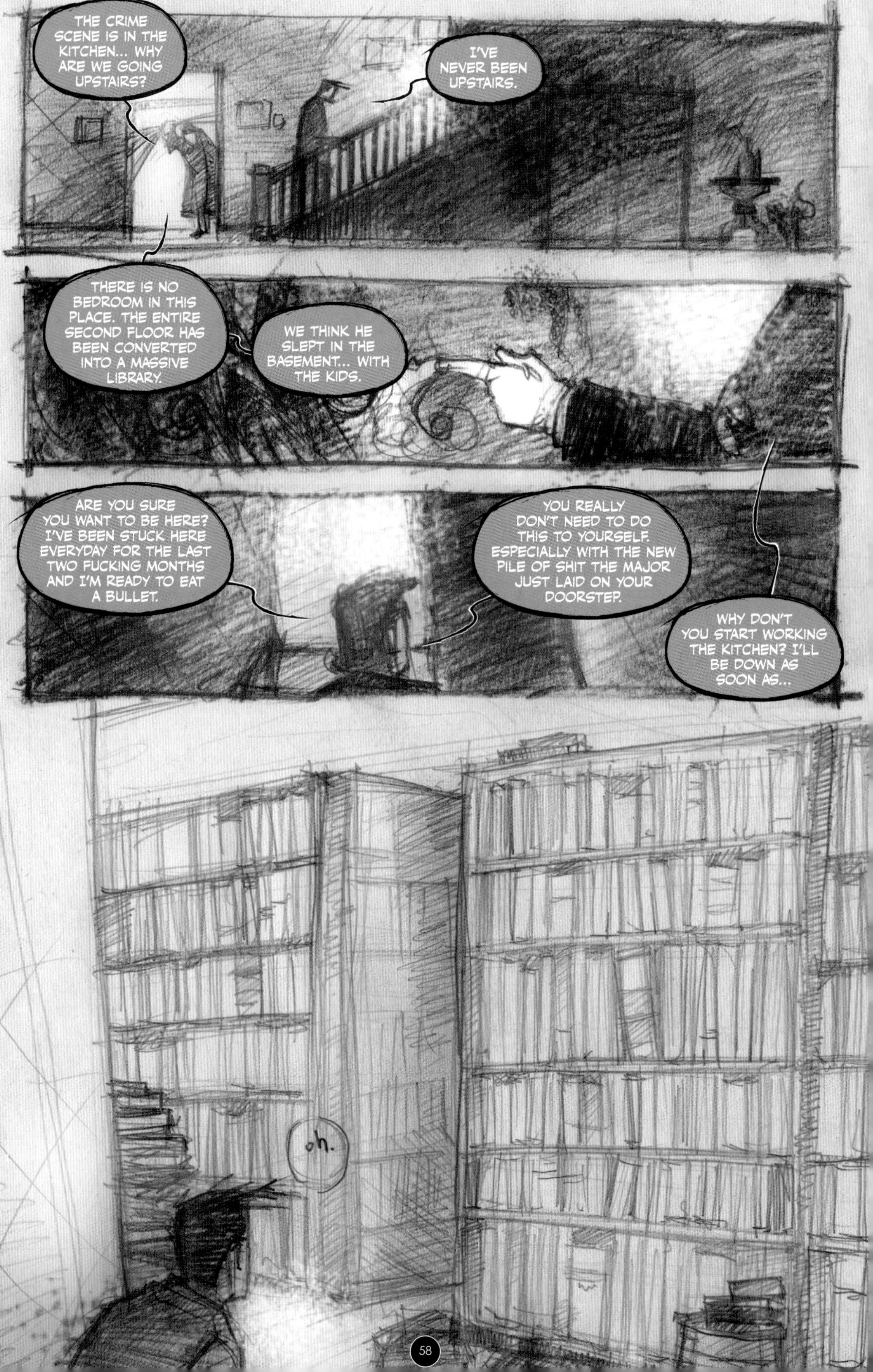
THE CRIME SCENE IS IN THE KITCHEN... WHY ARE WE GOING UPSTAIRS?
I'VE NEVER BEEN UPSTAIRS.
THERE IS NO BEDROOM IN THIS PLACE. THE ENTIRE SECOND FLOOR HAS BEEN CONVERTED INTO A MASSIVE LIBRARY.
WE THINK HE SLEPT IN THE BASEMENT... WITH THE KIDS.
ARE YOU SURE YOU WANT TO BE HERE? I'VE BEEN STUCK HERE EVERYDAY FOR THE LAST TWO FUCKING MONTHS AND I'M READY TO EAT A BULLET.
YOU REALLY DON'T NEED TO DO THIS TO YOURSELF. ESPECIALLY WITH THE NEW PILE OF SHIT THE MAJOR JUST LAID ON YOUR DOORSTEP.
WHY DON'T YOU START WORKING THE KITCHEN? I'LL BE DOWN AS SOON AS...
oh.

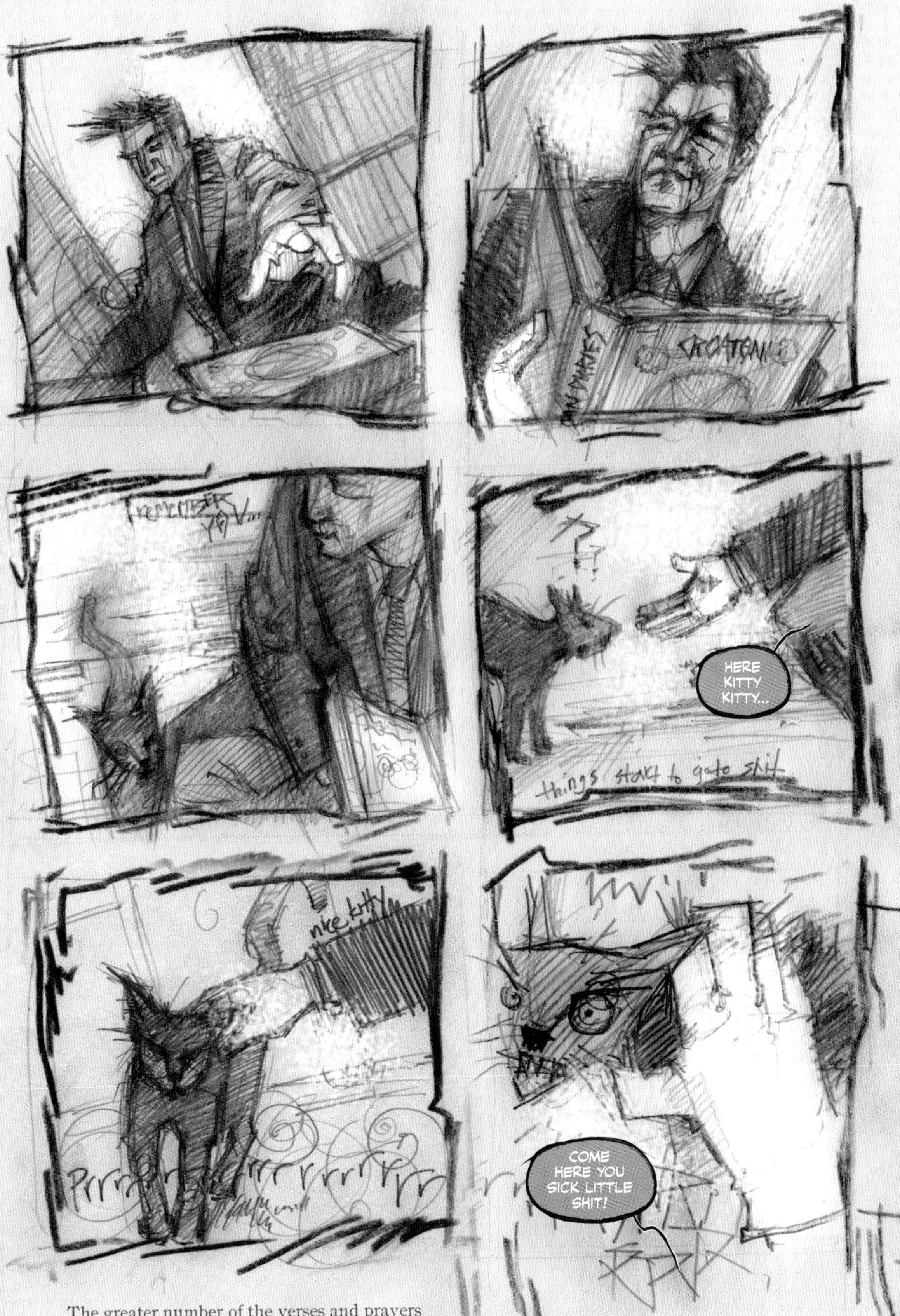
HERE KITTY KITTY...
things start to go to shit
nice kitty
COME HERE YOU SICK LITTLE SHIT!

The greater number of the verses and prayers in this book have been in use among the children for many years, and have already encouraged and edified many young hearts.

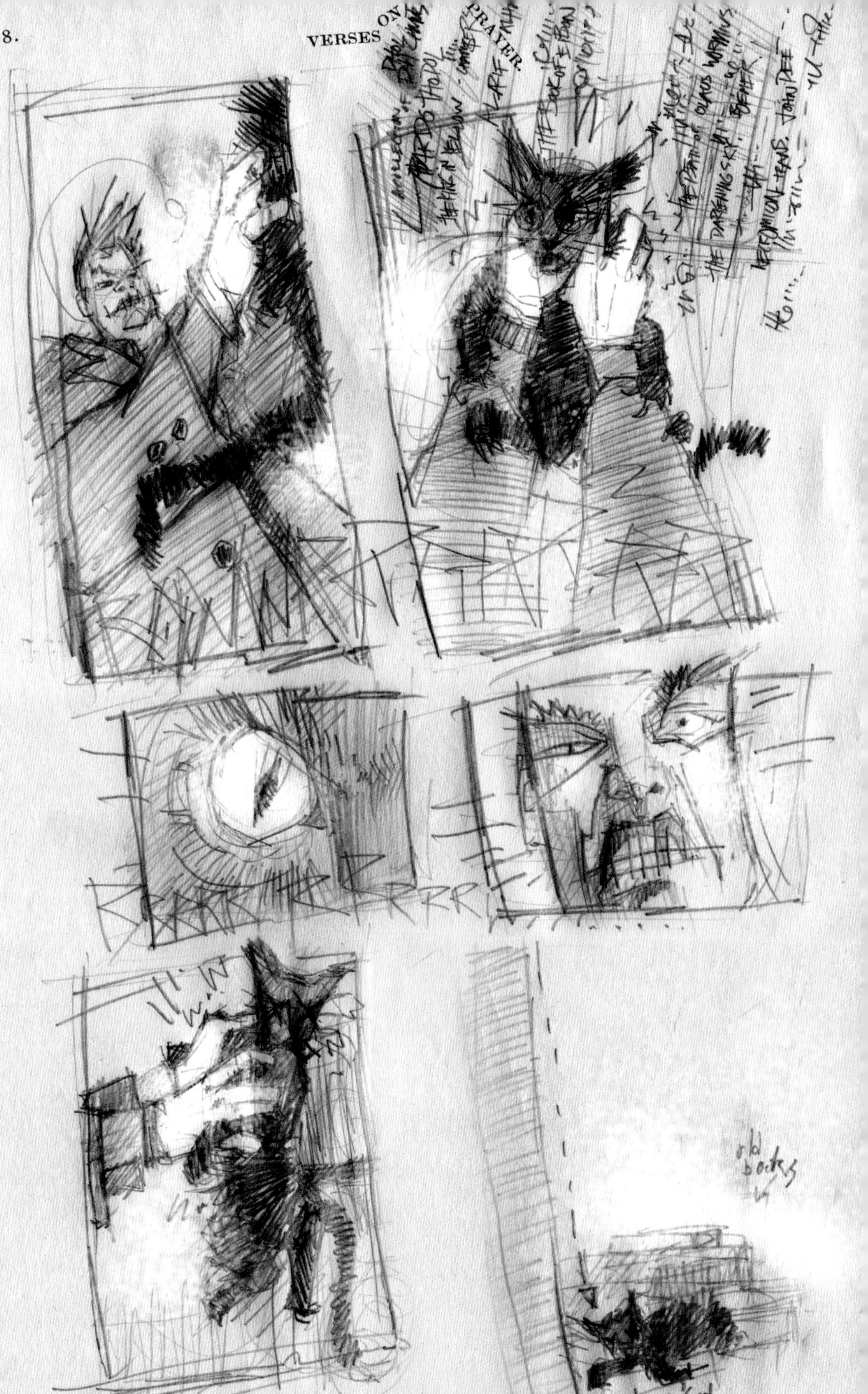
old books
dead cat

prayers are printed in larger type and always close with *Amen*; the verses are printed in smaller type and have no *Amen*.

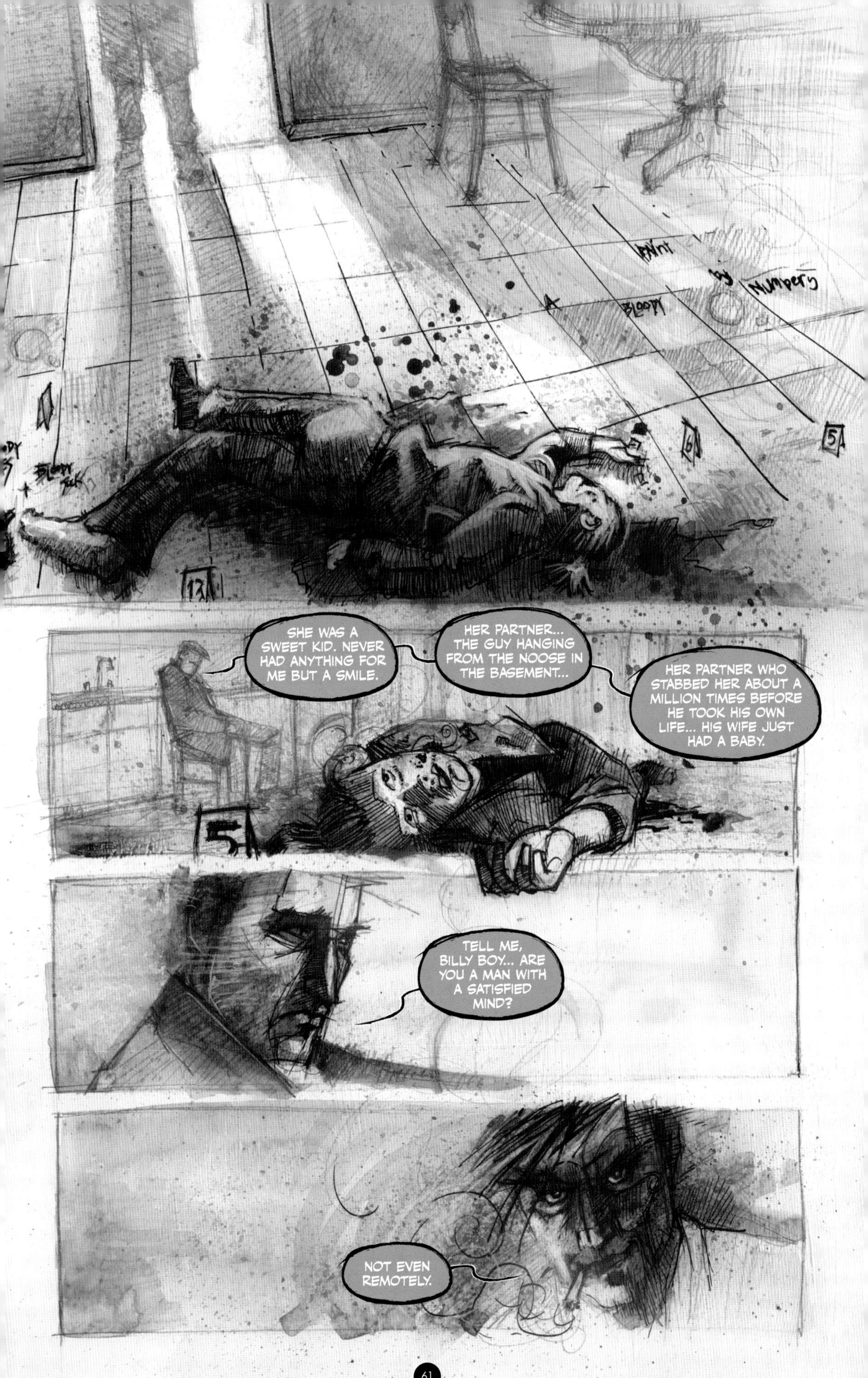
SHE WAS A SWEET KID. NEVER HAD ANYTHING FOR ME BUT A SMILE.
HER PARTNER... THE GUY HANGING FROM THE NOOSE IN THE BASEMENT...
HER PARTNER WHO STABBED HER ABOUT A MILLION TIMES BEFORE HE TOOK HIS OWN LIFE... HIS WIFE JUST HAD A BABY.
TELL ME, BILLY BOY... ARE YOU A MAN WITH A SATISFIED MIND?
NOT EVEN REMOTELY.

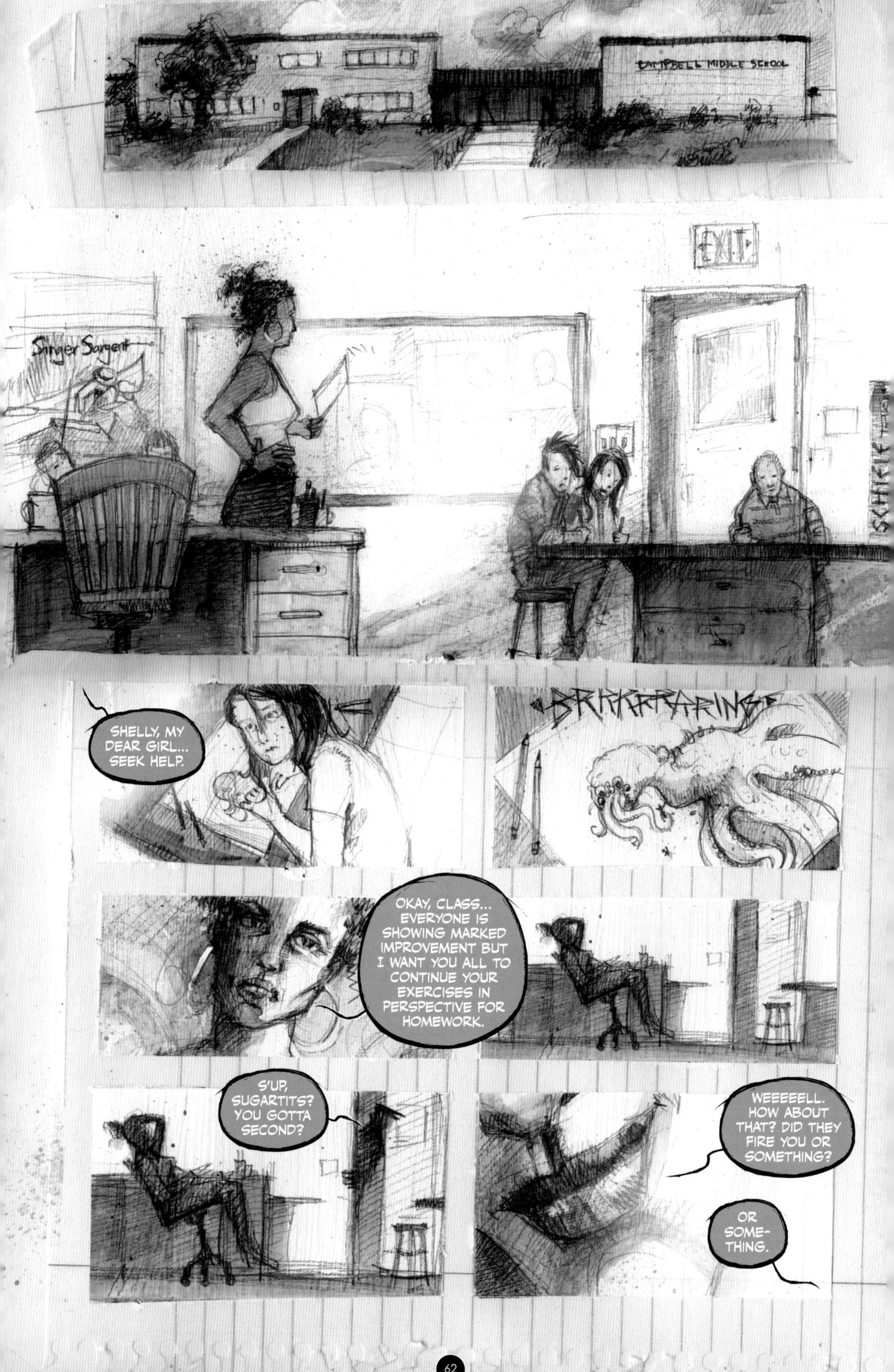
CAMPBELL MIDDLE SCHOOL
Singer Sargent
EXIT
SCHIELE
SHELLY, MY DEAR GIRL... SEEK HELP.
OKAY, CLASS... EVERYONE IS SHOWING MARKED IMPROVEMENT BUT I WANT YOU ALL TO CONTINUE YOUR EXERCISES IN PERSPECTIVE FOR HOMEWORK.
S'UP, SUGARTITS? YOU GOTTA SECOND?
WEEEEELL. HOW ABOUT THAT? DID THEY FIRE YOU OR SOMETHING?
OR SOME-THING.

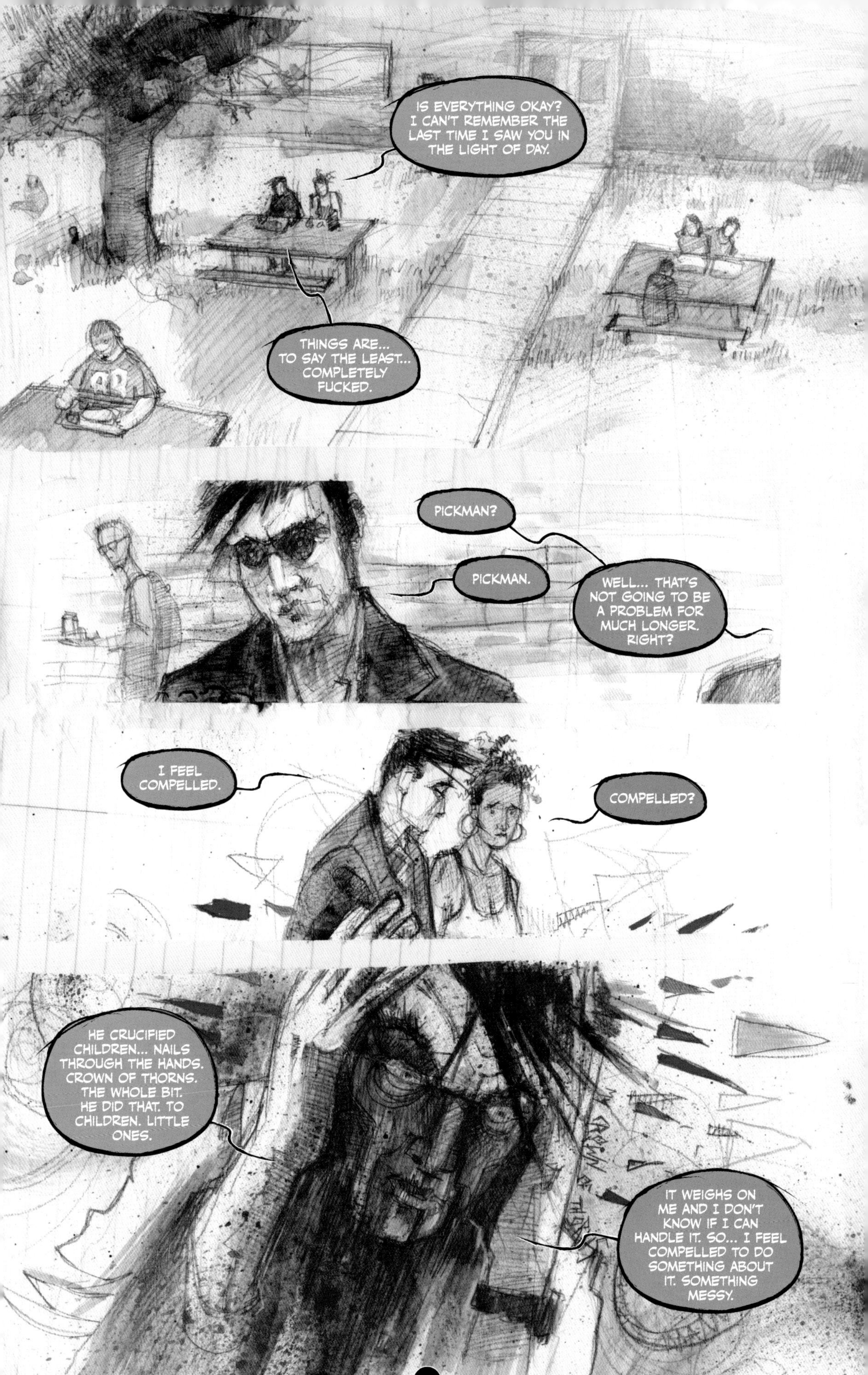
IS EVERYTHING OKAY? I CAN'T REMEMBER THE LAST TIME I SAW YOU IN THE LIGHT OF DAY.
THINGS ARE... TO SAY THE LEAST... COMPLETELY FUCKED.
PICKMAN?
PICKMAN.
WELL... THAT'S NOT GOING TO BE A PROBLEM FOR MUCH LONGER. RIGHT?
I FEEL COMPELLED.
COMPELLED?
HE CRUCIFIED CHILDREN... NAILS THROUGH THE HANDS. CROWN OF THORNS. THE WHOLE BIT. HE DID THAT. TO CHILDREN. LITTLE ONES.
IT WEIGHS ON ME AND I DON'T KNOW IF I CAN HANDLE IT. SO... I FEEL COMPELLED TO DO SOMETHING ABOUT IT. SOMETHING MESSY.

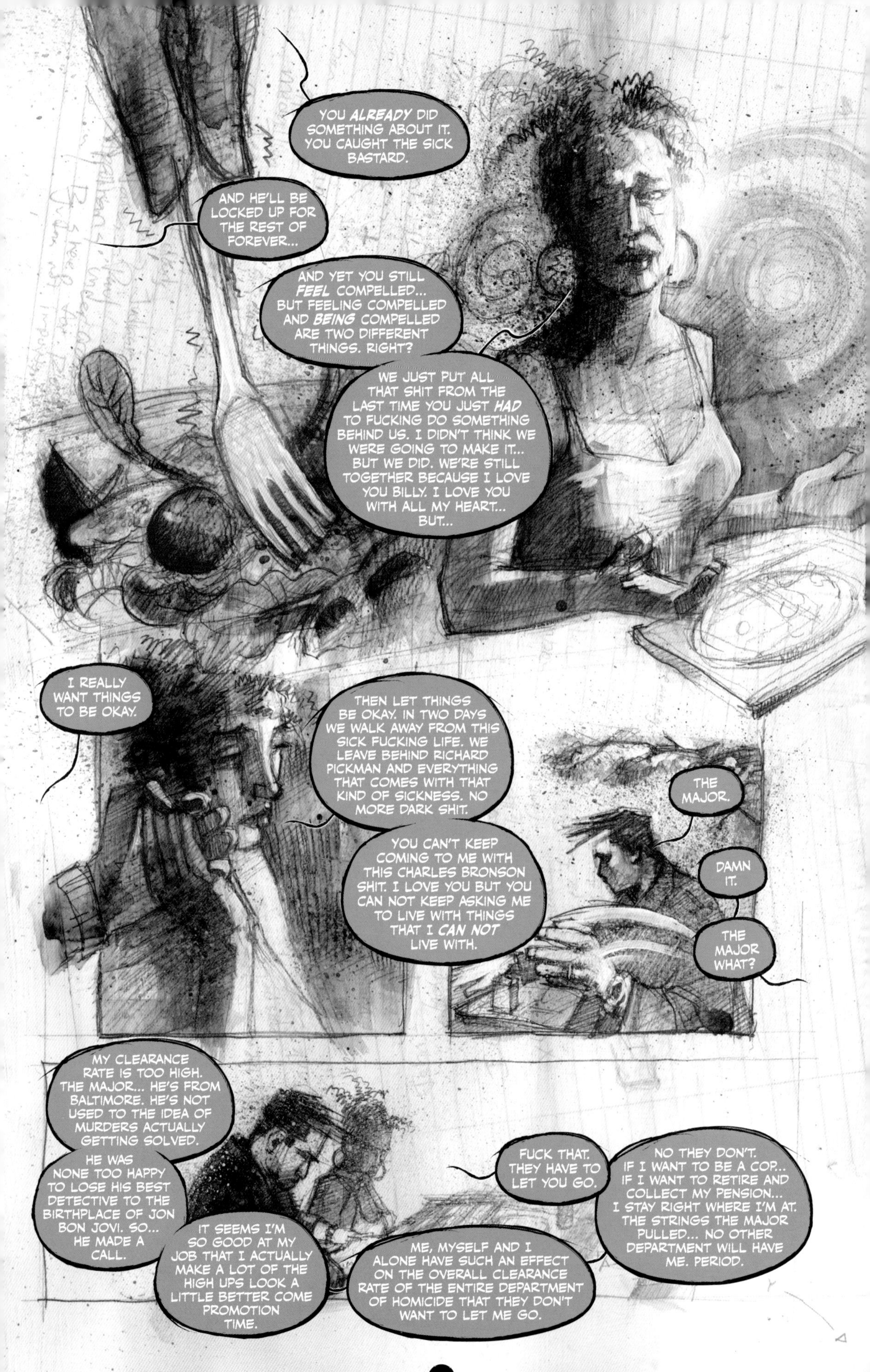
YOU ALREADY DID SOMETHING ABOUT IT. YOU CAUGHT THE SICK BASTARD.
AND HE'LL BE LOCKED UP FOR THE REST OF FOREVER...
AND YET YOU STILL FEEL COMPELLED... BUT FEELING COMPELLED AND BEING COMPELLED ARE TWO DIFFERENT THINGS. RIGHT?
WE JUST PUT ALL THAT SHIT FROM THE LAST TIME YOU JUST HAD TO FUCKING DO SOMETHING BEHIND US. I DIDN'T THINK WE WERE GOING TO MAKE IT... BUT WE DID. WE'RE STILL TOGETHER BECAUSE I LOVE YOU BILLY. I LOVE YOU WITH ALL MY HEART... BUT...
I REALLY WANT THINGS TO BE OKAY.
THEN LET THINGS BE OKAY. IN TWO DAYS WE WALK AWAY FROM THIS SICK FUCKING LIFE. WE LEAVE BEHIND RICHARD PICKMAN AND EVERYTHING THAT COMES WITH THAT KIND OF SICKNESS. NO MORE DARK SHIT.
YOU CAN'T KEEP COMING TO ME WITH THIS CHARLES BRONSON SHIT. I LOVE YOU BUT YOU CAN NOT KEEP ASKING ME TO LIVE WITH THINGS THAT I CAN NOT LIVE WITH.
THE MAJOR.
DAMN IT.
THE MAJOR WHAT?
MY CLEARANCE RATE IS TOO HIGH. THE MAJOR... HE'S FROM BALTIMORE. HE'S NOT USED TO THE IDEA OF MURDERS ACTUALLY GETTING SOLVED.
HE WAS NONE TOO HAPPY TO LOSE HIS BEST DETECTIVE TO THE BIRTHPLACE OF JON BON JOVI. SO... HE MADE A CALL.
IT SEEMS I'M SO GOOD AT MY JOB THAT I ACTUALLY MAKE A LOT OF THE HIGH UPS LOOK A LITTLE BETTER COME PROMOTION TIME.
ME, MYSELF AND I ALONE HAVE SUCH AN EFFECT ON THE OVERALL CLEARANCE RATE OF THE ENTIRE DEPARTMENT OF HOMICIDE THAT THEY DON'T WANT TO LET ME GO.
FUCK THAT. THEY HAVE TO LET YOU GO.
NO THEY DON'T. IF I WANT TO BE A COP... IF I WANT TO RETIRE AND COLLECT MY PENSION... I STAY RIGHT WHERE I'M AT. THE STRINGS THE MAJOR PULLED... NO OTHER DEPARTMENT WILL HAVE ME. PERIOD.

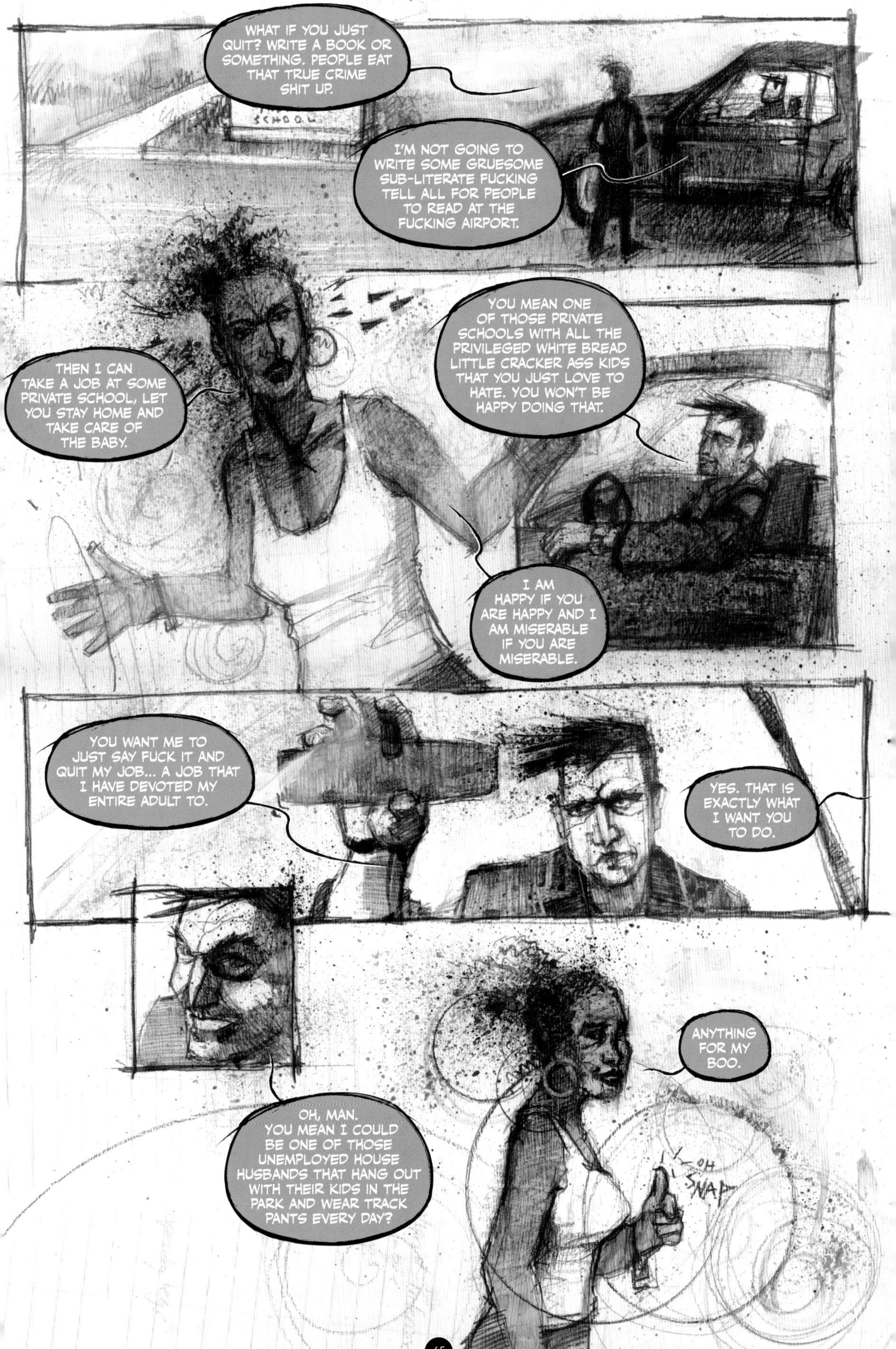
SCHOOL
WHAT IF YOU JUST QUIT? WRITE A BOOK OR SOMETHING. PEOPLE EAT THAT TRUE CRIME SHIT UP.
I'M NOT GOING TO WRITE SOME GRUESOME SUB-LITERATE FUCKING TELL ALL FOR PEOPLE TO READ AT THE FUCKING AIRPORT.
THEN I CAN TAKE A JOB AT SOME PRIVATE SCHOOL, LET YOU STAY HOME AND TAKE CARE OF THE BABY.
YOU MEAN ONE OF THOSE PRIVATE SCHOOLS WITH ALL THE PRIVILEGED WHITE BREAD LITTLE CRACKER ASS KIDS THAT YOU JUST LOVE TO HATE. YOU WON'T BE HAPPY DOING THAT.
I AM HAPPY IF YOU ARE HAPPY AND I AM MISERABLE IF YOU ARE MISERABLE.
YOU WANT ME TO JUST SAY FUCK IT AND QUIT MY JOB... A JOB THAT I HAVE DEVOTED MY ENTIRE ADULT TO.
YES. THAT IS EXACTLY WHAT I WANT YOU TO DO.
OH, MAN. YOU MEAN I COULD BE ONE OF THOSE UNEMPLOYED HOUSE HUSBANDS THAT HANG OUT WITH THEIR KIDS IN THE PARK AND WEAR TRACK PANTS EVERY DAY?
ANYTHING FOR MY BOO.
OH SNAP

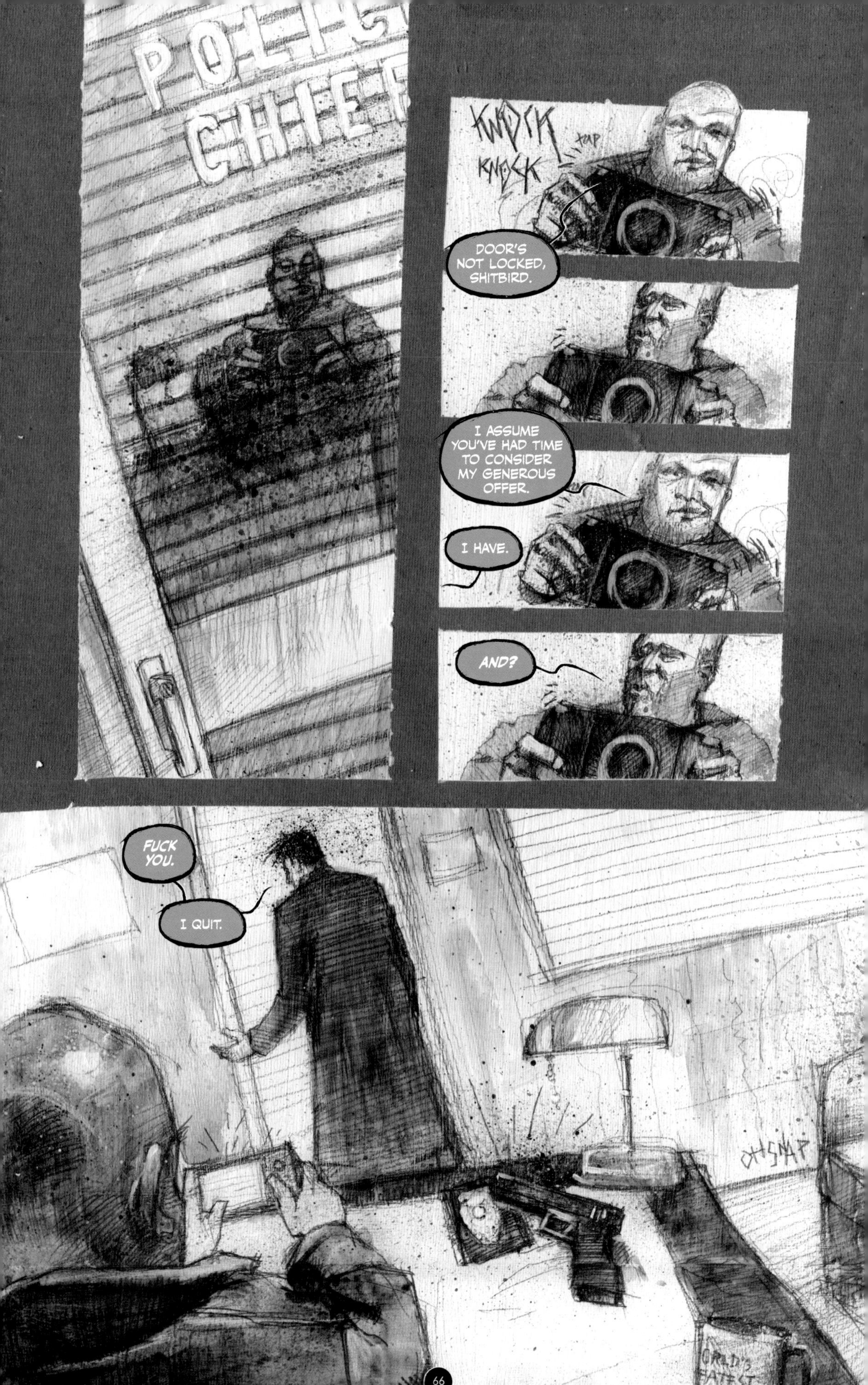
KNOCK
tap
KNOCK
DOOR'S NOT LOCKED, SHITBIRD.
I ASSUME YOU'VE HAD TIME TO CONSIDER MY GENEROUS OFFER.
I HAVE.
AND?
FUCK YOU.
I QUIT.

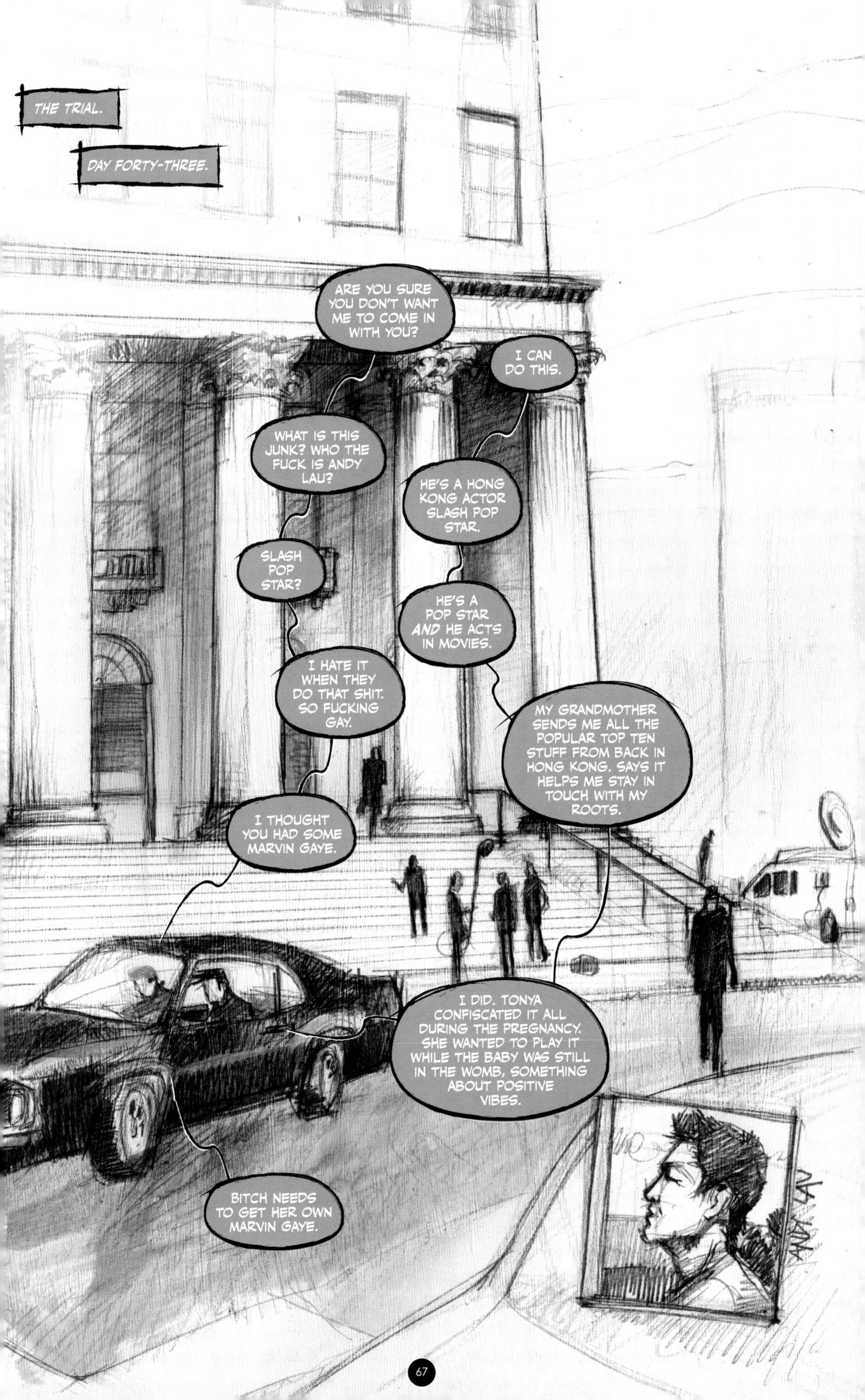
THE TRIAL.
DAY FORTY-THREE.
ARE YOU SURE YOU DON'T WANT ME TO COME IN WITH YOU?
I CAN DO THIS.
WHAT IS THIS JUNK? WHO THE FUCK IS ANDY LAU?
HE'S A HONG KONG ACTOR SLASH POP STAR.
SLASH POP STAR?
HE'S A POP STAR *AND* HE ACTS IN MOVIES.
I HATE IT WHEN THEY DO THAT SHIT. SO FUCKING GAY.
MY GRANDMOTHER SENDS ME ALL THE POPULAR TOP TEN STUFF FROM BACK IN HONG KONG. SAYS IT HELPS ME STAY IN TOUCH WITH MY ROOTS.
I THOUGHT YOU HAD SOME MARVIN GAYE.
I DID. TONYA CONFISCATED IT ALL DURING THE PREGNANCY. SHE WANTED TO PLAY IT WHILE THE BABY WAS STILL IN THE WOMB, SOMETHING ABOUT POSITIVE VIBES.
BITCH NEEDS TO GET HER OWN MARVIN GAYE.
ANDY LAU

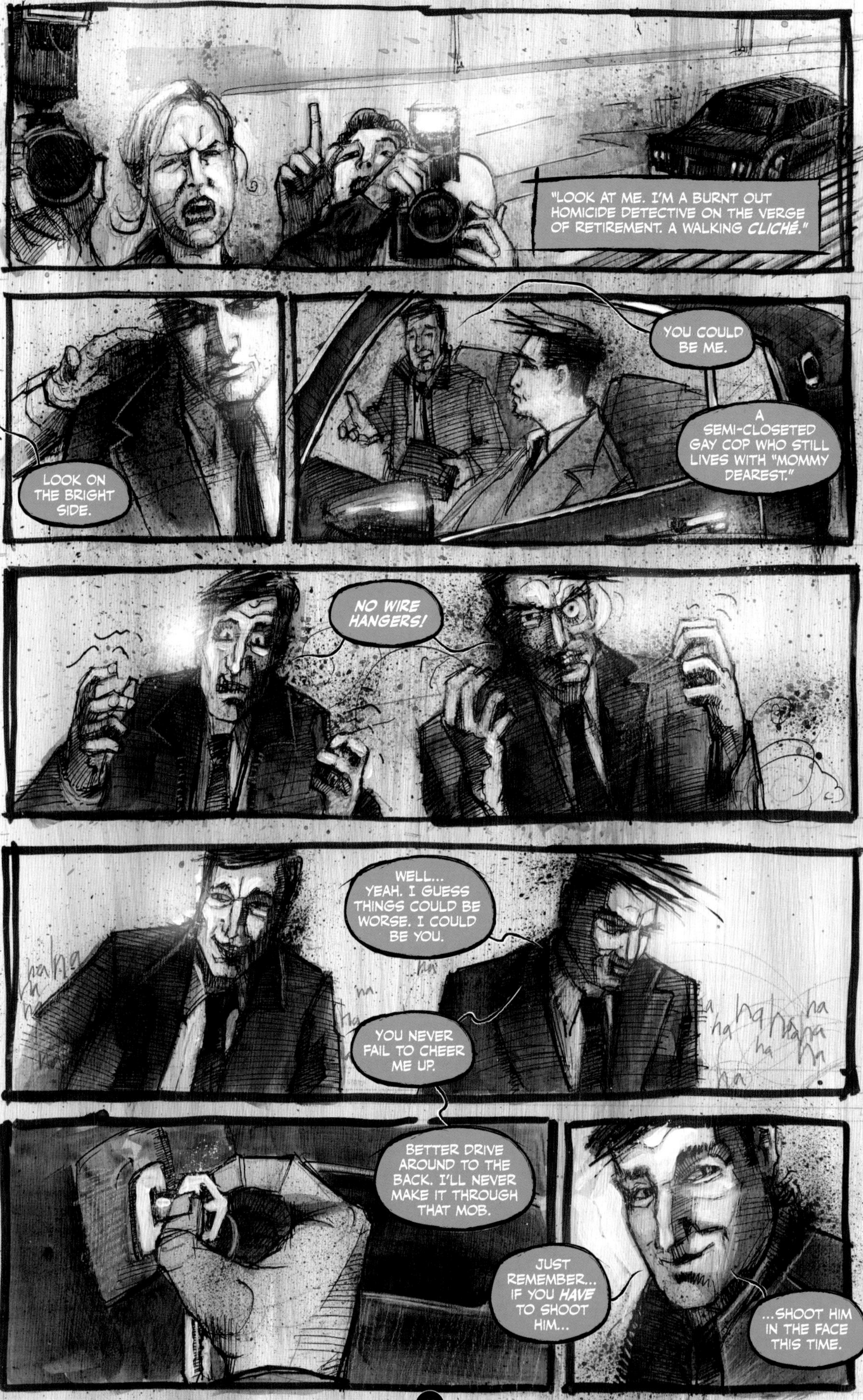
"LOOK AT ME. I'M A BURNT OUT HOMICIDE DETECTIVE ON THE VERGE OF RETIREMENT. A WALKING *CLICHÉ.*"
LOOK ON THE BRIGHT SIDE.
YOU COULD BE ME.
A SEMI-CLOSETED GAY COP WHO STILL LIVES WITH "MOMMY DEAREST."
NO WIRE HANGERS!
WELL... YEAH. I GUESS THINGS COULD BE WORSE. I COULD BE YOU.
YOU NEVER FAIL TO CHEER ME UP.
ha ha ha
ha ha ha ha ha ha ha
BETTER DRIVE AROUND TO THE BACK. I'LL NEVER MAKE IT THROUGH THAT MOB.
JUST REMEMBER... IF YOU *HAVE* TO SHOOT HIM...
...SHOOT HIM IN THE FACE THIS TIME.

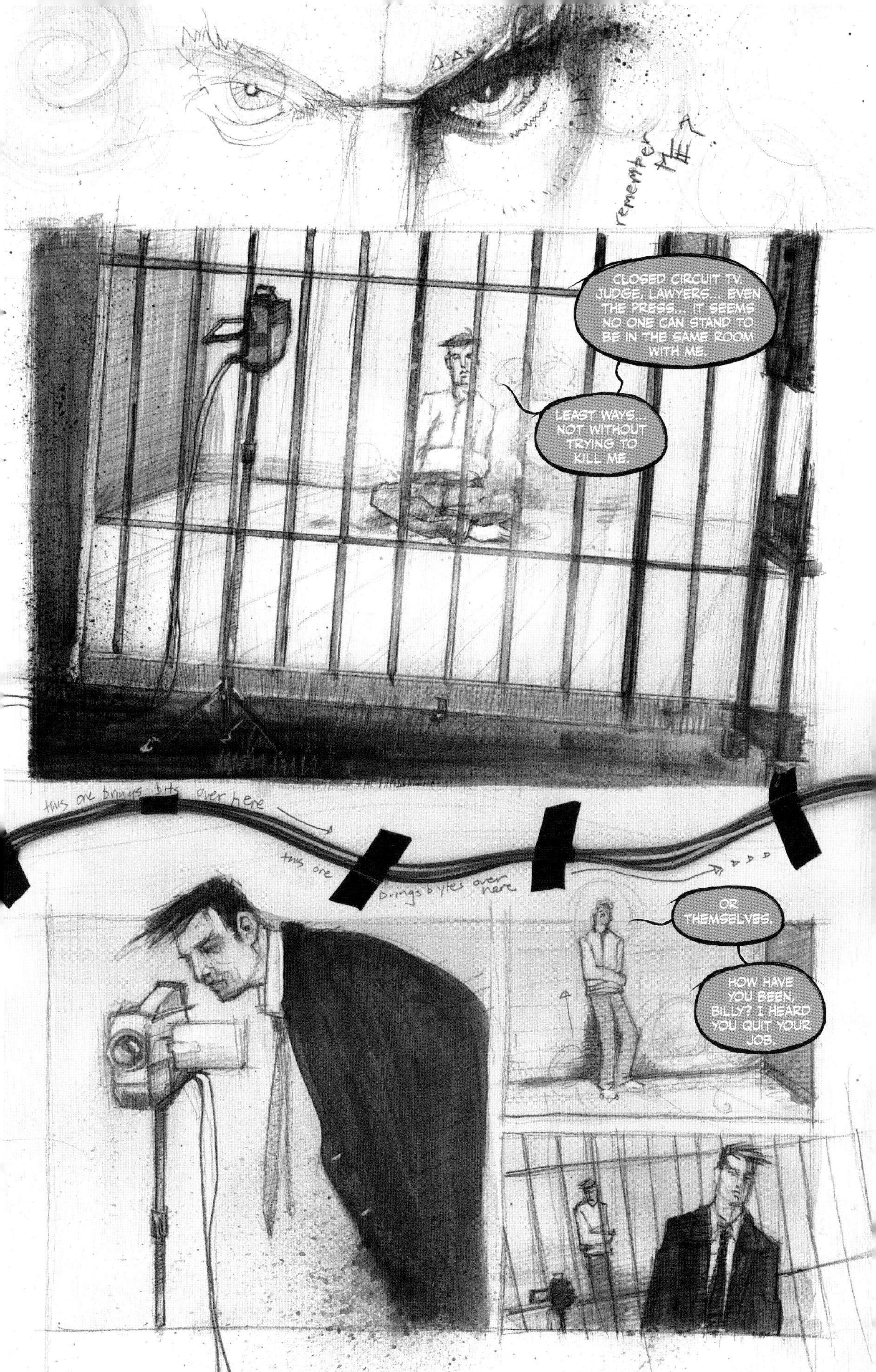
remember ME?
CLOSED CIRCUIT TV. JUDGE, LAWYERS... EVEN THE PRESS... IT SEEMS NO ONE CAN STAND TO BE IN THE SAME ROOM WITH ME.
LEAST WAYS... NOT WITHOUT TRYING TO KILL ME.
this one brings bits over here
this one brings bytes over here
OR THEMSELVES.
HOW HAVE YOU BEEN, BILLY? I HEARD YOU QUIT YOUR JOB.

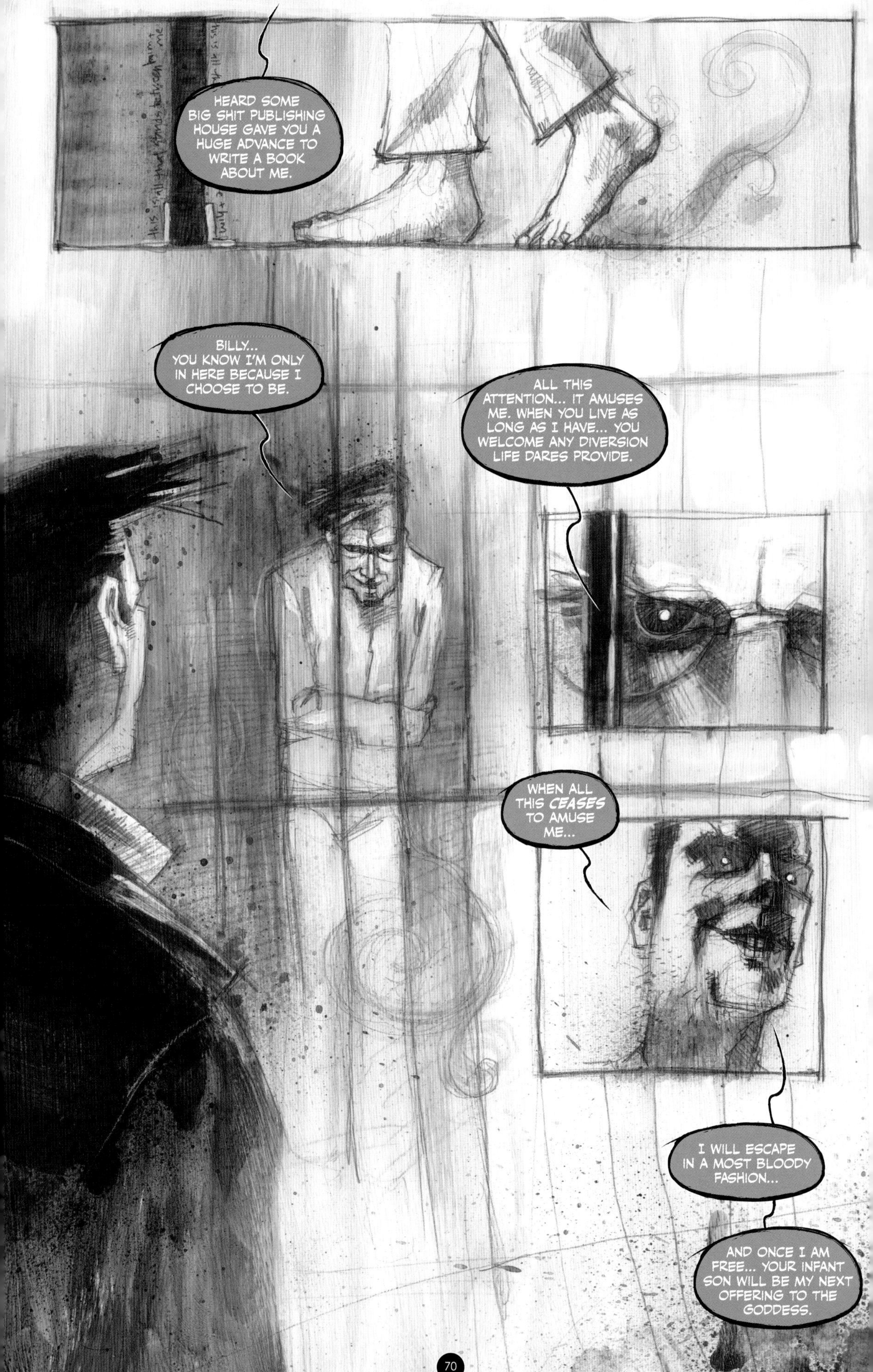
this is all that stands between him + me
HEARD SOME BIG SHIT PUBLISHING HOUSE GAVE YOU A HUGE ADVANCE TO WRITE A BOOK ABOUT ME.
BILLY... YOU KNOW I'M ONLY IN HERE BECAUSE I CHOOSE TO BE.
ALL THIS ATTENTION... IT AMUSES ME. WHEN YOU LIVE AS LONG AS I HAVE... YOU WELCOME ANY DIVERSION LIFE DARES PROVIDE.
WHEN ALL THIS *CEASES* TO AMUSE ME...
I WILL ESCAPE IN A MOST BLOODY FASHION...
AND ONCE I AM FREE... YOUR INFANT SON WILL BE MY NEXT OFFERING TO THE GODDESS.

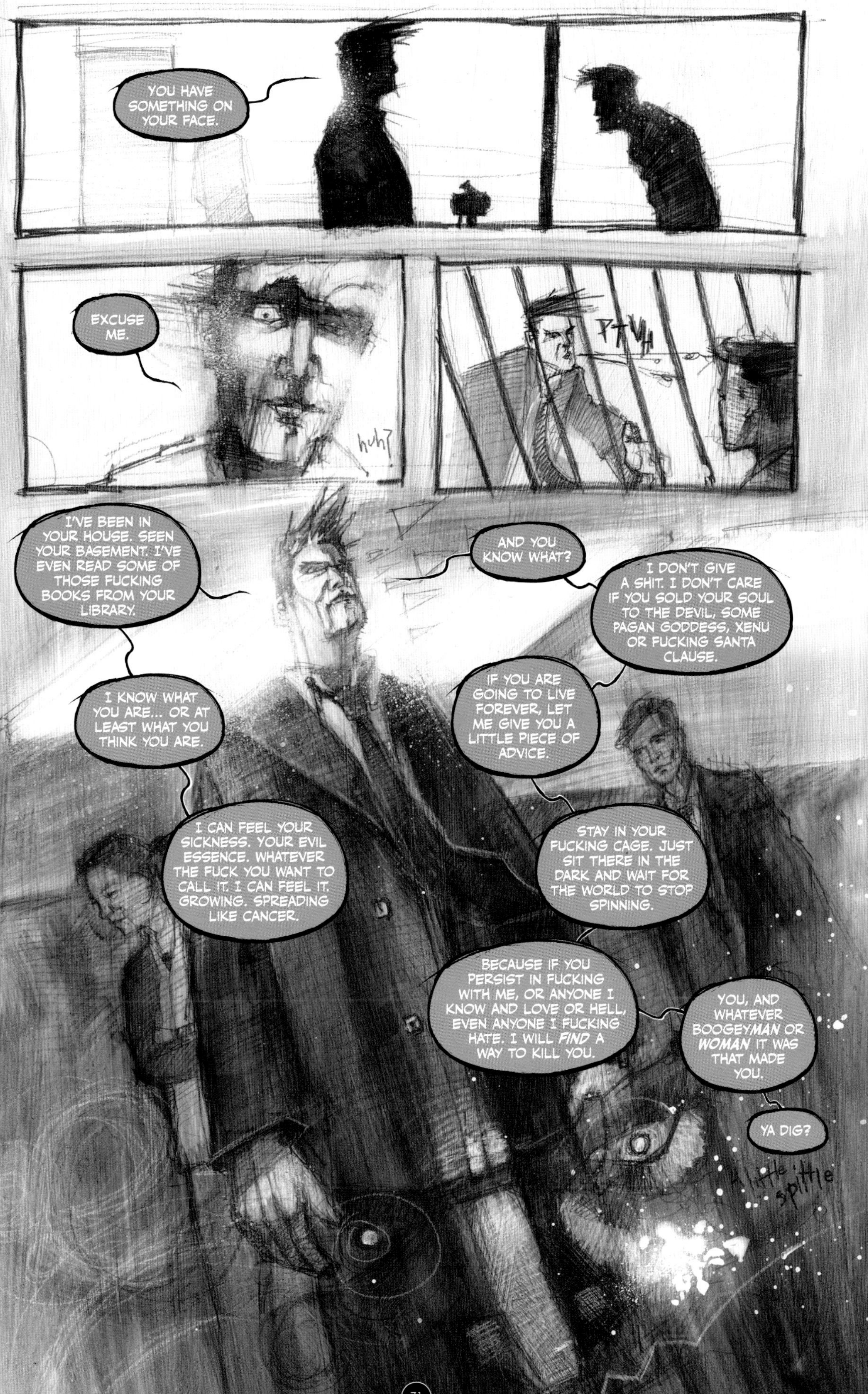
YOU HAVE SOMETHING ON YOUR FACE.
EXCUSE ME.
huh?
PTVUH
I'VE BEEN IN YOUR HOUSE. SEEN YOUR BASEMENT. I'VE EVEN READ SOME OF THOSE FUCKING BOOKS FROM YOUR LIBRARY.
I KNOW WHAT YOU ARE... OR AT LEAST WHAT YOU THINK YOU ARE.
I CAN FEEL YOUR SICKNESS. YOUR EVIL ESSENCE. WHATEVER THE FUCK YOU WANT TO CALL IT. I CAN FEEL IT. GROWING. SPREADING LIKE CANCER.
AND YOU KNOW WHAT?
I DON'T GIVE A SHIT. I DON'T CARE IF YOU SOLD YOUR SOUL TO THE DEVIL, SOME PAGAN GODDESS, XENU OR FUCKING SANTA CLAUSE.
IF YOU ARE GOING TO LIVE FOREVER, LET ME GIVE YOU A LITTLE PIECE OF ADVICE.
STAY IN YOUR FUCKING CAGE. JUST SIT THERE IN THE DARK AND WAIT FOR THE WORLD TO STOP SPINNING.
BECAUSE IF YOU PERSIST IN FUCKING WITH ME, OR ANYONE I KNOW AND LOVE OR HELL, EVEN ANYONE I FUCKING HATE. I WILL *FIND* A WAY TO KILL YOU.
YOU, AND WHATEVER BOOGEY*MAN* OR *WOMAN* IT WAS THAT MADE YOU.
YA DIG?
a little spittle

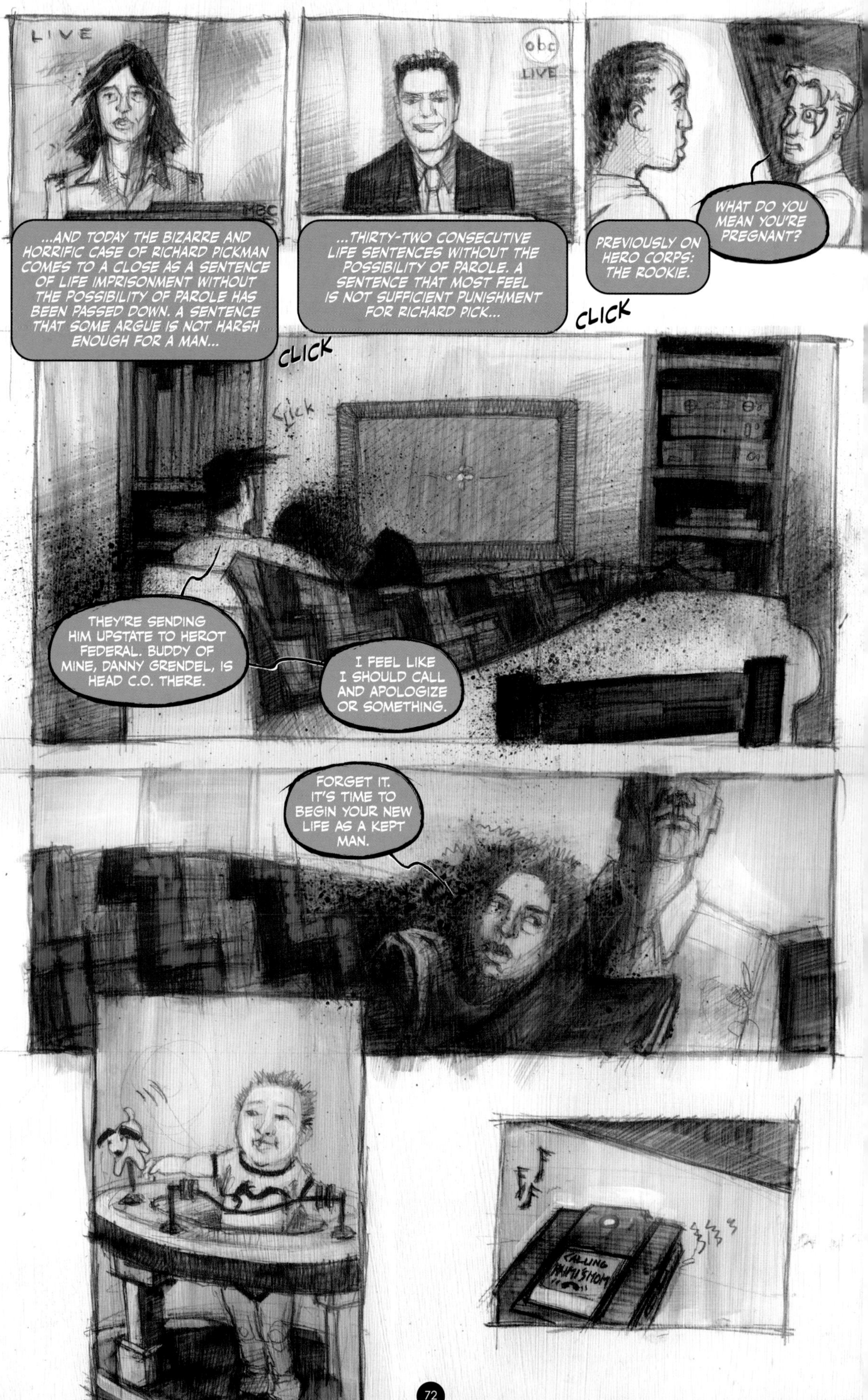
LIVE
...AND TODAY THE BIZARRE AND HORRIFIC CASE OF RICHARD PICKMAN COMES TO A CLOSE AS A SENTENCE OF LIFE IMPRISONMENT WITHOUT THE POSSIBILITY OF PAROLE HAS BEEN PASSED DOWN. A SENTENCE THAT SOME ARGUE IS NOT HARSH ENOUGH FOR A MAN...
CLICK
LIVE
...THIRTY-TWO CONSECUTIVE LIFE SENTENCES WITHOUT THE POSSIBILITY OF PAROLE. A SENTENCE THAT MOST FEEL IS NOT SUFFICIENT PUNISHMENT FOR RICHARD PICK...
CLICK
PREVIOUSLY ON HERO CORPS: THE ROOKIE.
WHAT DO YOU MEAN YOU'RE PREGNANT?
THEY'RE SENDING HIM UPSTATE TO HEROT FEDERAL. BUDDY OF MINE, DANNY GRENDEL, IS HEAD C.O. THERE.
I FEEL LIKE I SHOULD CALL AND APOLOGIZE OR SOMETHING.
FORGET IT. IT'S TIME TO BEGIN YOUR NEW LIFE AS A KEPT MAN.

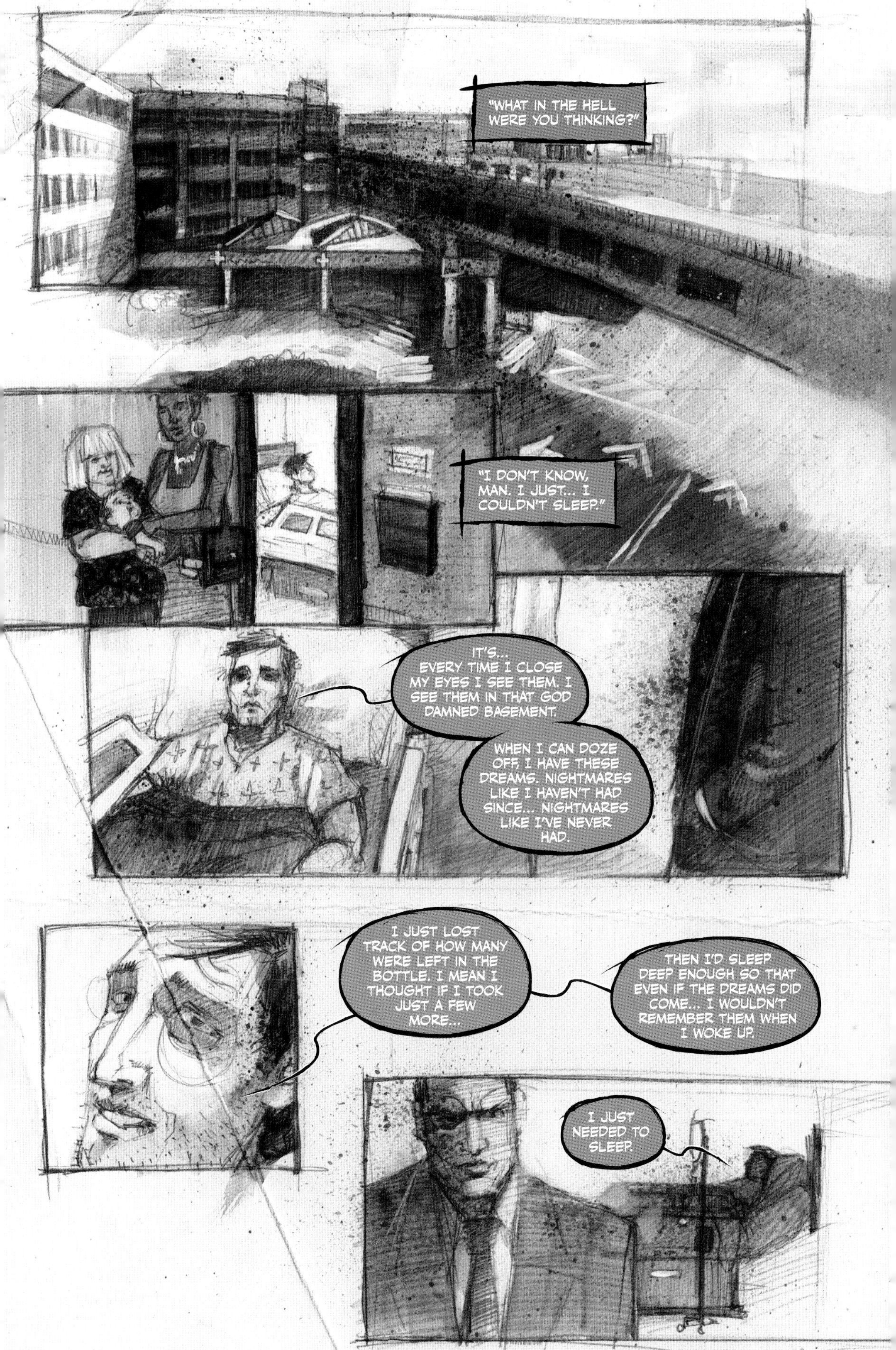
"WHAT IN THE HELL WERE YOU THINKING?"
"I DON'T KNOW, MAN. I JUST... I COULDN'T SLEEP."
IT'S... EVERY TIME I CLOSE MY EYES I SEE THEM. I SEE THEM IN THAT GOD DAMNED BASEMENT.
WHEN I CAN DOZE OFF, I HAVE THESE DREAMS. NIGHTMARES LIKE I HAVEN'T HAD SINCE... NIGHTMARES LIKE I'VE NEVER HAD.
I JUST LOST TRACK OF HOW MANY WERE LEFT IN THE BOTTLE. I MEAN I THOUGHT IF I TOOK JUST A FEW MORE...
THEN I'D SLEEP DEEP ENOUGH SO THAT EVEN IF THE DREAMS DID COME... I WOULDN'T REMEMBER THEM WHEN I WOKE UP.
I JUST NEEDED TO SLEEP.

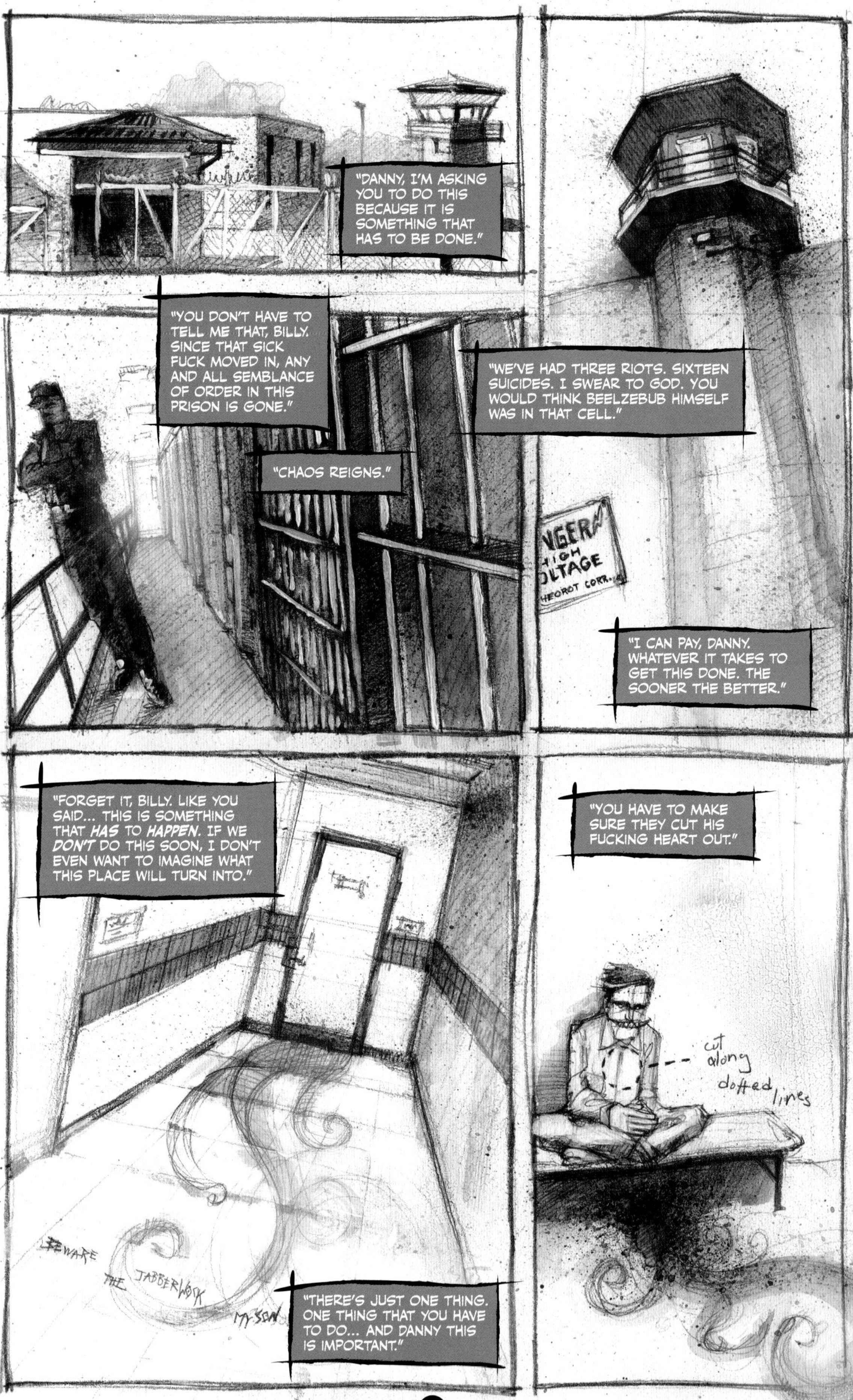
"DANNY, I'M ASKING YOU TO DO THIS BECAUSE IT IS SOMETHING THAT HAS TO BE DONE."
"WE'VE HAD THREE RIOTS. SIXTEEN SUICIDES. I SWEAR TO GOD. YOU WOULD THINK BEELZEBUB HIMSELF WAS IN THAT CELL."
"YOU DON'T HAVE TO TELL ME THAT, BILLY. SINCE THAT SICK FUCK MOVED IN, ANY AND ALL SEMBLANCE OF ORDER IN THIS PRISON IS GONE."
"CHAOS REIGNS."
HIGH
HEOROT CORR.
"I CAN PAY, DANNY. WHATEVER IT TAKES TO GET THIS DONE. THE SOONER THE BETTER."
"FORGET IT, BILLY. LIKE YOU SAID... THIS IS SOMETHING THAT ***HAS*** TO ***HAPPEN***. IF WE ***DON'T*** DO THIS SOON, I DON'T EVEN WANT TO IMAGINE WHAT THIS PLACE WILL TURN INTO."
BEWARE THE JABBERWOCK MY SON
"THERE'S JUST ONE THING. ONE THING THAT YOU HAVE TO DO... AND DANNY THIS IS IMPORTANT."
"YOU HAVE TO MAKE SURE THEY CUT HIS FUCKING HEART OUT."
cut along dotted lines

ATONYA

JONAFA

chapter four

HARM AND HATRED

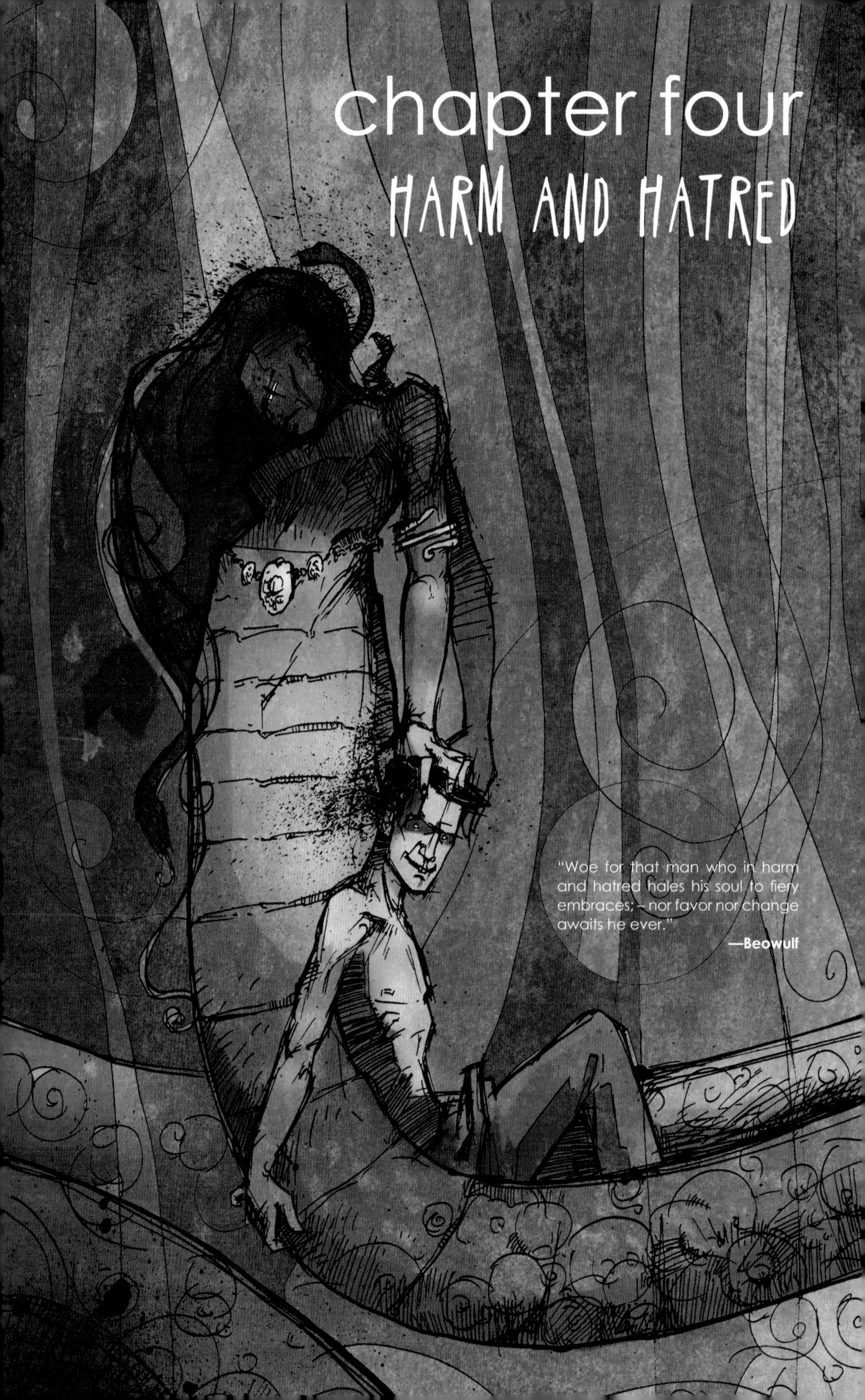

"Woe for that man who in harm and hatred hales his soul to fiery embraces; – nor favor nor change awaits he ever."

—**Beowulf**

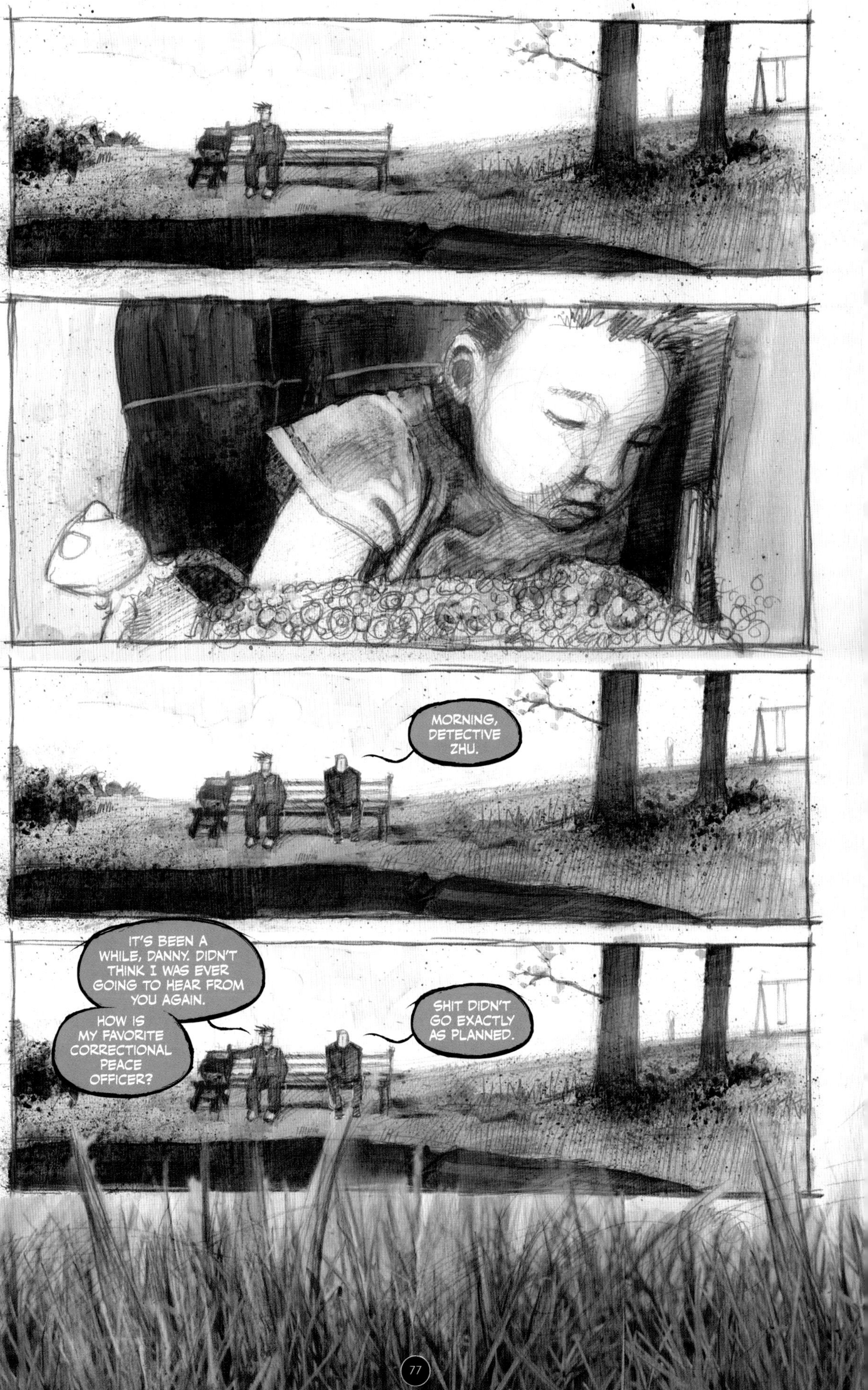
MORNING, DETECTIVE ZHU.
IT'S BEEN A WHILE, DANNY. DIDN'T THINK I WAS EVER GOING TO HEAR FROM YOU AGAIN.
HOW IS MY FAVORITE CORRECTIONAL PEACE OFFICER?
SHIT DIDN'T GO EXACTLY AS PLANNED.

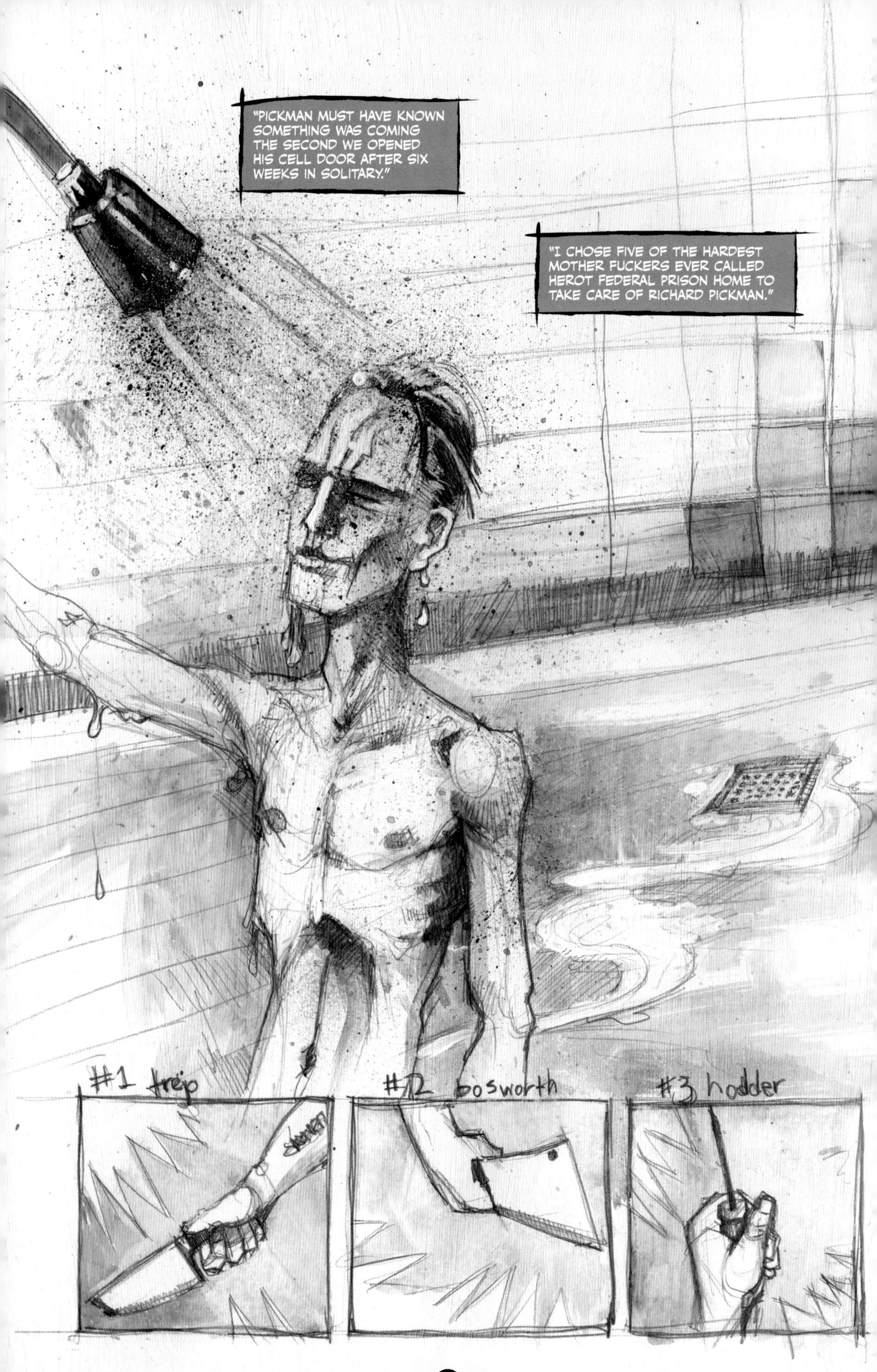
"PICKMAN MUST HAVE KNOWN SOMETHING WAS COMING THE SECOND WE OPENED HIS CELL DOOR AFTER SIX WEEKS IN SOLITARY."
"I CHOSE FIVE OF THE HARDEST MOTHER FUCKERS EVER CALLED HEROT FEDERAL PRISON HOME TO TAKE CARE OF RICHARD PICKMAN."
#1 trejo
#2 bosworth
#3 hodder

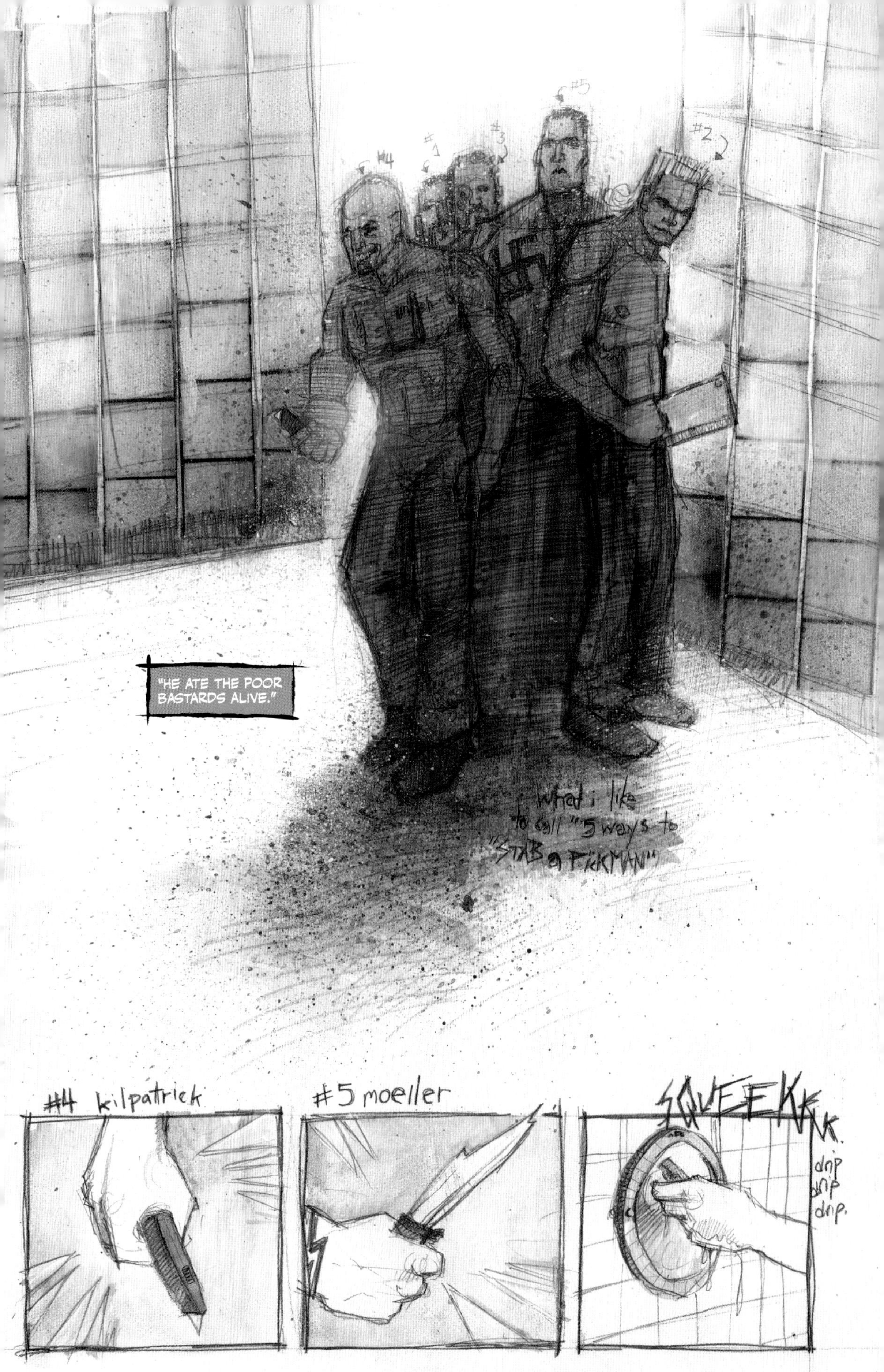
#4
#1
#3
#5
#2
"HE ATE THE POOR BASTARDS ALIVE."
what i like to call "5 ways to "STAB a PICKMAN""
#4 kilpatrick
#5 moeller
SQUEEKK.
drip
drip
drip.

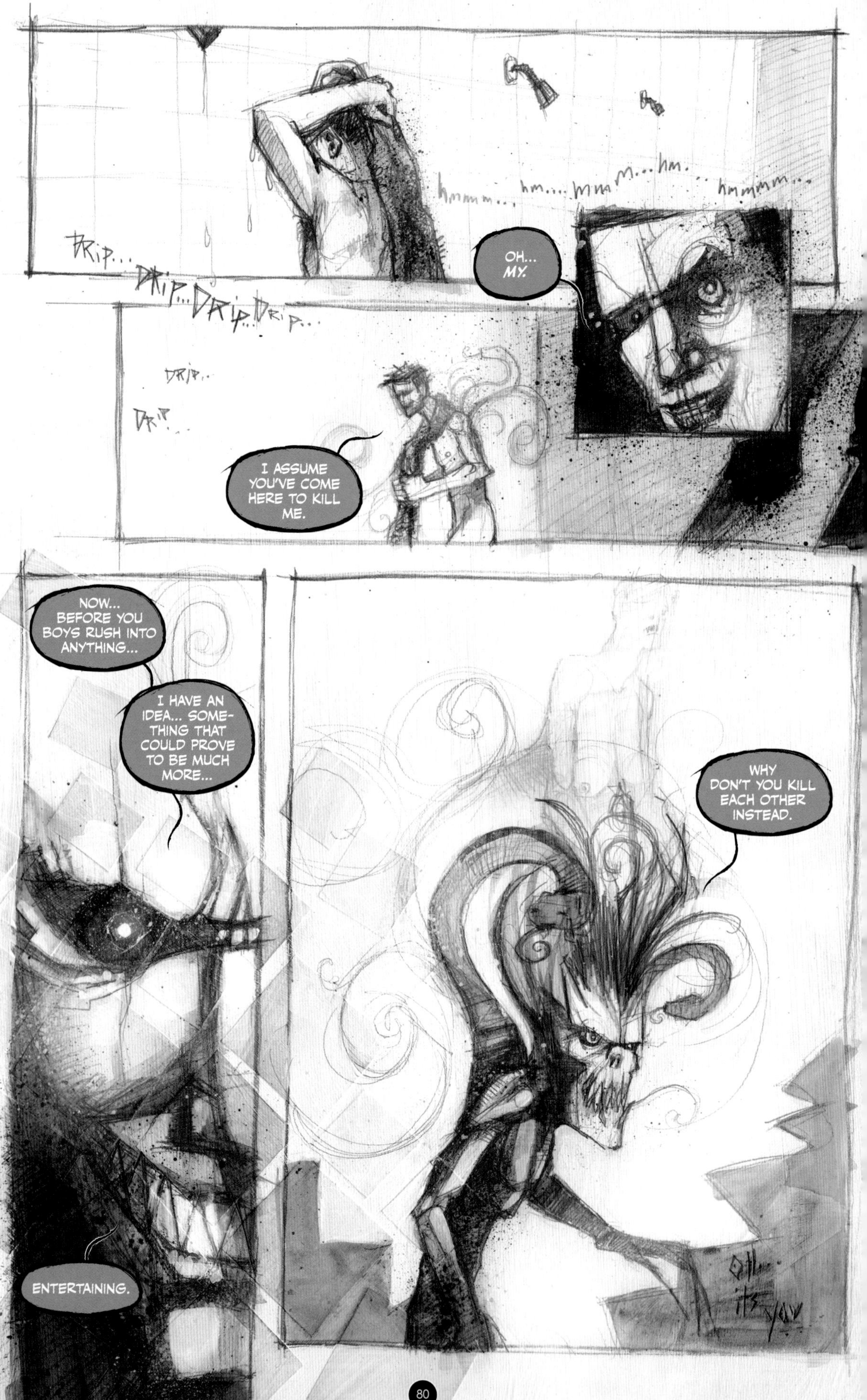
DRIP... DRIP... DRIP... DRIP...
OH... MY.
DRIP...
DRIP...
I ASSUME YOU'VE COME HERE TO KILL ME.
NOW... BEFORE YOU BOYS RUSH INTO ANYTHING...
I HAVE AN IDEA... SOMETHING THAT COULD PROVE TO BE MUCH MORE...
ENTERTAINING.
WHY DON'T YOU KILL EACH OTHER INSTEAD.

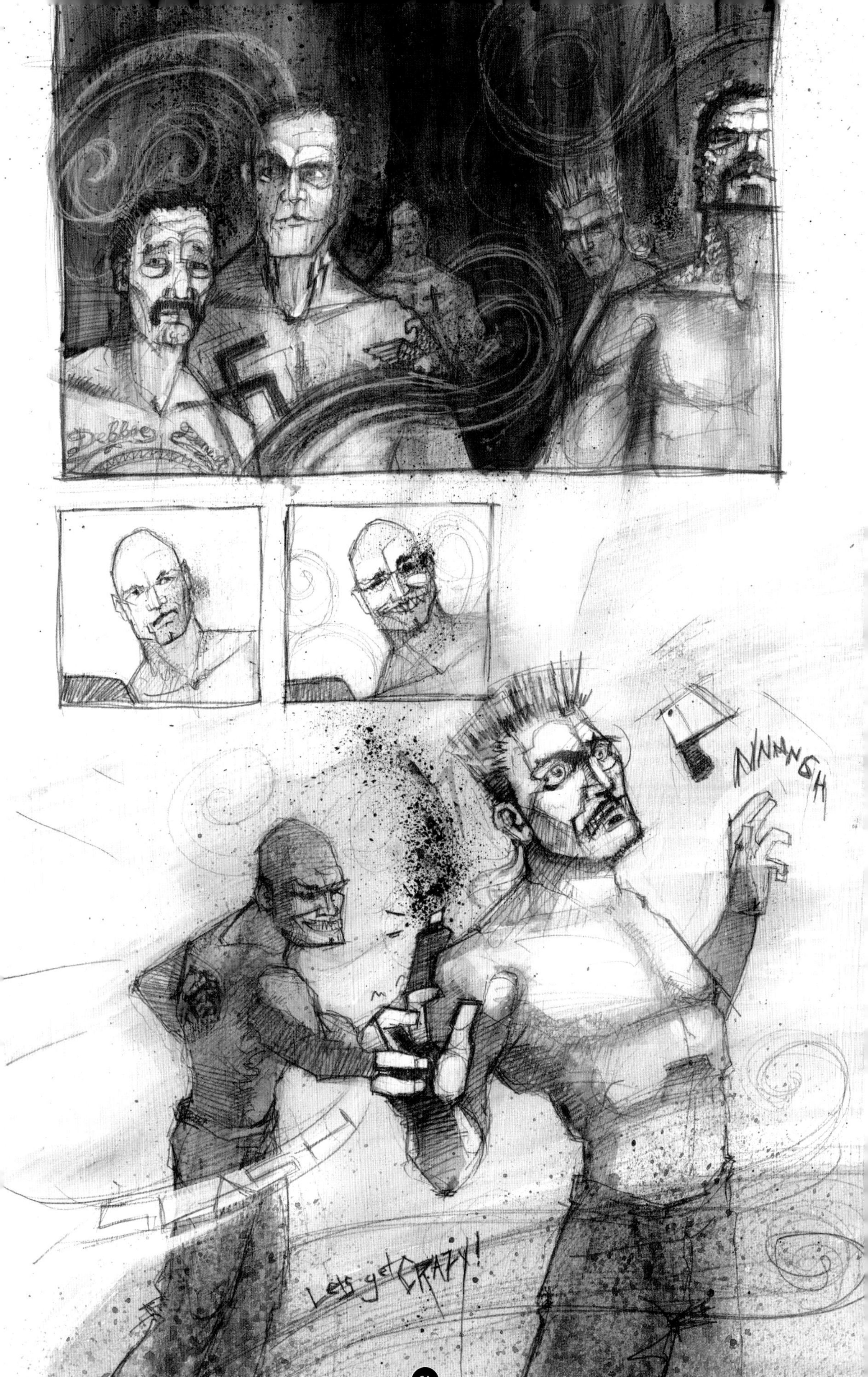
Debbie
NNNNNGH
Lets get CRAZY!

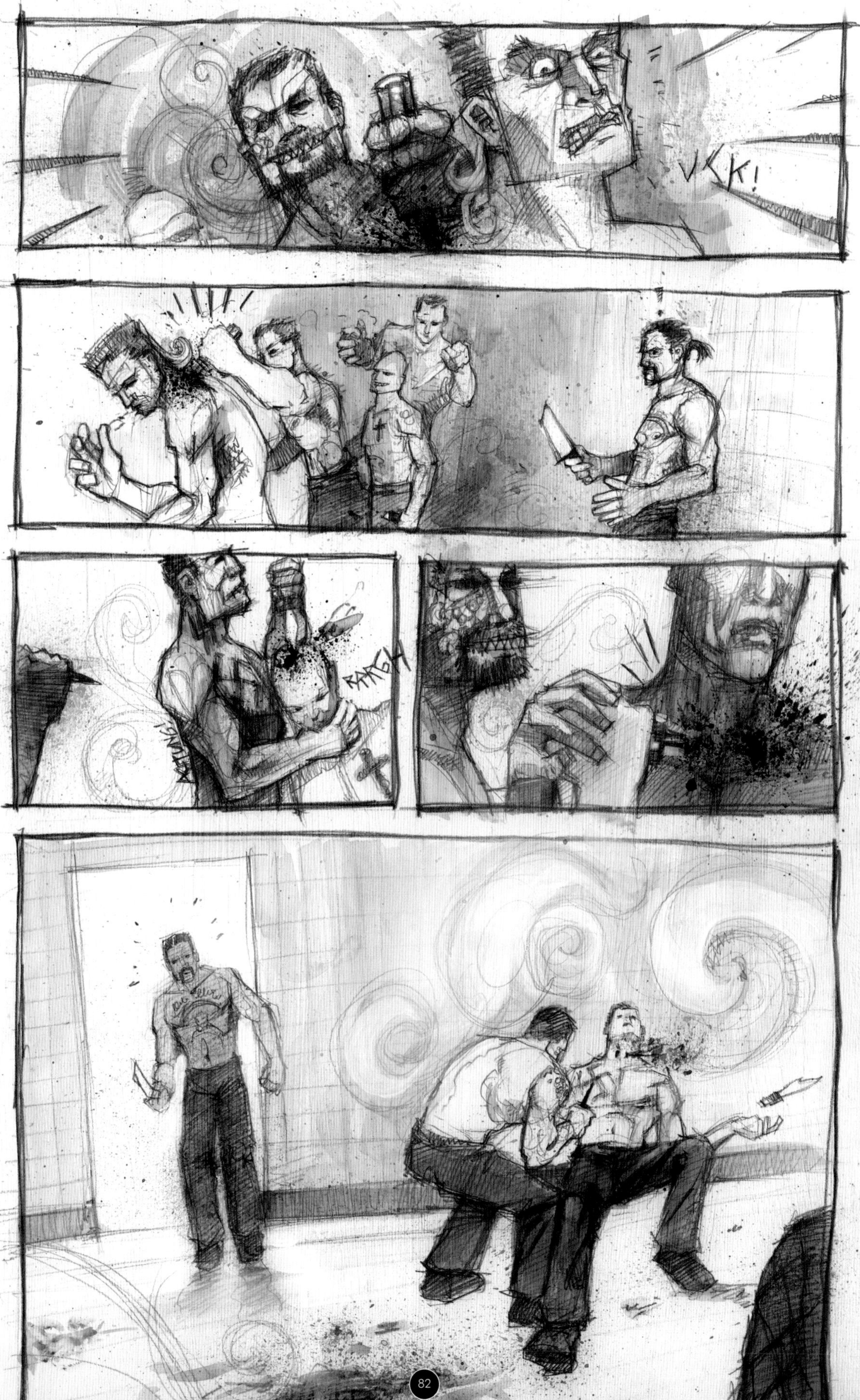
UCK!
RARGH

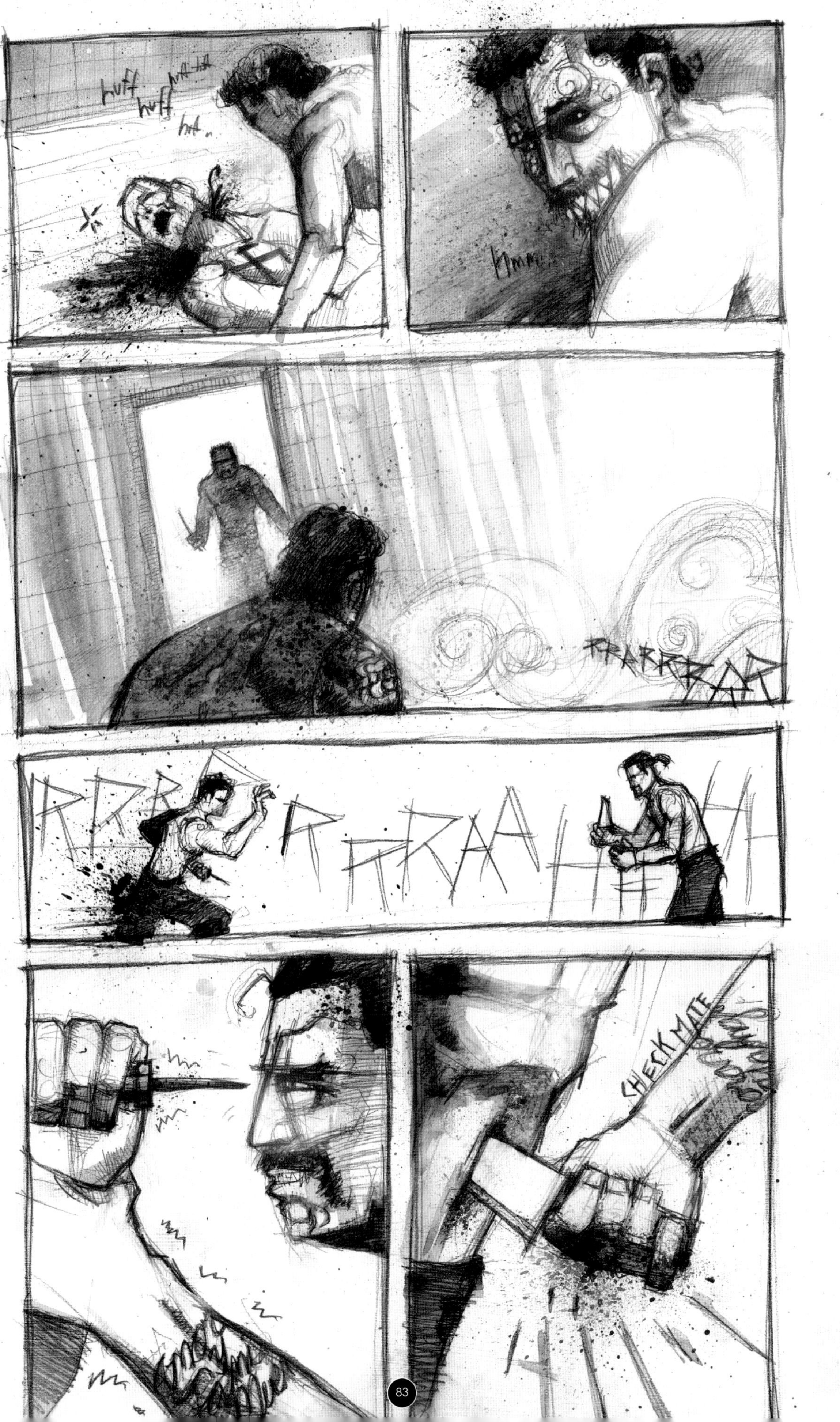
huff
huff
Hmm...
CHECKMATE

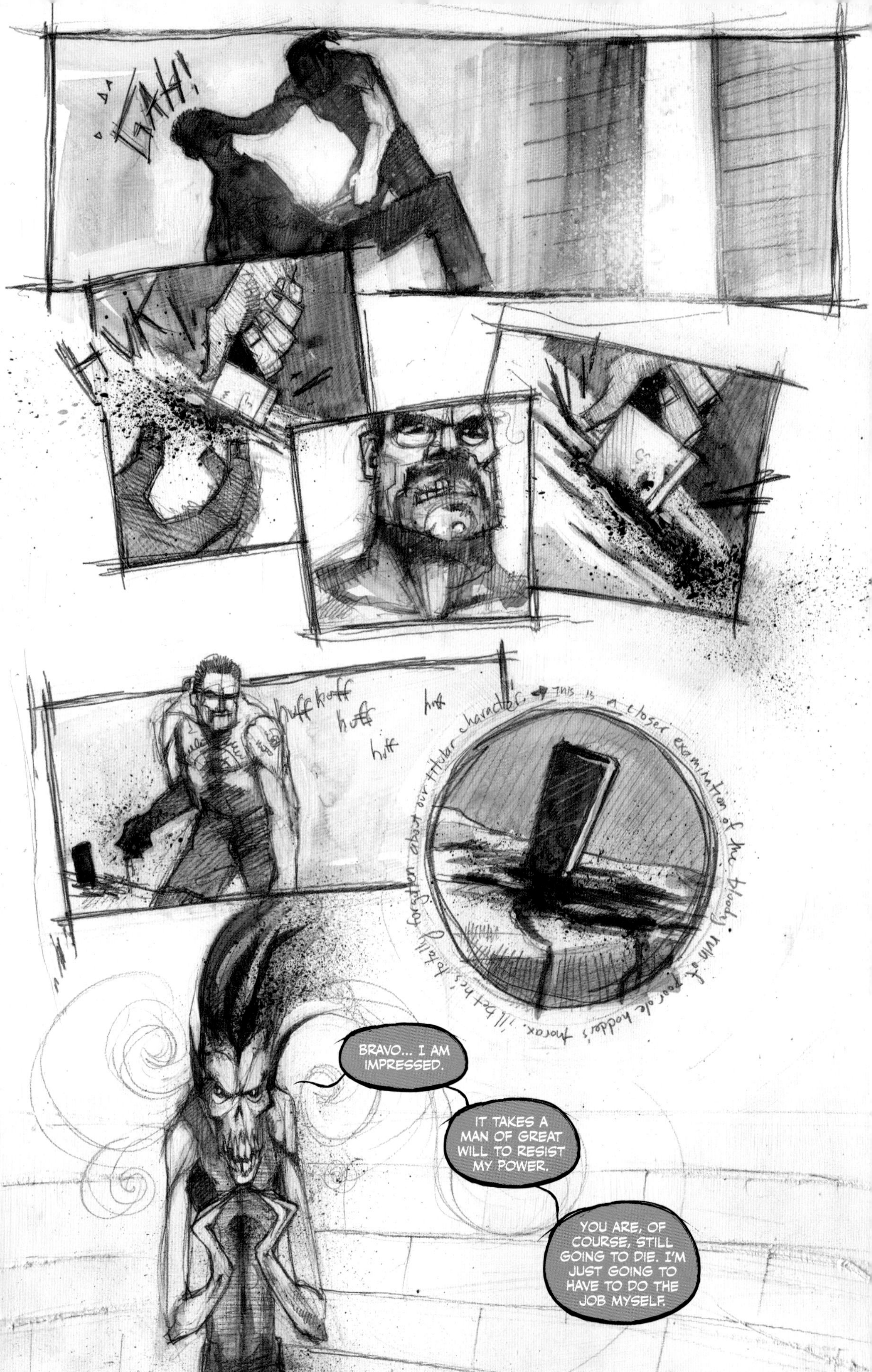
GAH!
HUK!
huff huff
huff
huff
huff
This is a closer examination of the bloody ruin of poor ole hodder's thorax. i'll bet he's totally forgotten about our titular character.
BRAVO... I AM IMPRESSED.
IT TAKES A MAN OF GREAT WILL TO RESIST MY POWER.
YOU ARE, OF COURSE, STILL GOING TO DIE. I'M JUST GOING TO HAVE TO DO THE JOB MYSELF.

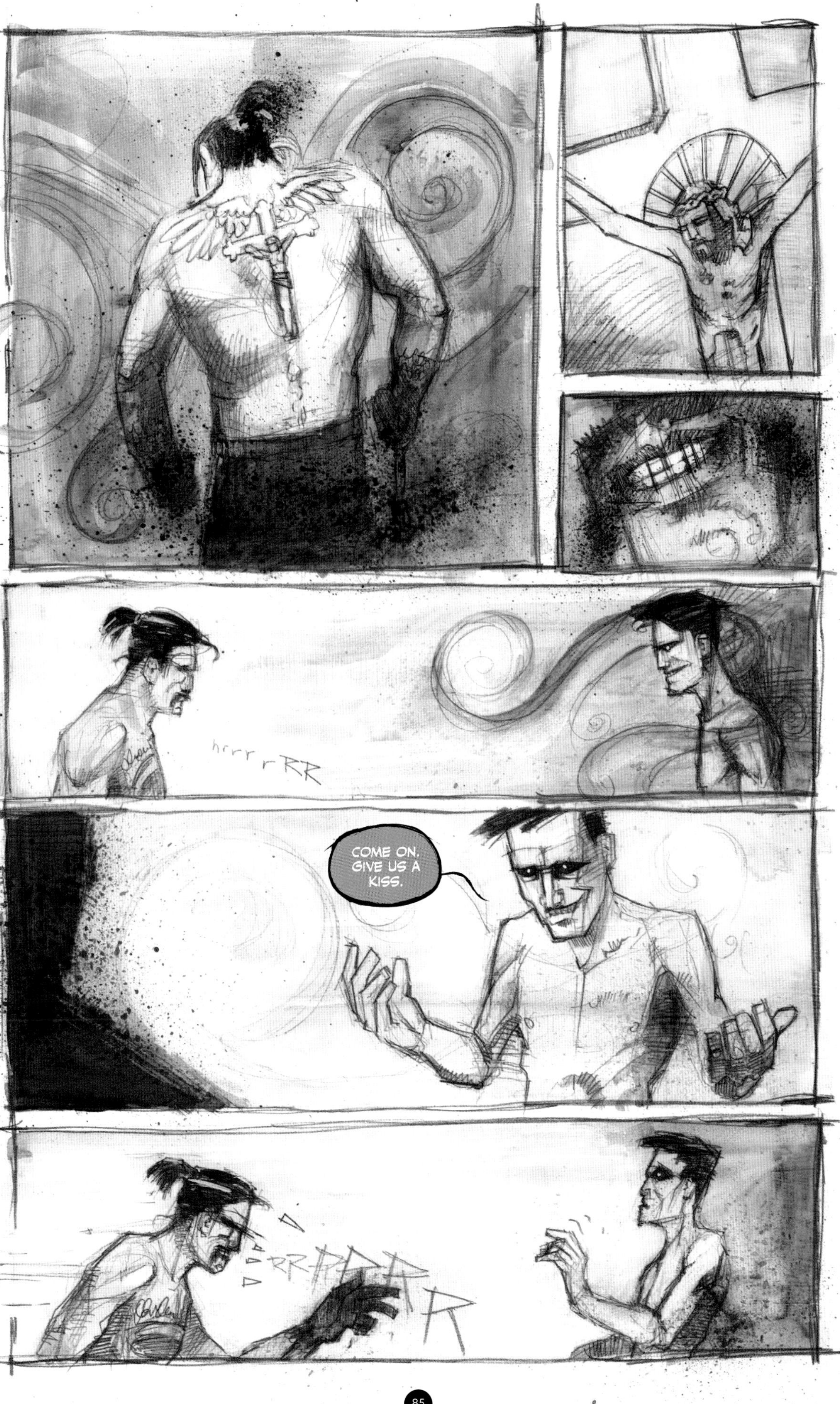
hrrr r RR
COME ON. GIVE US A KISS.

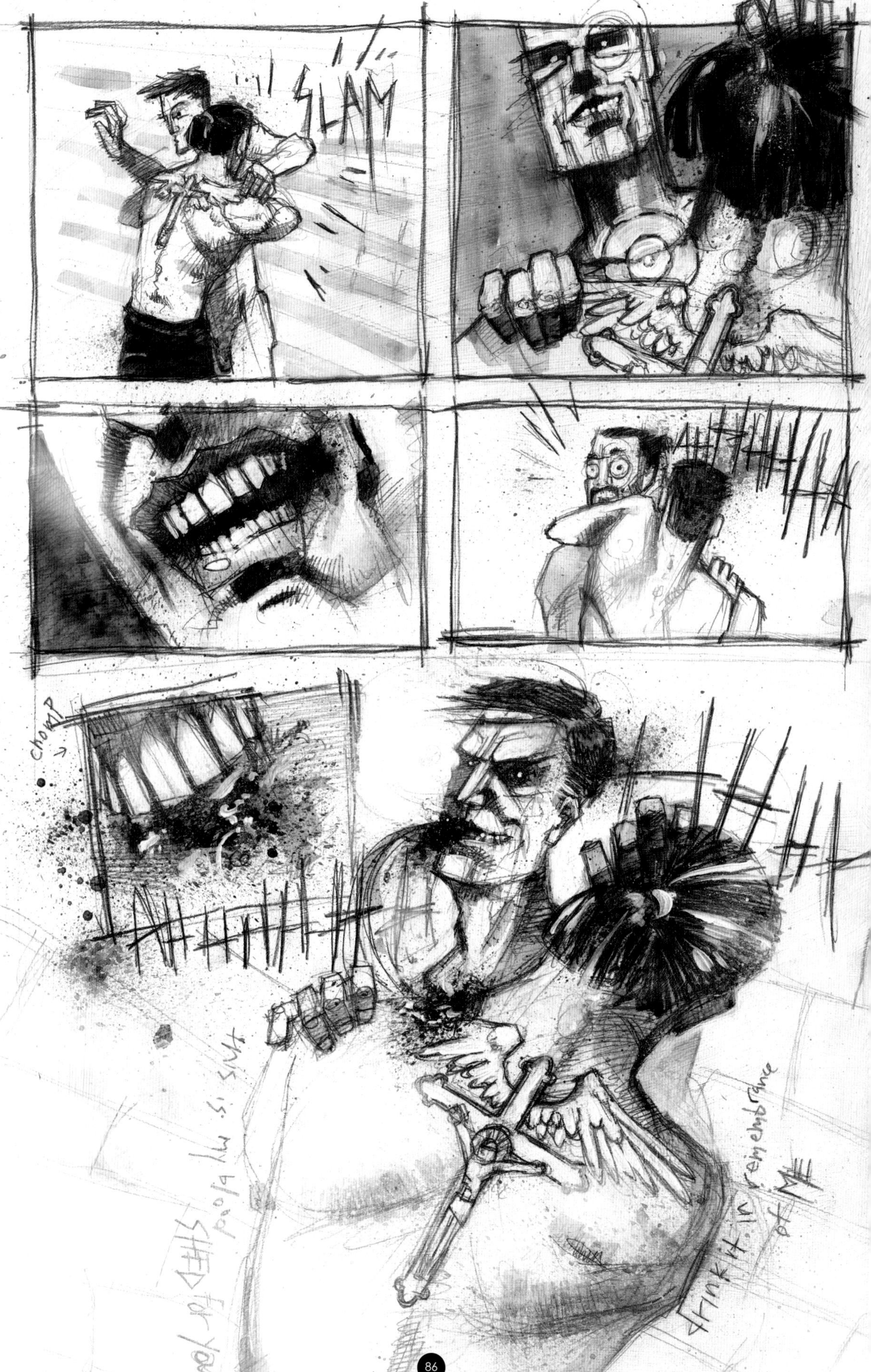
SLAM
chomp
this is my blood
SHED for you
drink it in remembrance
of ME

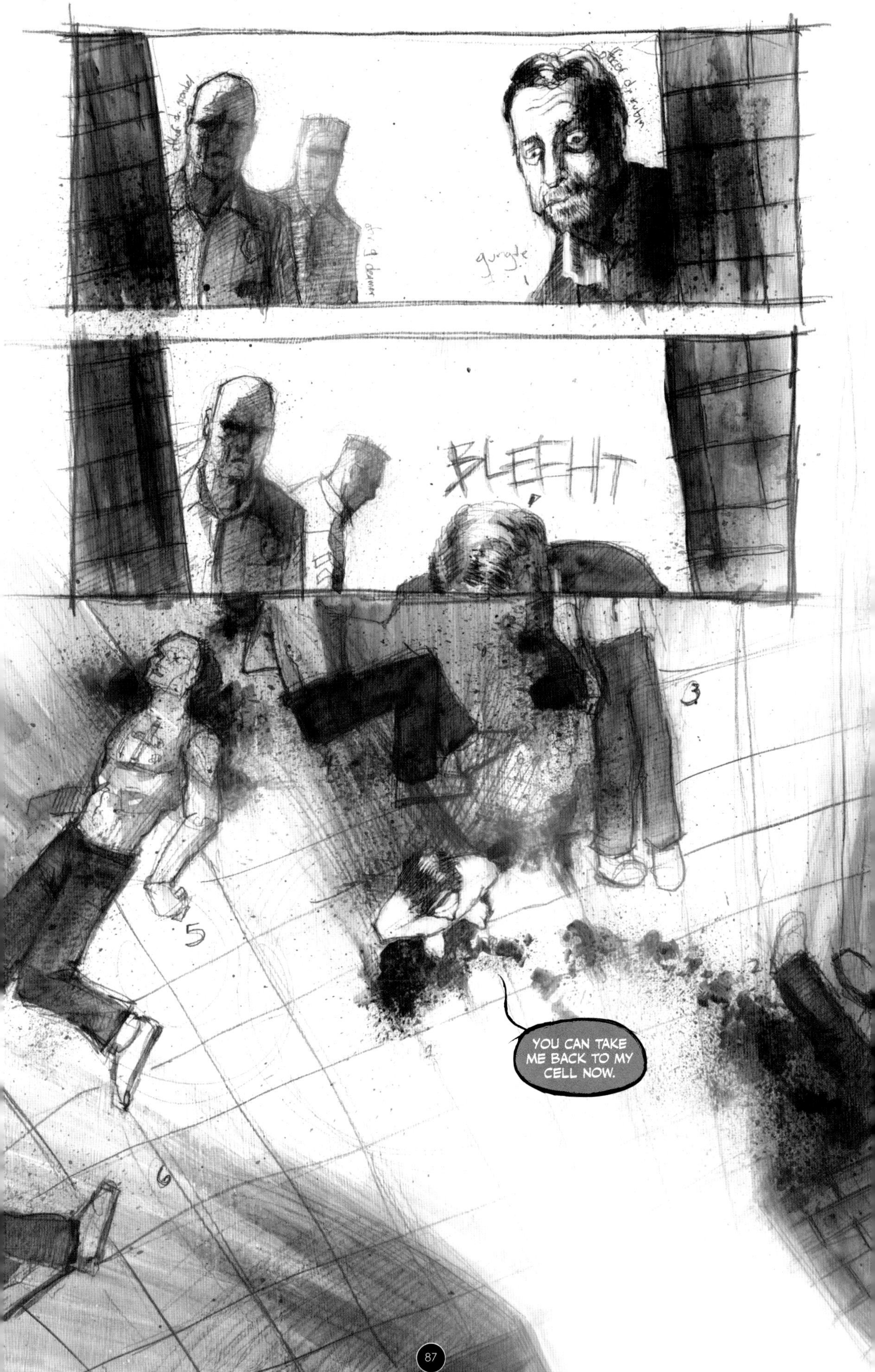
BLEEHT
YOU CAN TAKE ME BACK TO MY CELL NOW.

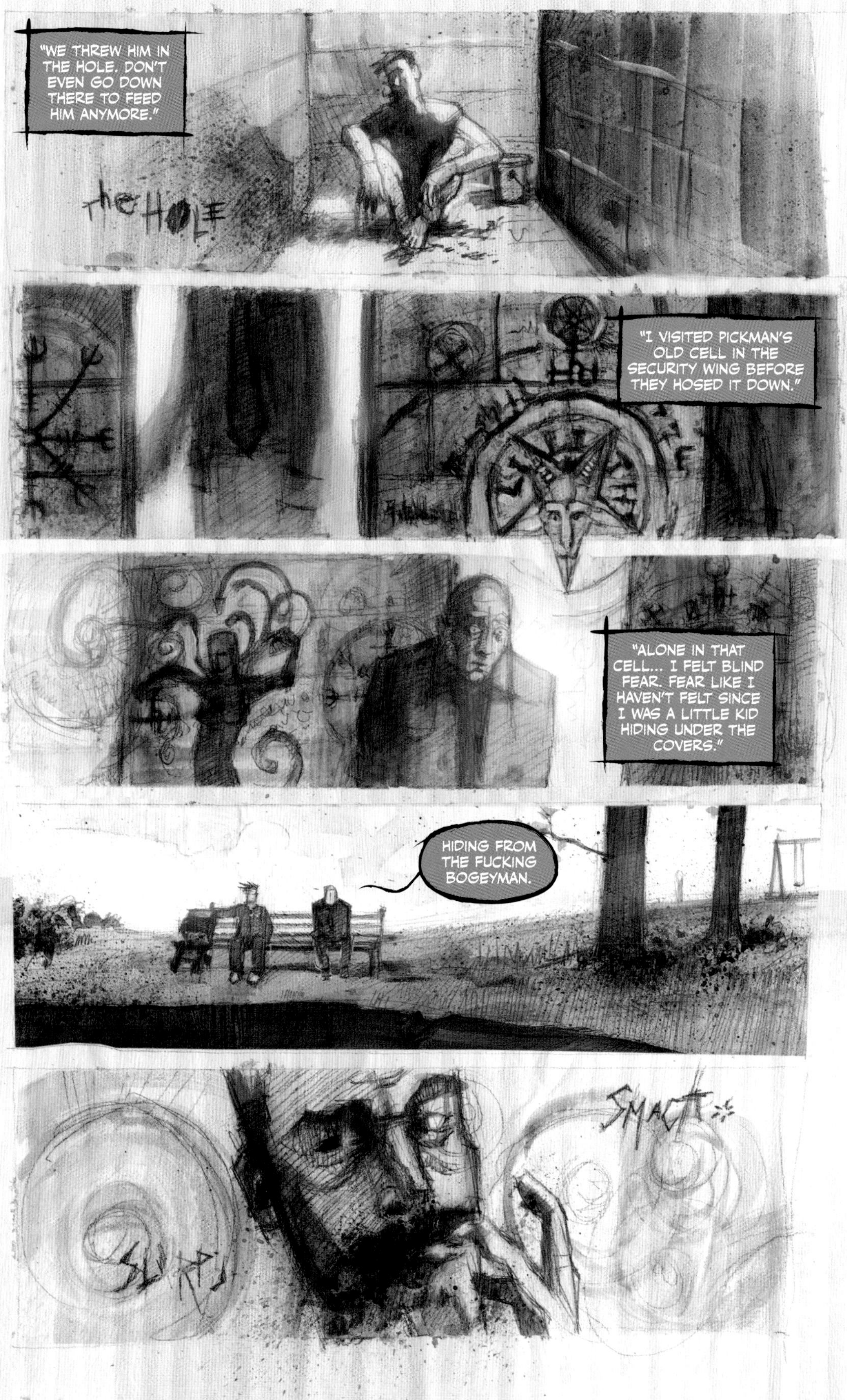
"WE THREW HIM IN THE HOLE. DON'T EVEN GO DOWN THERE TO FEED HIM ANYMORE."
the HOLE
"I VISITED PICKMAN'S OLD CELL IN THE SECURITY WING BEFORE THEY HOSED IT DOWN."
"ALONE IN THAT CELL... I FELT BLIND FEAR. FEAR LIKE I HAVEN'T FELT SINCE I WAS A LITTLE KID HIDING UNDER THE COVERS."
HIDING FROM THE FUCKING BOGEYMAN.
SMACK
SLURP

UGH. I AM FUCKING BORED.
MOTHER. I AM READY TO LEAVE.
MOTHER? ARE YOU LISTENING? I AM READY TO LEAVE THIS PLACE.
THIS PLACE IS FUCKING BORING.
I WOULD LIKE TO GO HOME NOW.
SILENCE.

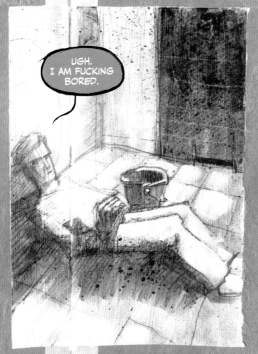

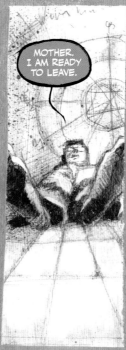

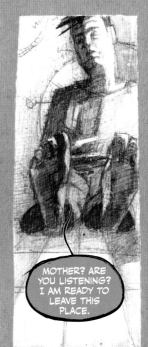

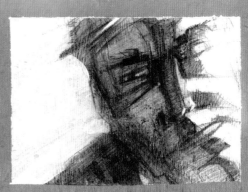

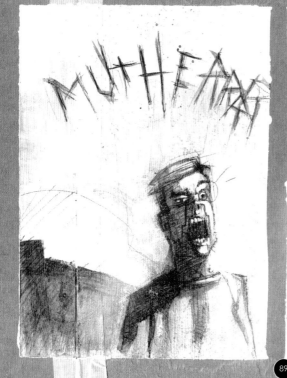

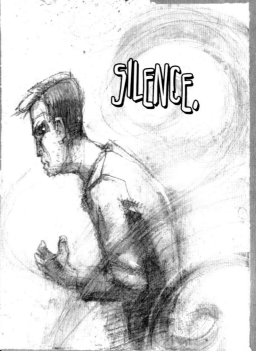

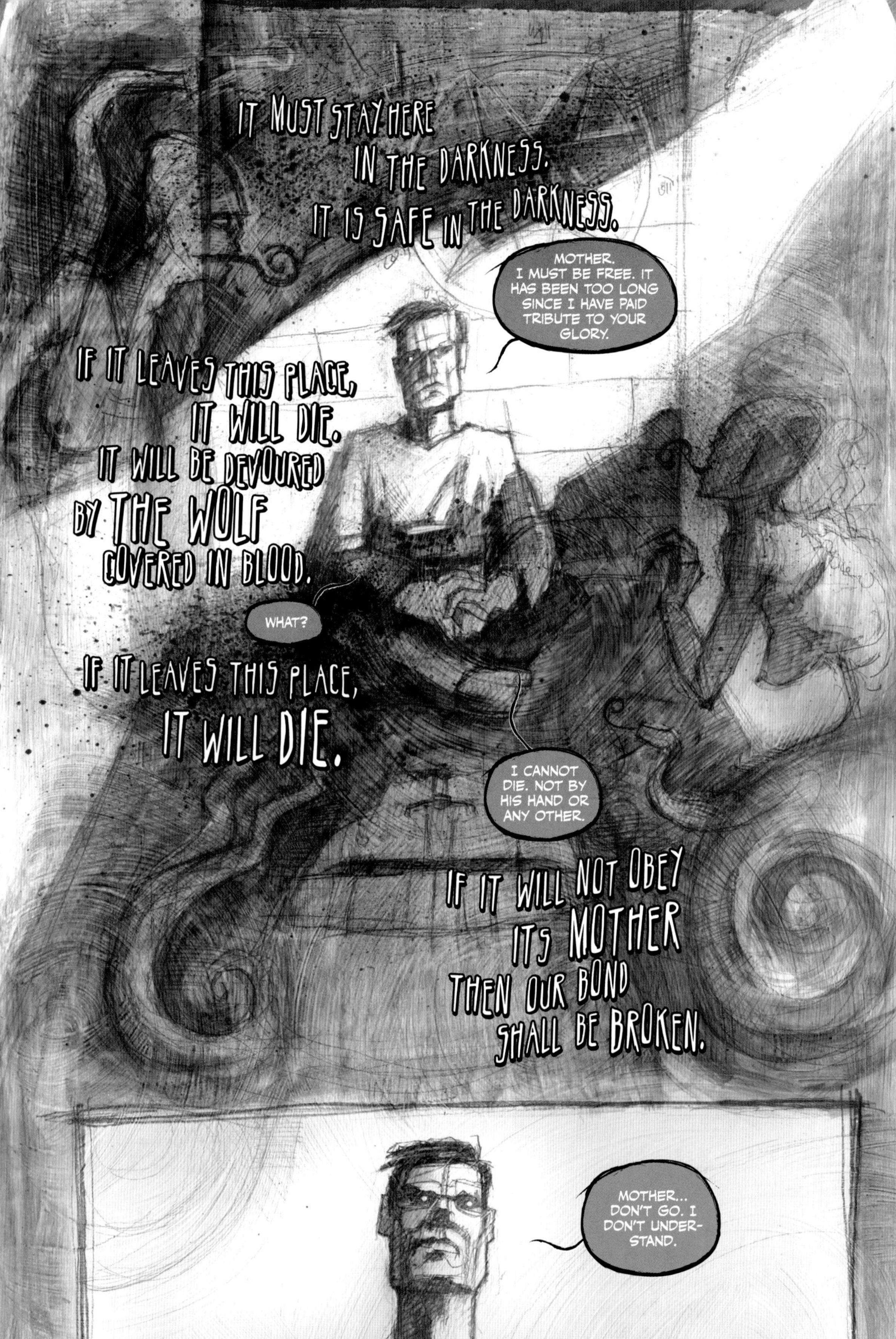
IT MUST STAY HERE IN THE DARKNESS.
IT IS SAFE IN THE DARKNESS.
MOTHER. I MUST BE FREE. IT HAS BEEN TOO LONG SINCE I HAVE PAID TRIBUTE TO YOUR GLORY.
IF IT LEAVES THIS PLACE, IT WILL DIE. IT WILL BE DEVOURED BY THE WOLF COVERED IN BLOOD.
WHAT?
IF IT LEAVES THIS PLACE, IT WILL DIE.
I CANNOT DIE. NOT BY HIS HAND OR ANY OTHER.
IF IT WILL NOT OBEY ITS MOTHER THEN OUR BOND SHALL BE BROKEN.
MOTHER... DON'T GO. I DON'T UNDER-STAND.

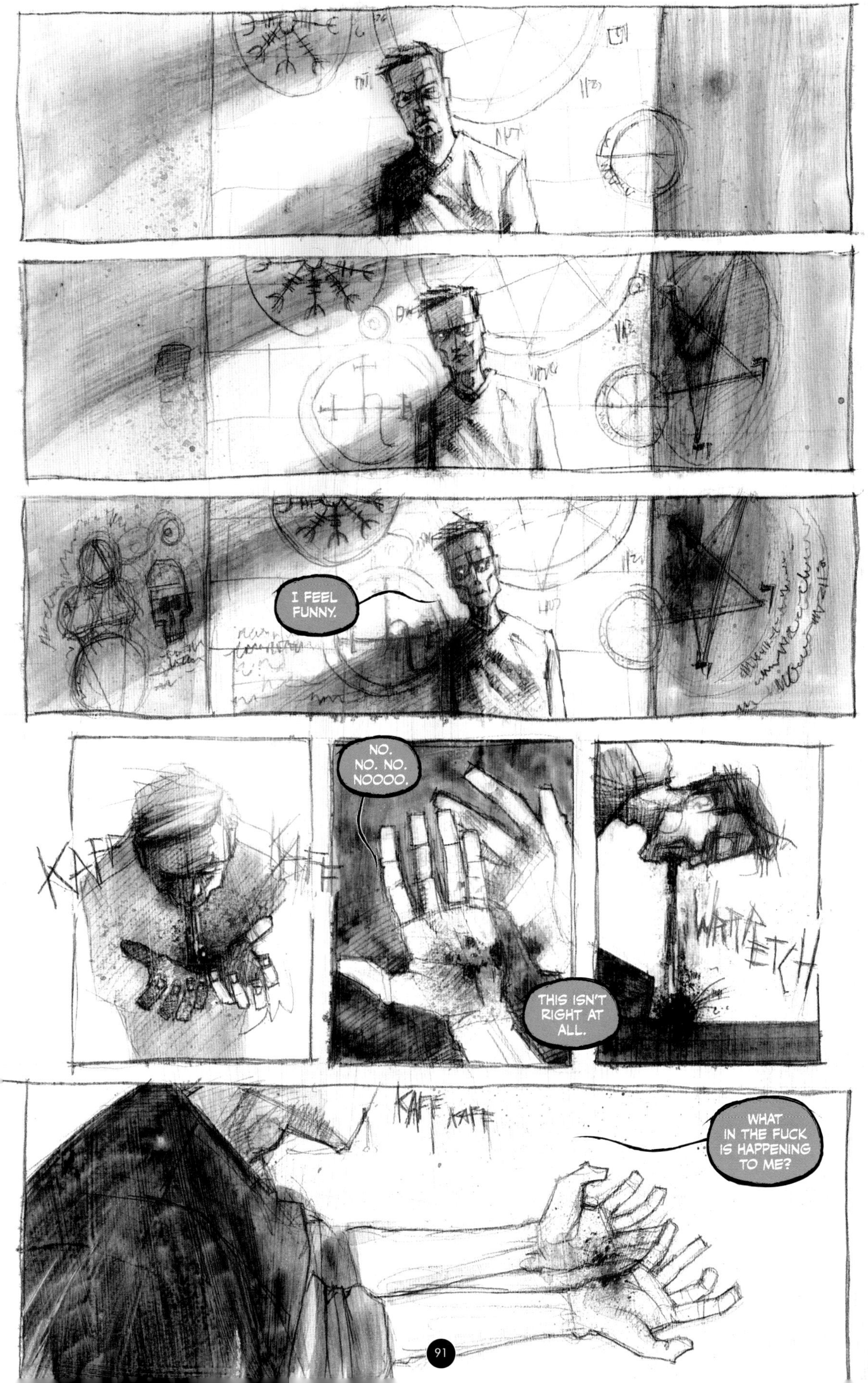
I FEEL FUNNY.
KAFF KAFF
NO. NO. NO. NOOOO.
THIS ISN'T RIGHT AT ALL.
WRRRETCH
KAFF KAFF
WHAT IN THE FUCK IS HAPPENING TO ME?

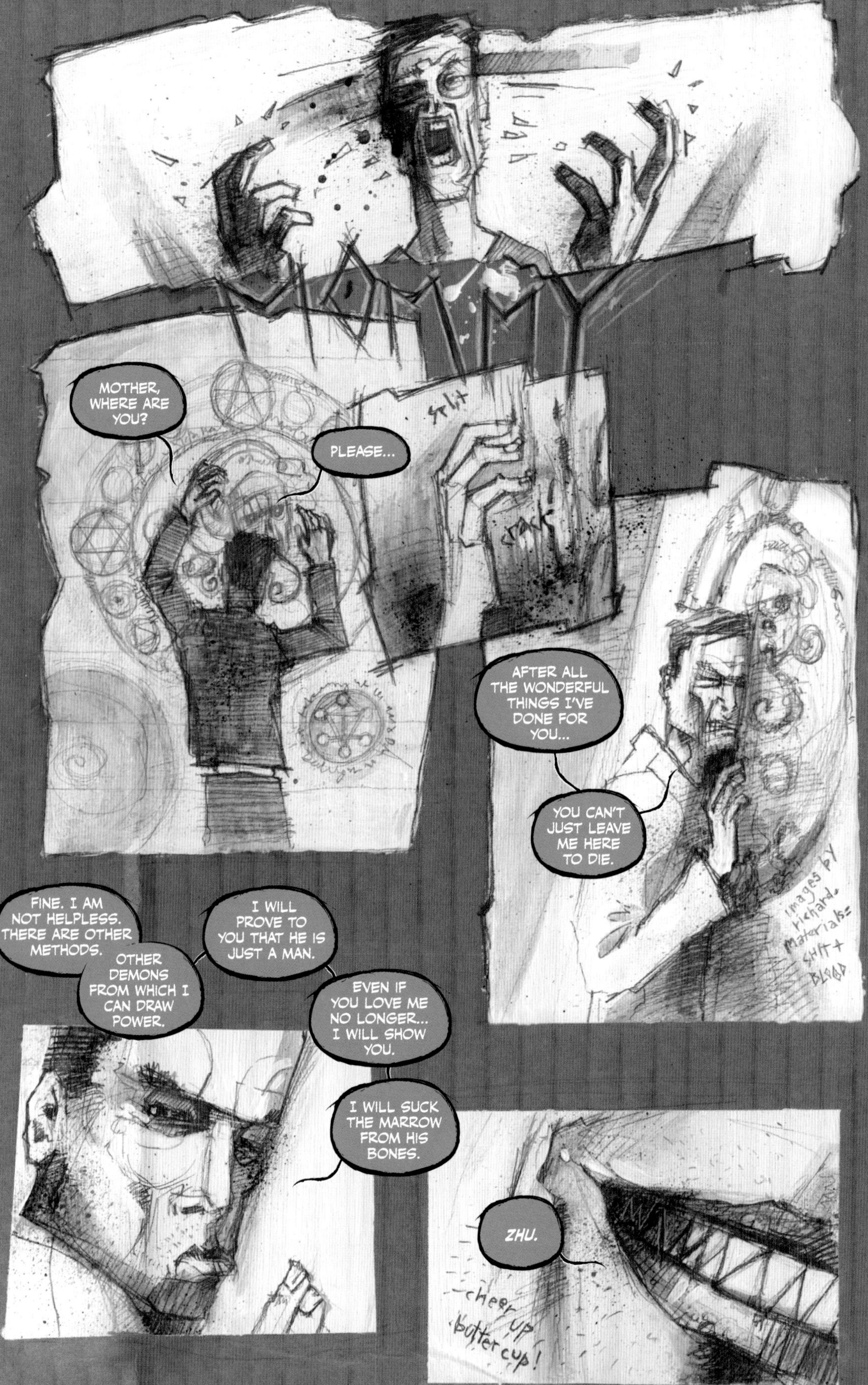

MOTHER, WHERE ARE YOU?
PLEASE...
split
crack
AFTER ALL THE WONDERFUL THINGS I'VE DONE FOR YOU...
YOU CAN'T JUST LEAVE ME HERE TO DIE.
images by richard. materials= SHIT + BLOOD
FINE. I AM NOT HELPLESS. THERE ARE OTHER METHODS.
OTHER DEMONS FROM WHICH I CAN DRAW POWER.
I WILL PROVE TO YOU THAT HE IS JUST A MAN.
EVEN IF YOU LOVE ME NO LONGER... I WILL SHOW YOU.
I WILL SUCK THE MARROW FROM HIS BONES.
ZHU.
cheer up butter cup!

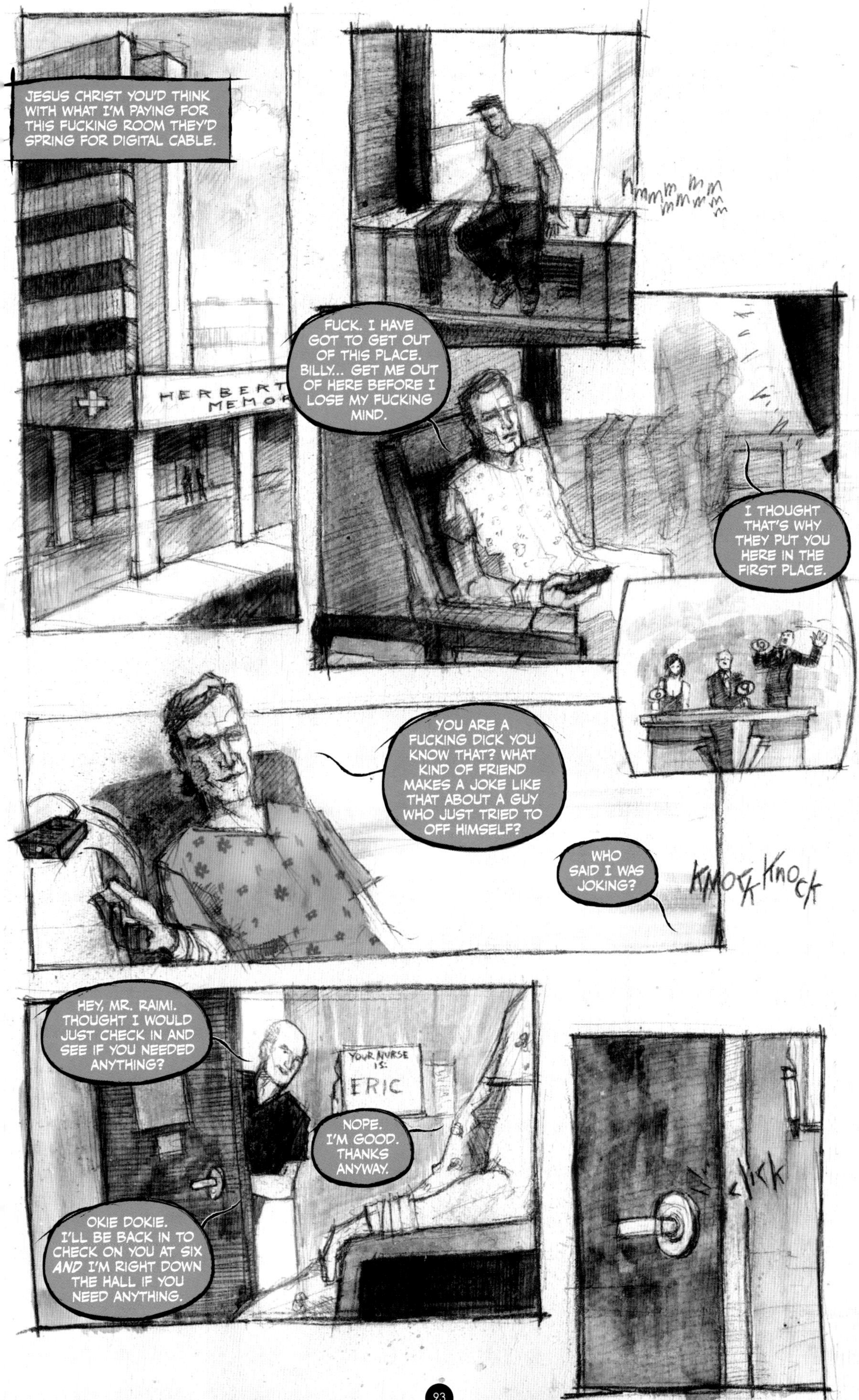
JESUS CHRIST YOU'D THINK WITH WHAT I'M PAYING FOR THIS FUCKING ROOM THEY'D SPRING FOR DIGITAL CABLE.
HERBERT MEMOR
mmmm mm mmmm m
FUCK. I HAVE GOT TO GET OUT OF THIS PLACE. BILLY... GET ME OUT OF HERE BEFORE I LOSE MY FUCKING MIND.
I THOUGHT THAT'S WHY THEY PUT YOU HERE IN THE FIRST PLACE.
YOU ARE A FUCKING DICK YOU KNOW THAT? WHAT KIND OF FRIEND MAKES A JOKE LIKE THAT ABOUT A GUY WHO JUST TRIED TO OFF HIMSELF?
WHO SAID I WAS JOKING?
KNOCK KNOCK
HEY, MR. RAIMI. THOUGHT I WOULD JUST CHECK IN AND SEE IF YOU NEEDED ANYTHING?
YOUR NURSE IS: ERIC
NOPE. I'M GOOD. THANKS ANYWAY.
OKIE DOKIE. I'LL BE BACK IN TO CHECK ON YOU AT SIX AND I'M RIGHT DOWN THE HALL IF YOU NEED ANYTHING.
click

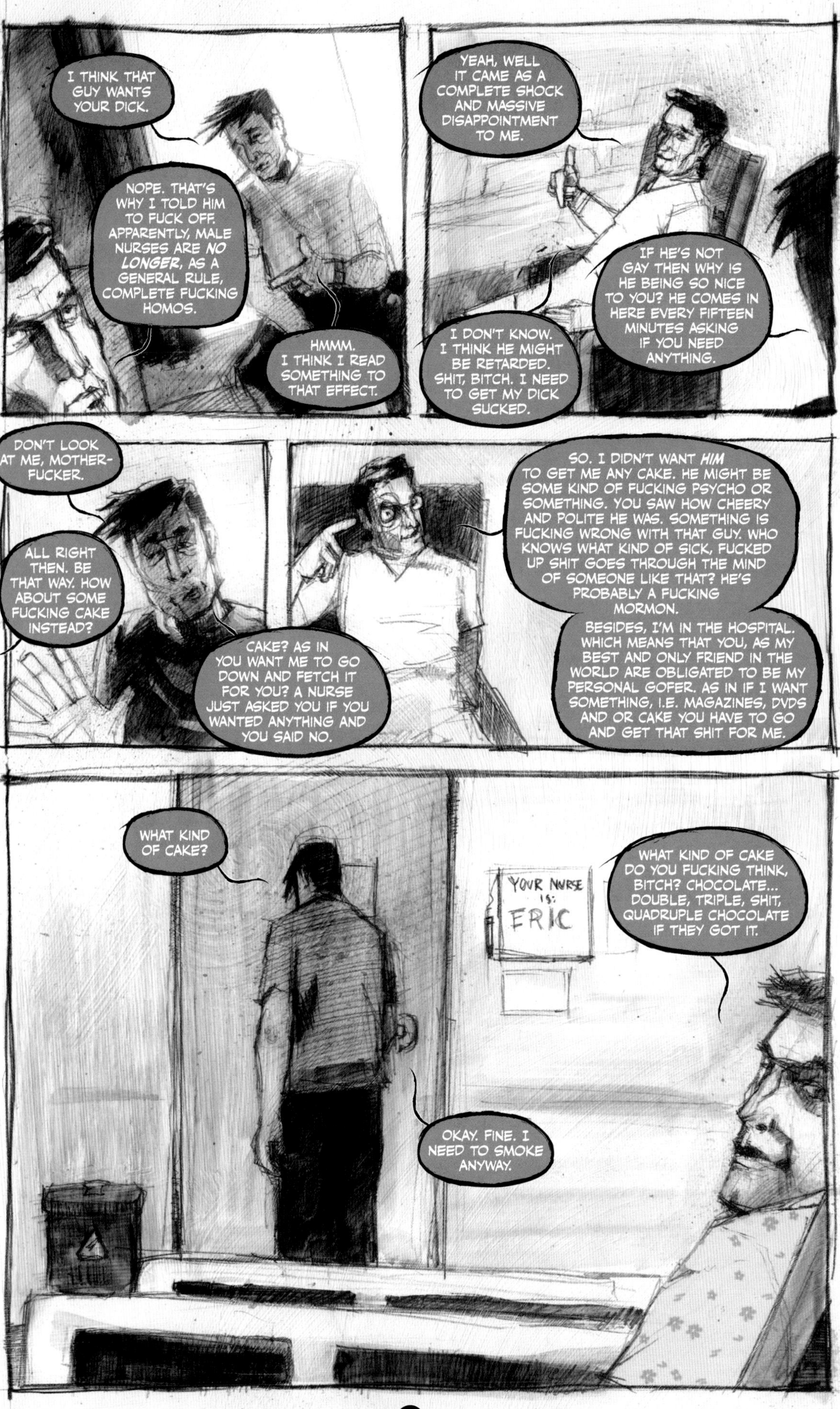
I THINK THAT GUY WANTS YOUR DICK.
NOPE. THAT'S WHY I TOLD HIM TO FUCK OFF. APPARENTLY, MALE NURSES ARE *NO LONGER*, AS A GENERAL RULE, COMPLETE FUCKING HOMOS.
HMMM. I THINK I READ SOMETHING TO THAT EFFECT.
YEAH, WELL IT CAME AS A COMPLETE SHOCK AND MASSIVE DISAPPOINTMENT TO ME.
IF HE'S NOT GAY THEN WHY IS HE BEING SO NICE TO YOU? HE COMES IN HERE EVERY FIFTEEN MINUTES ASKING IF YOU NEED ANYTHING.
I DON'T KNOW. I THINK HE MIGHT BE RETARDED. SHIT, BITCH. I NEED TO GET MY DICK SUCKED.
DON'T LOOK AT ME, MOTHER-FUCKER.
ALL RIGHT THEN. BE THAT WAY. HOW ABOUT SOME FUCKING CAKE INSTEAD?
CAKE? AS IN YOU WANT ME TO GO DOWN AND FETCH IT FOR YOU? A NURSE JUST ASKED YOU IF YOU WANTED ANYTHING AND YOU SAID NO.
SO. I DIDN'T WANT *HIM* TO GET ME ANY CAKE. HE MIGHT BE SOME KIND OF FUCKING PSYCHO OR SOMETHING. YOU SAW HOW CHEERY AND POLITE HE WAS. SOMETHING IS FUCKING WRONG WITH THAT GUY. WHO KNOWS WHAT KIND OF SICK, FUCKED UP SHIT GOES THROUGH THE MIND OF SOMEONE LIKE THAT? HE'S PROBABLY A FUCKING MORMON.
BESIDES, I'M IN THE HOSPITAL. WHICH MEANS THAT YOU, AS MY BEST AND ONLY FRIEND IN THE WORLD ARE OBLIGATED TO BE MY PERSONAL GOFER. AS IN IF I WANT SOMETHING, I.E. MAGAZINES, DVDS AND OR CAKE YOU HAVE TO GO AND GET THAT SHIT FOR ME.
WHAT KIND OF CAKE?
YOUR NURSE IS: ERIC
WHAT KIND OF CAKE DO YOU FUCKING THINK, BITCH? CHOCOLATE... DOUBLE, TRIPLE, SHIT, QUADRUPLE CHOCOLATE IF THEY GOT IT.
OKAY. FINE. I NEED TO SMOKE ANYWAY.

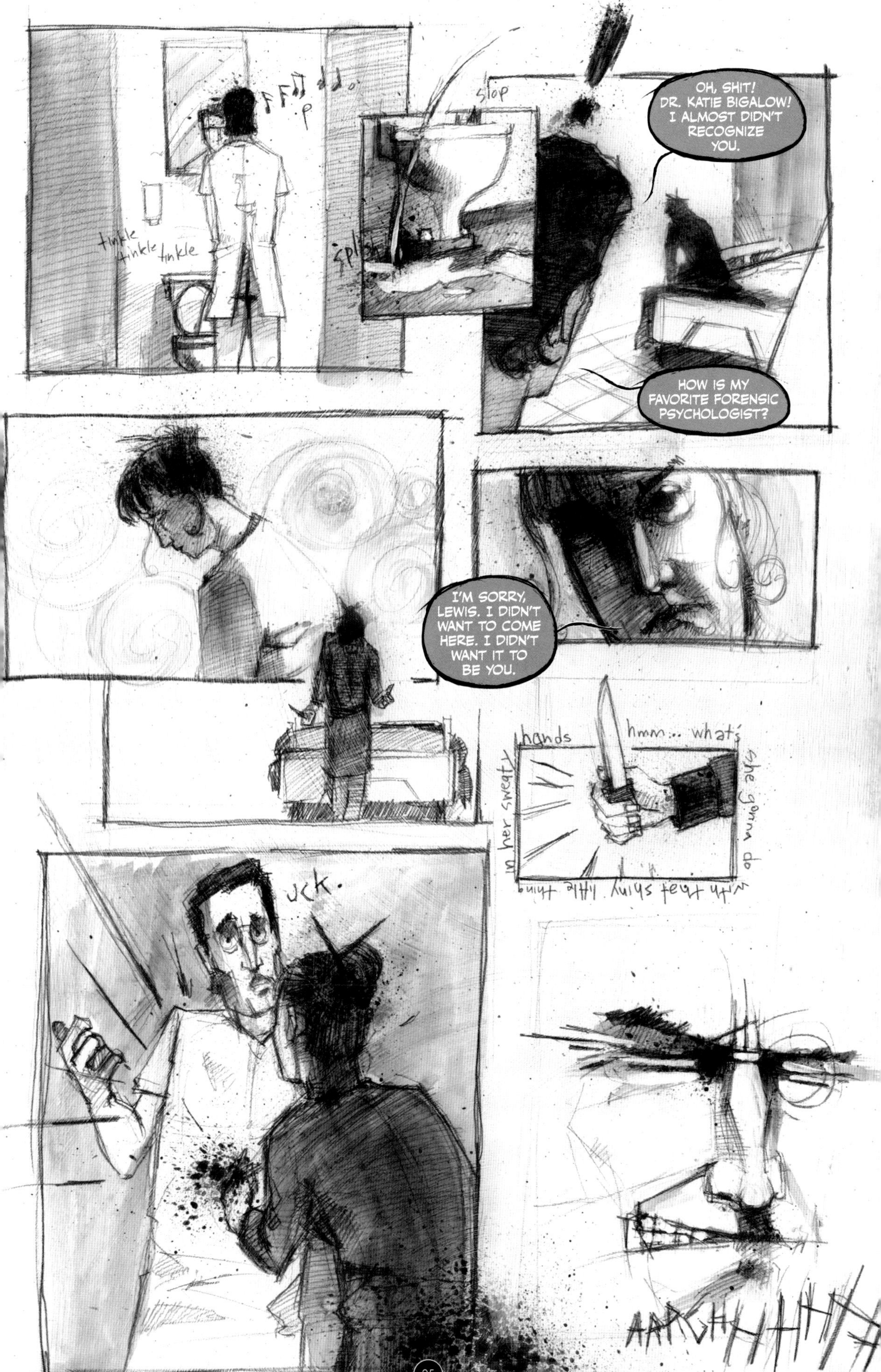
tinkle tinkle tinkle
slop
splish
OH, SHIT! DR. KATIE BIGALOW! I ALMOST DIDN'T RECOGNIZE YOU.
HOW IS MY FAVORITE FORENSIC PSYCHOLOGIST?
I'M SORRY, LEWIS. I DIDN'T WANT TO COME HERE. I DIDN'T WANT IT TO BE YOU.
hmm... what's she gonna do with that shiny little thing in her sweaty hands
uck
AARGHHHHHH

- coats from dry cleaner
- call danny g.
- call raimi
- tylenol for marvin
- card for mom
- refill ambien
- call for inspection
- email new draft to publisher
- kill Pickman ✖✖✖

chapter five

FEUD AND CRIME

"Anew began ruthless murder; he recked no whit, firm in
his guilt, of the feud and crime. They were easy to find
who elsewhere sought in room remote their rest at night,
bed in the bowers, when that bale was shown, was seen
in sooth, with surest token, -- the hall-thane's hate. Such
held themselves far and fast who the fiend outran! Thus
ruled unrighteous and raged his fill one against all;."
—Beowulf

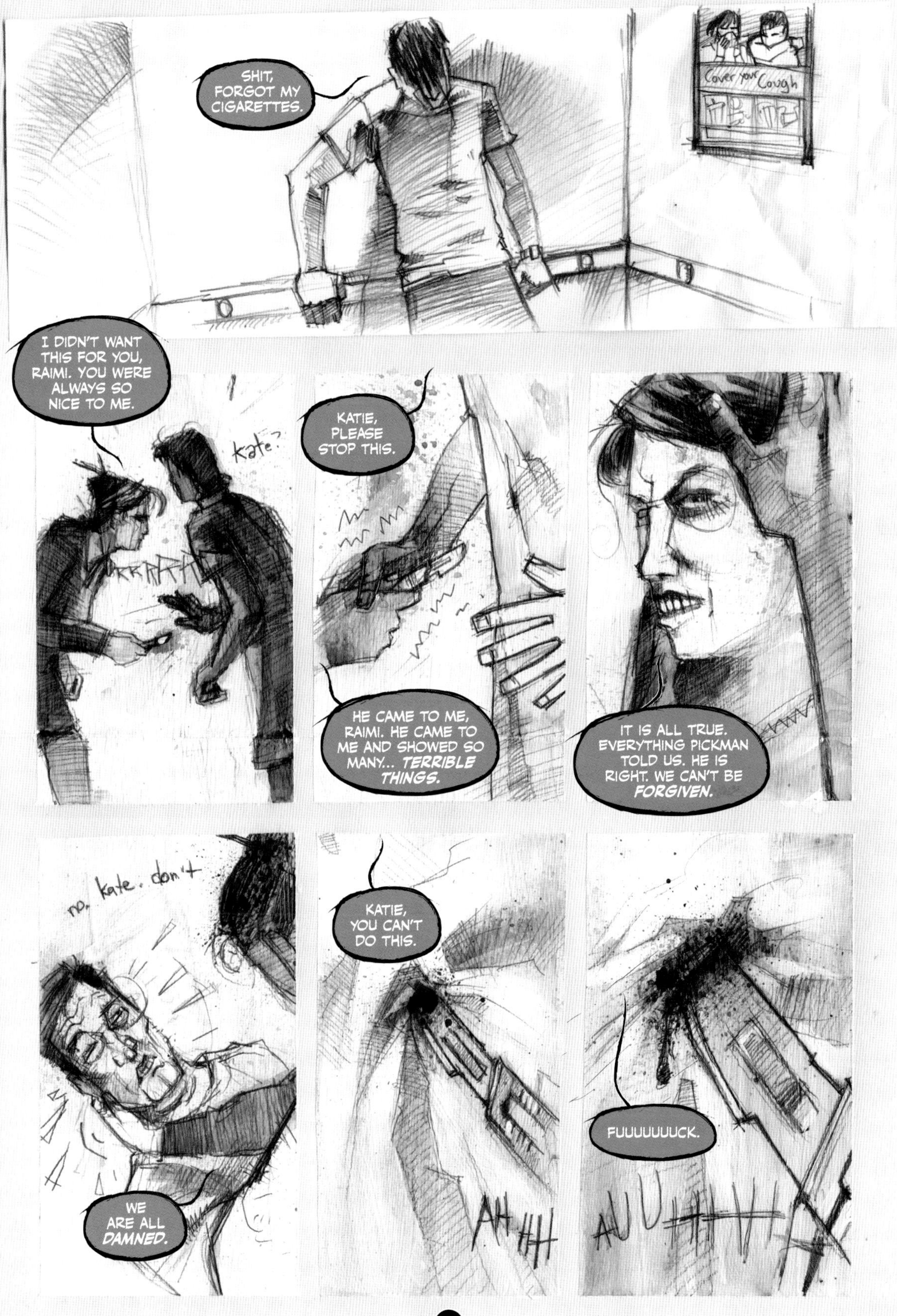
SHIT, FORGOT MY CIGARETTES.
Cover your Cough
I DIDN'T WANT THIS FOR YOU, RAIMI. YOU WERE ALWAYS SO NICE TO ME.
kate?
KATIE, PLEASE STOP THIS.
HE CAME TO ME, RAIMI. HE CAME TO ME AND SHOWED SO MANY... *TERRIBLE THINGS.*
IT IS ALL TRUE. EVERYTHING PICKMAN TOLD US. HE IS RIGHT. WE CAN'T BE *FORGIVEN.*
no. kate. don't
WE ARE ALL *DAMNED.*
KATIE, YOU CAN'T DO THIS.
FUUUUUUUCK.

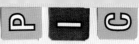

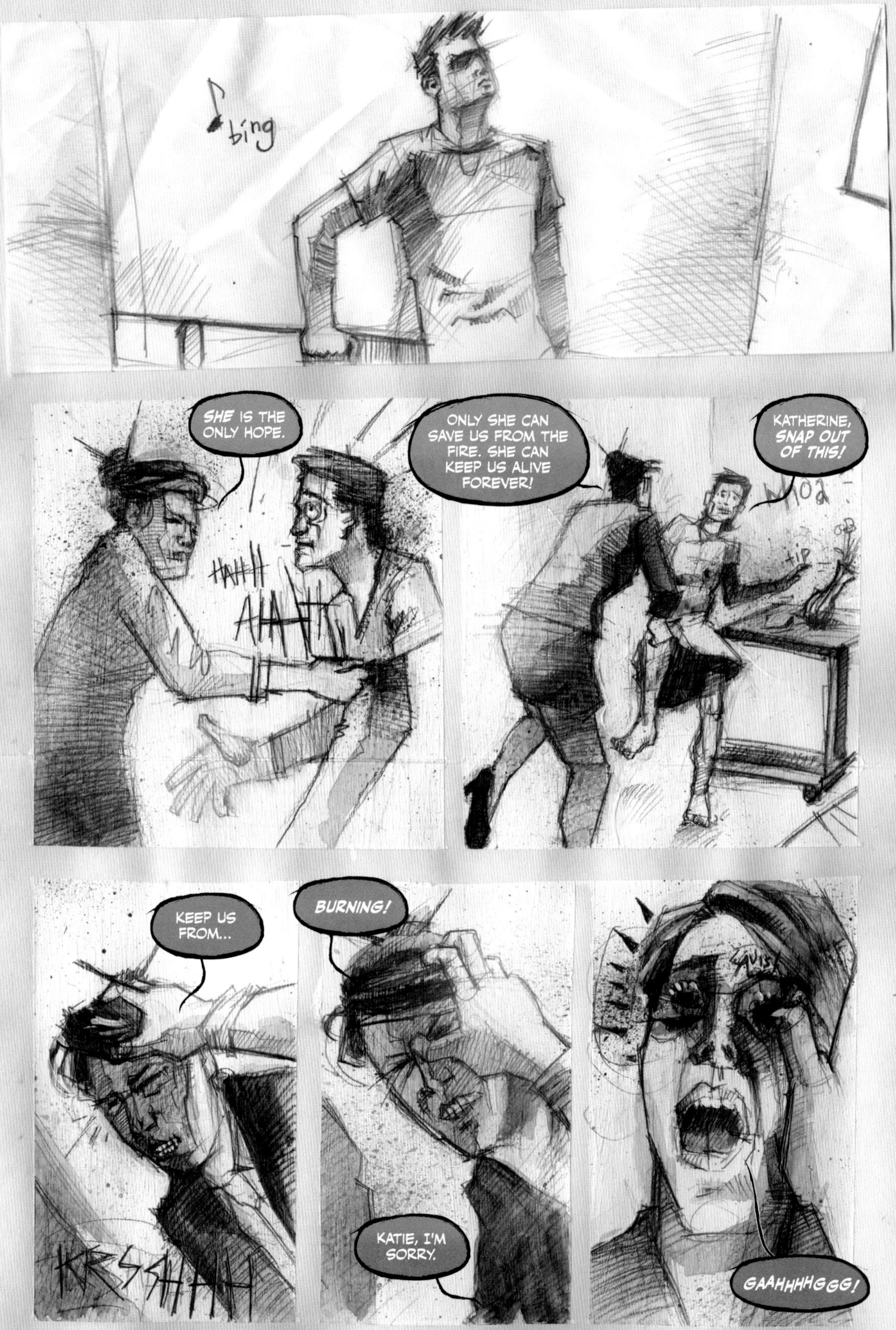
bing
SHE IS THE ONLY HOPE.
ONLY SHE CAN SAVE US FROM THE FIRE. SHE CAN KEEP US ALIVE FOREVER!
KATHERINE, SNAP OUT OF THIS!
KEEP US FROM...
BURNING!
KATIE, I'M SORRY.
GAAHHHHGGG!

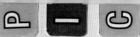

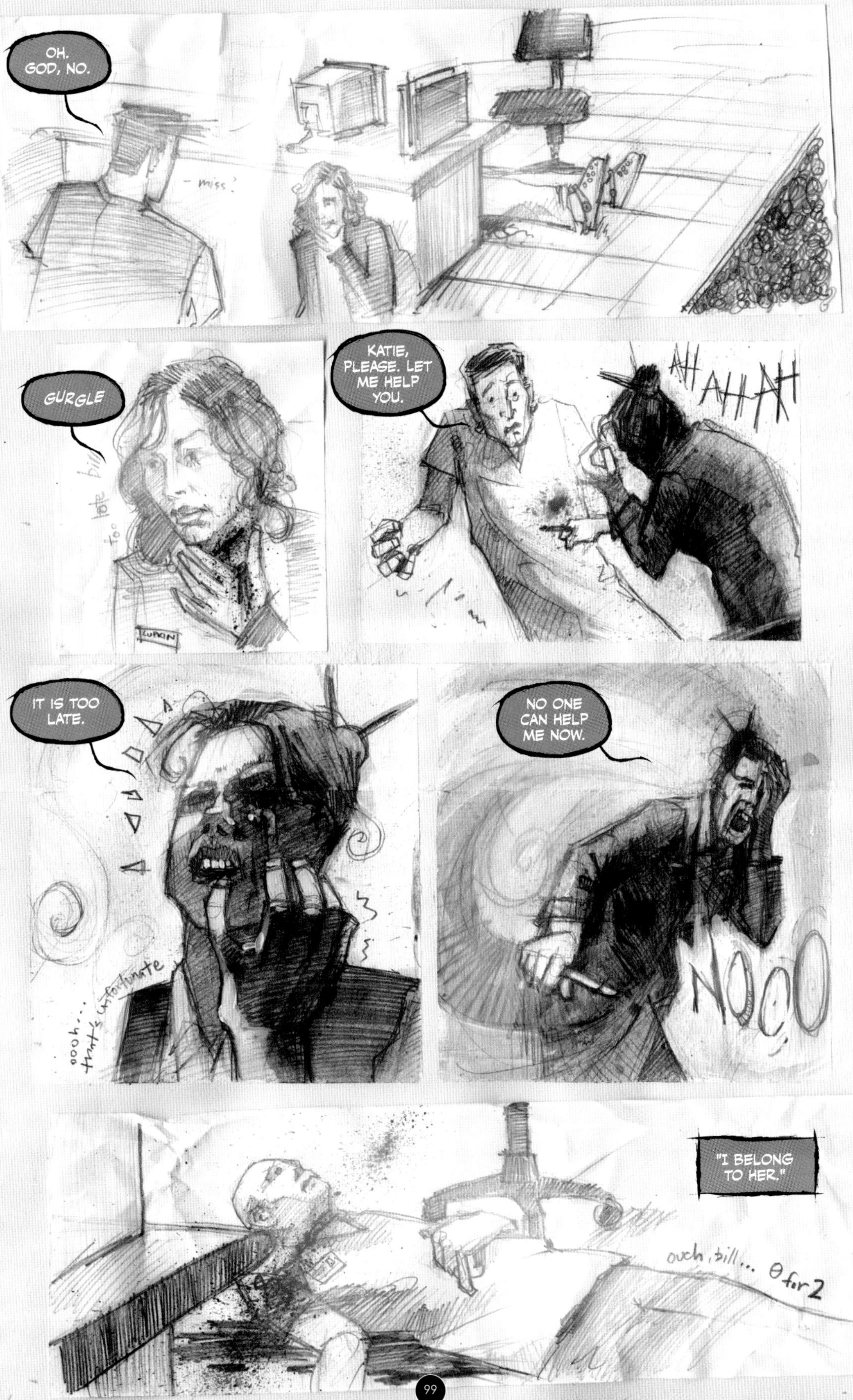
OH. GOD, NO.
- miss?
GURGLE
too late bill
KATIE, PLEASE. LET ME HELP YOU.
AH AH AH
IT IS TOO LATE.
ooh... that's unfortunate
NO ONE CAN HELP ME NOW.
NOOO
"I BELONG TO HER."
ouch, bill... 0 for 2

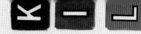

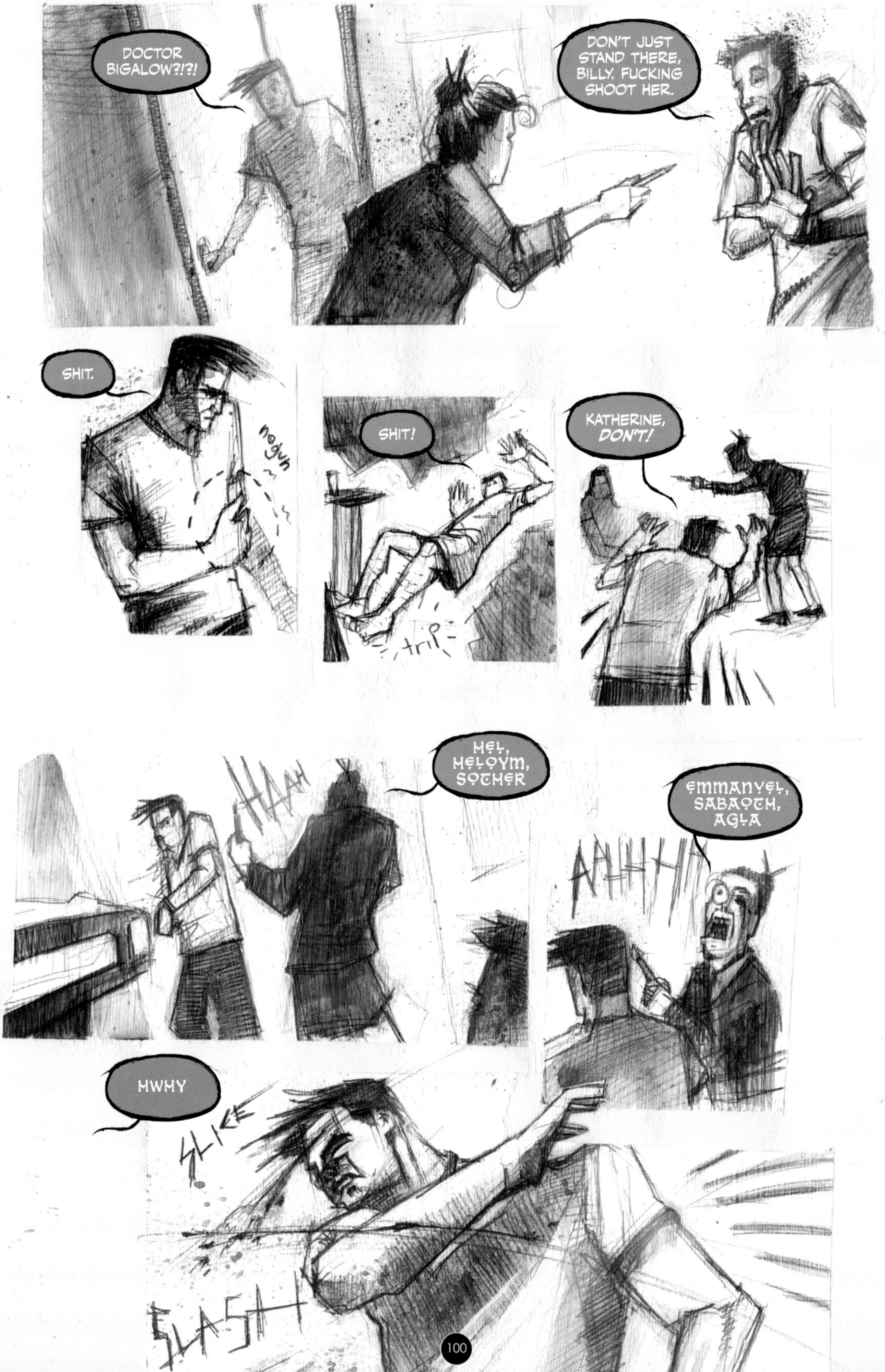

DOCTOR BIGALOW?!?!
DON'T JUST STAND THERE, BILLY. FUCKING SHOOT HER.
SHIT.
SHIT!
trip
KATHERINE, DON'T!
HAAH
HEL, HELOYM, SOTHER
EMMANUEL, SABAOTH, AGLA
AAHHH
HWHY
SLICE
SLASH

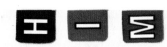

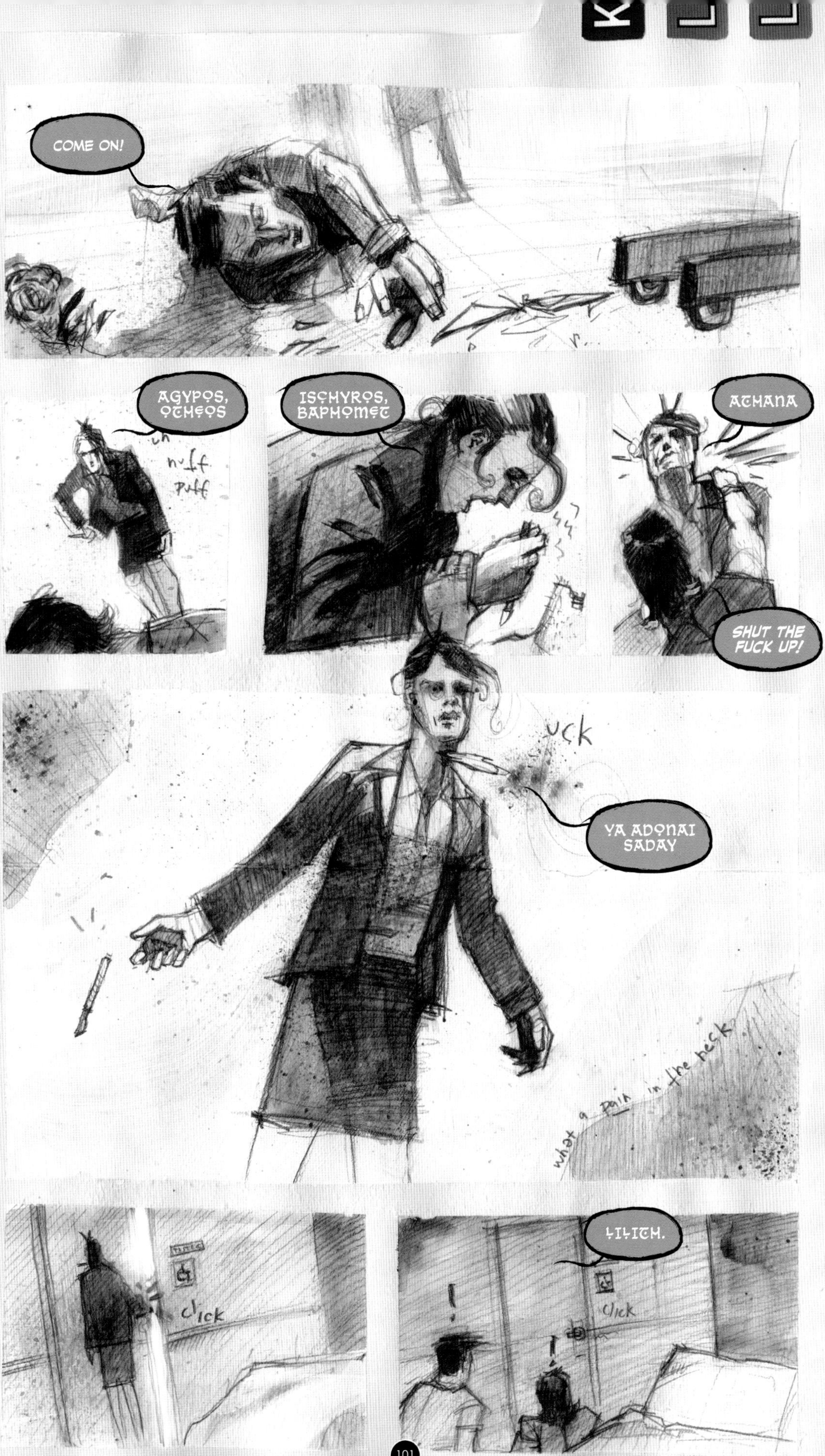
COME ON!
AGYPOS, OTHEOS
uh
nuff
puff
ISCHYROS, BAPHOMET
ATHANA
SHUT THE FUCK UP!
uck
YA ADONAI SADAY
what a pain in the neck
click
LILITH.
click

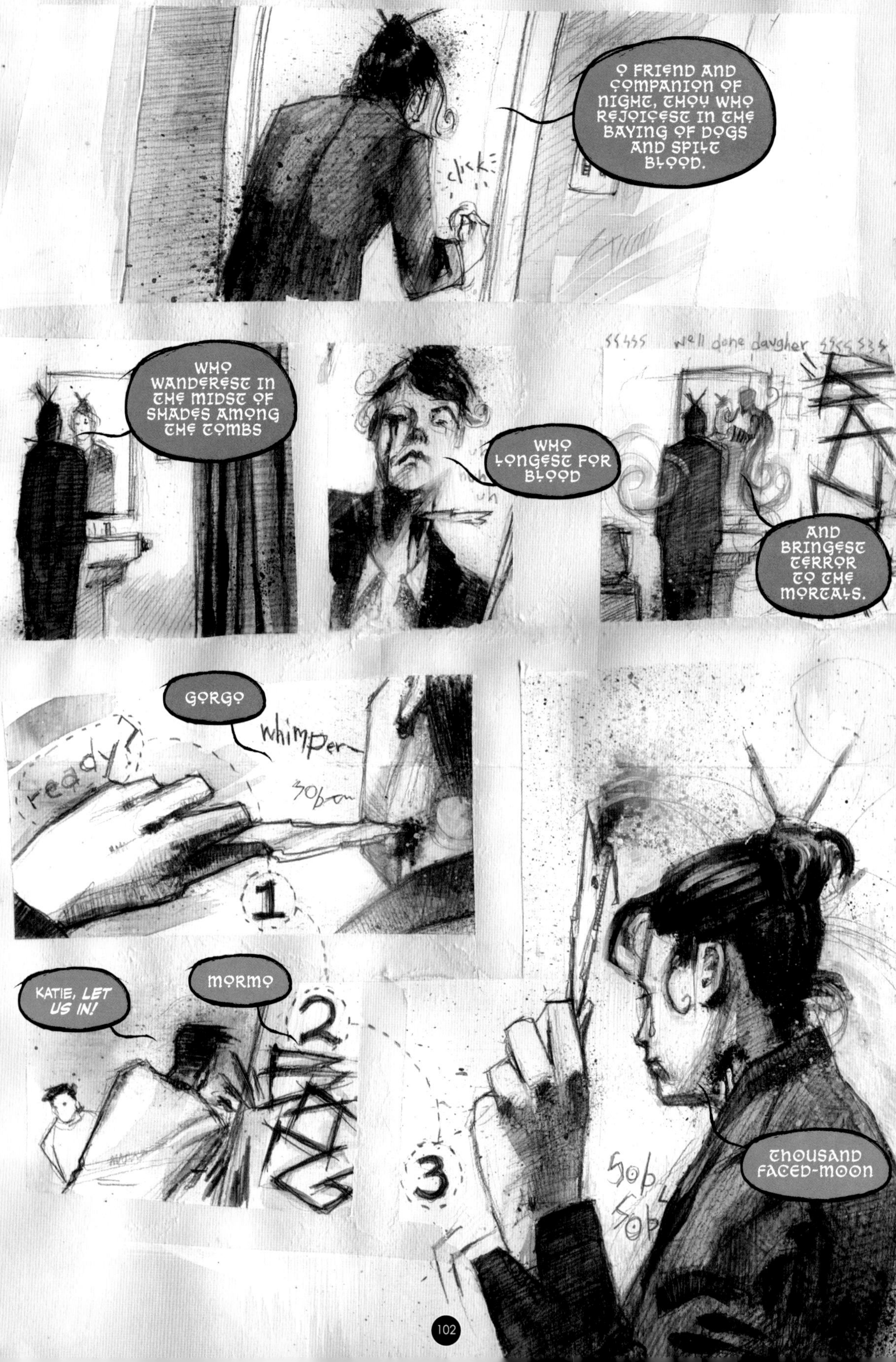
O FRIEND AND COMPANION OF NIGHT, THOU WHO REJOICEST IN THE BAYING OF DOGS AND SPILT BLOOD.
click
WHO WANDEREST IN THE MIDST OF SHADES AMONG THE TOMBS
WHO LONGEST FOR BLOOD
sssss well done daugher sssss
AND BRINGEST TERROR TO THE MORTALS.
GORGO
ready?
whimper
sob
1
KATIE, LET US IN!
MORMO
2
3
THOUSAND FACED-MOON
Sob
Sob

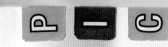

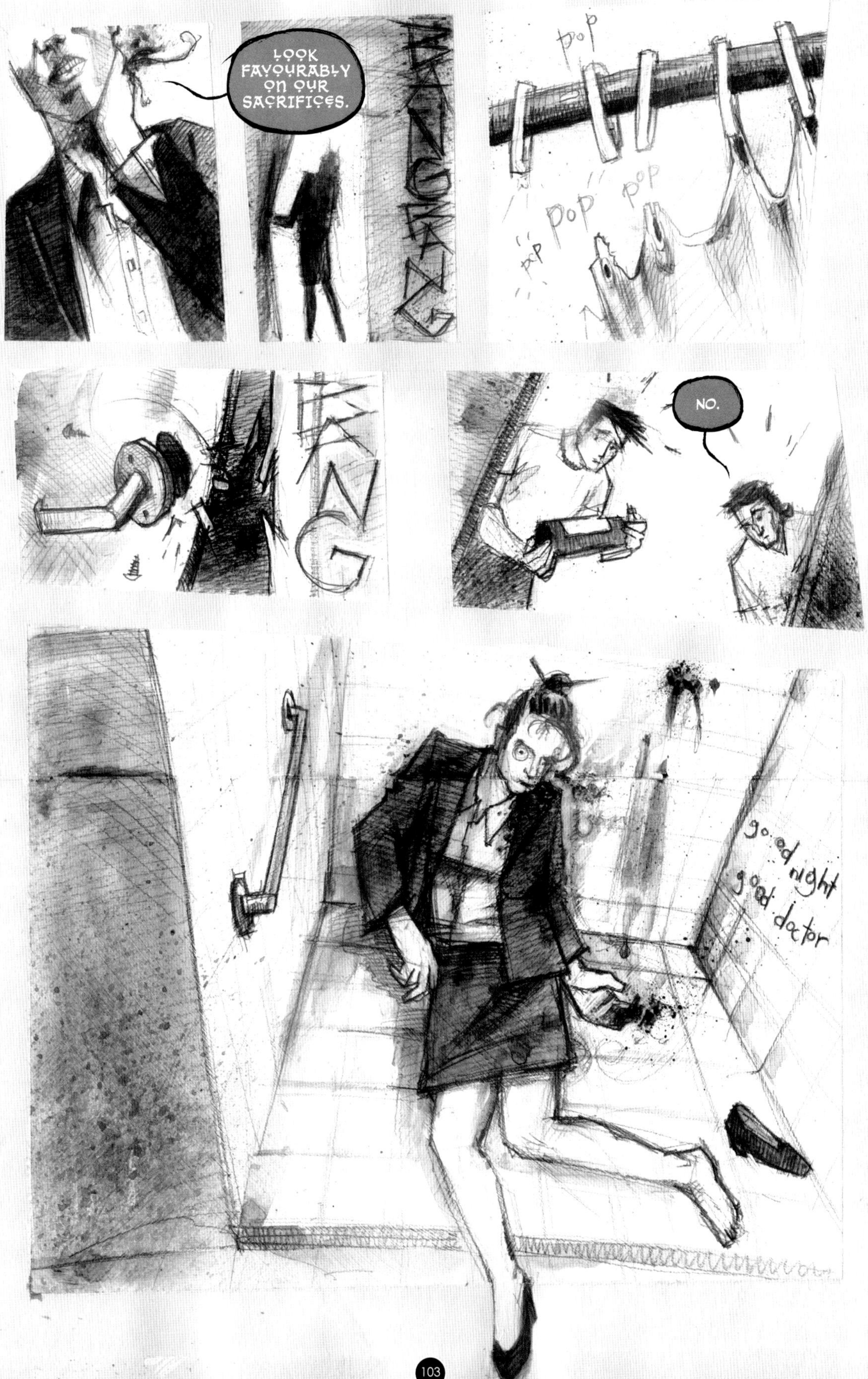
LOOK FAVOURABLY ON OUR SACRIFICES.
pop
pop pop pop pop
BANG
NO.
good night good doctor

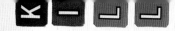

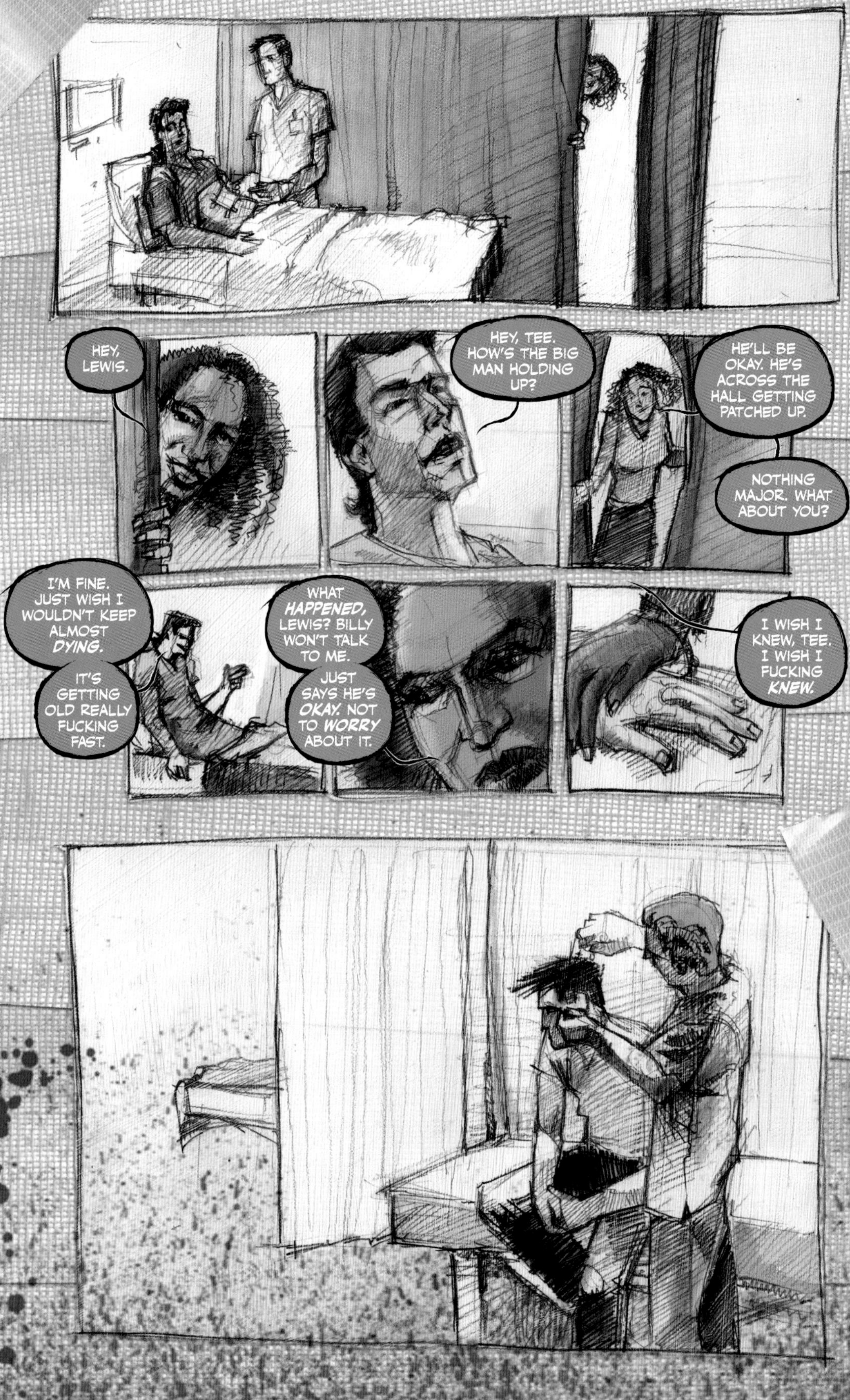
HEY, LEWIS.
HEY, TEE. HOW'S THE BIG MAN HOLDING UP?
HE'LL BE OKAY. HE'S ACROSS THE HALL GETTING PATCHED UP.
NOTHING MAJOR. WHAT ABOUT YOU?
I'M FINE. JUST WISH I WOULDN'T KEEP ALMOST *DYING.*
IT'S GETTING OLD REALLY FUCKING FAST.
WHAT *HAPPENED,* LEWIS? BILLY WON'T TALK TO ME.
JUST SAYS HE'S *OKAY.* NOT TO *WORRY* ABOUT IT.
I WISH I KNEW, TEE. I WISH I FUCKING *KNEW.*

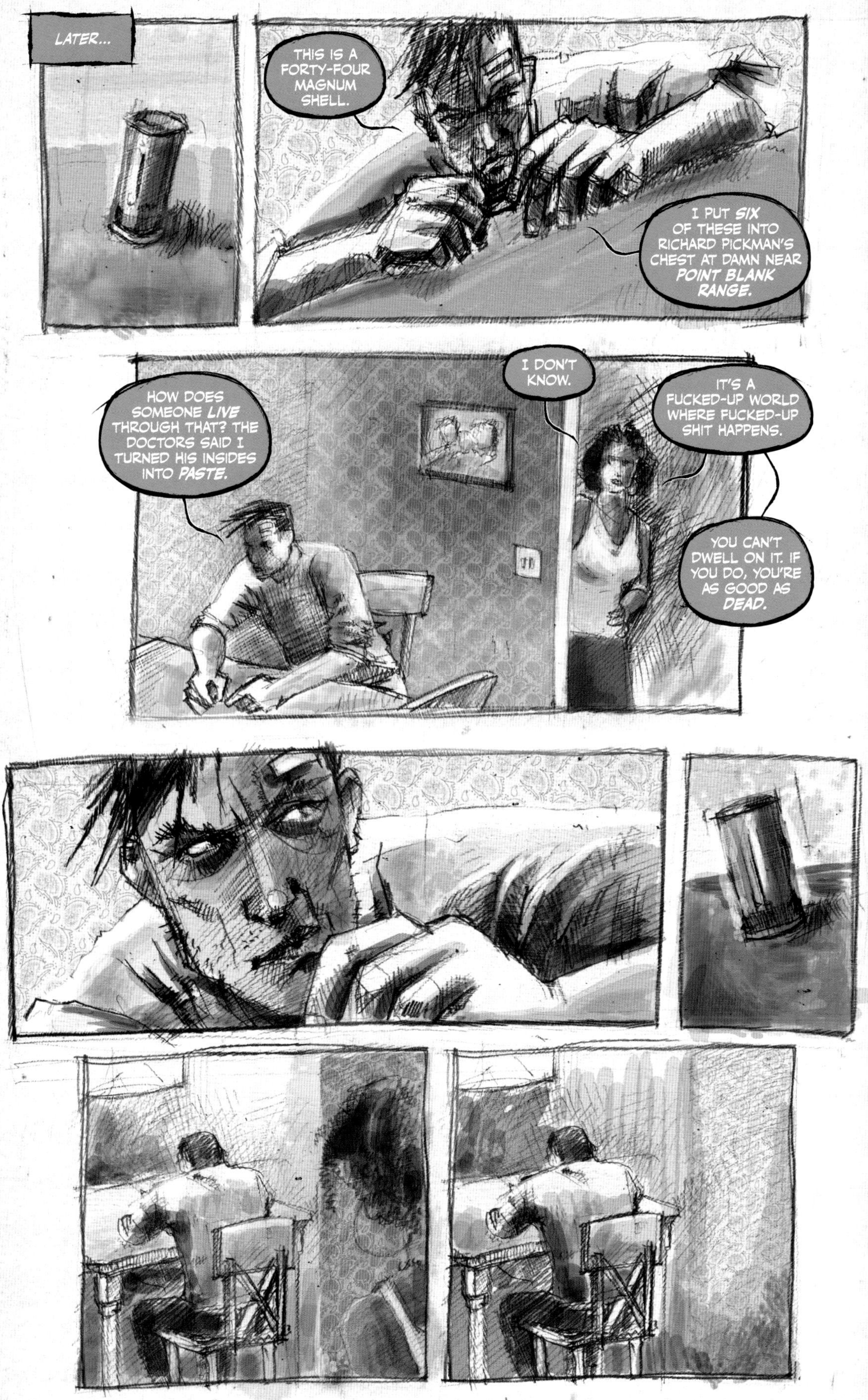
LATER...
THIS IS A FORTY-FOUR MAGNUM SHELL.
I PUT SIX OF THESE INTO RICHARD PICKMAN'S CHEST AT DAMN NEAR POINT BLANK RANGE.
HOW DOES SOMEONE LIVE THROUGH THAT? THE DOCTORS SAID I TURNED HIS INSIDES INTO PASTE.
I DON'T KNOW.
IT'S A FUCKED-UP WORLD WHERE FUCKED-UP SHIT HAPPENS.
YOU CAN'T DWELL ON IT. IF YOU DO, YOU'RE AS GOOD AS DEAD.

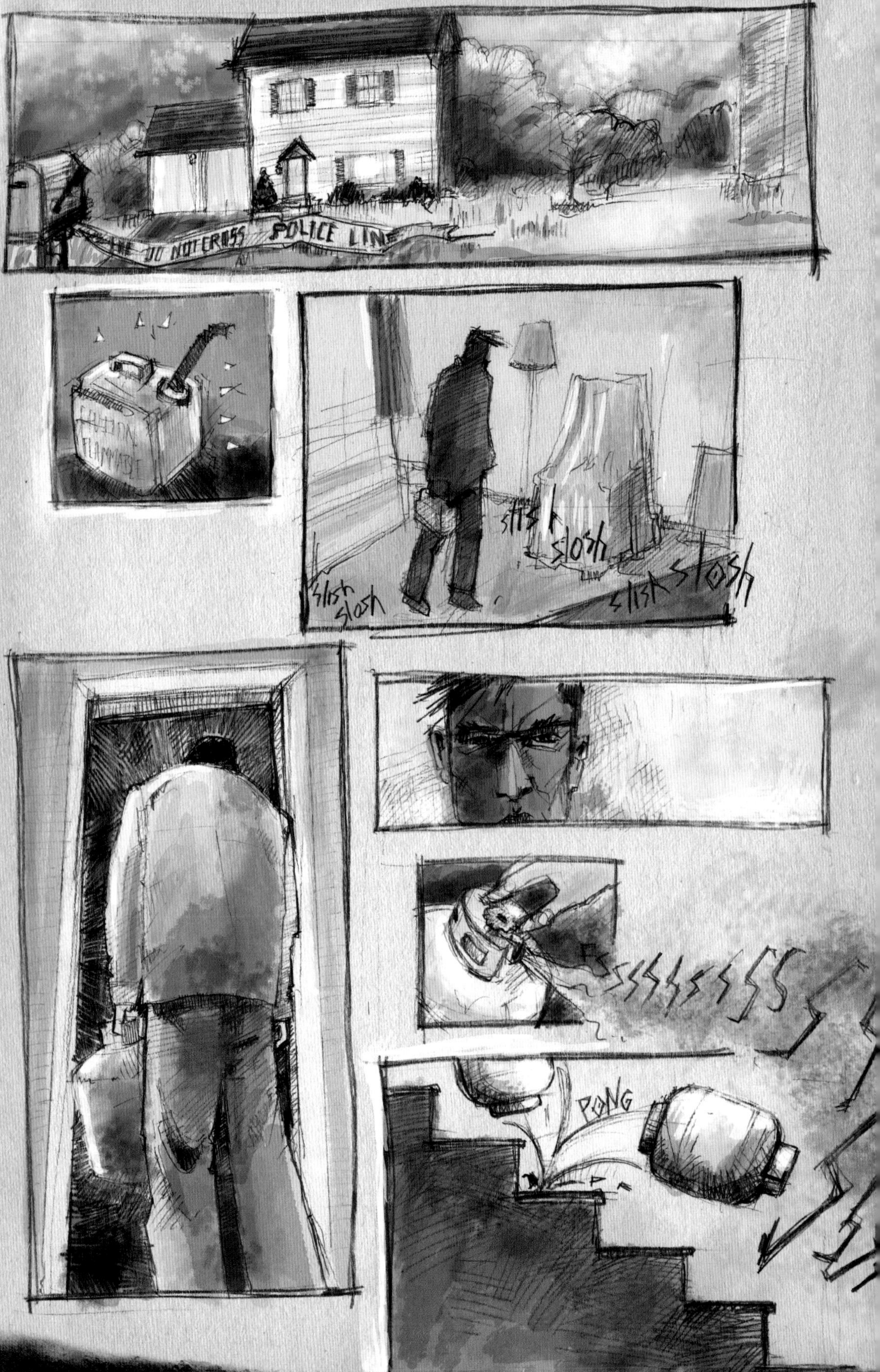
DO NOT CROSS
POLICE LINE
FLAMMABLE
slish slosh
slish slosh
slish slosh
slish slosh
SSSSSSSSSS
PONG

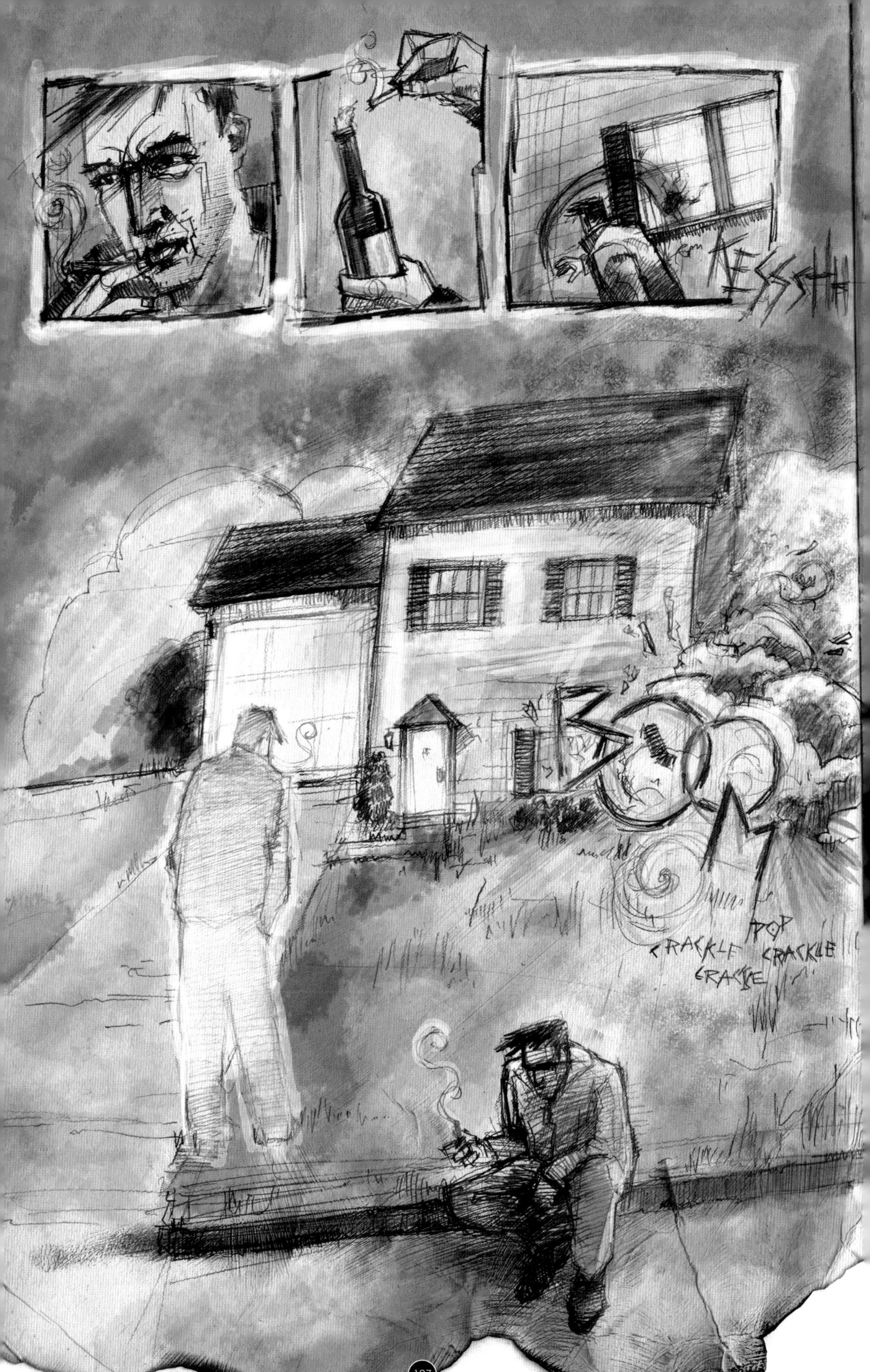
BOOM
POP
CRACKLE
CRACKLE
CRACKLE

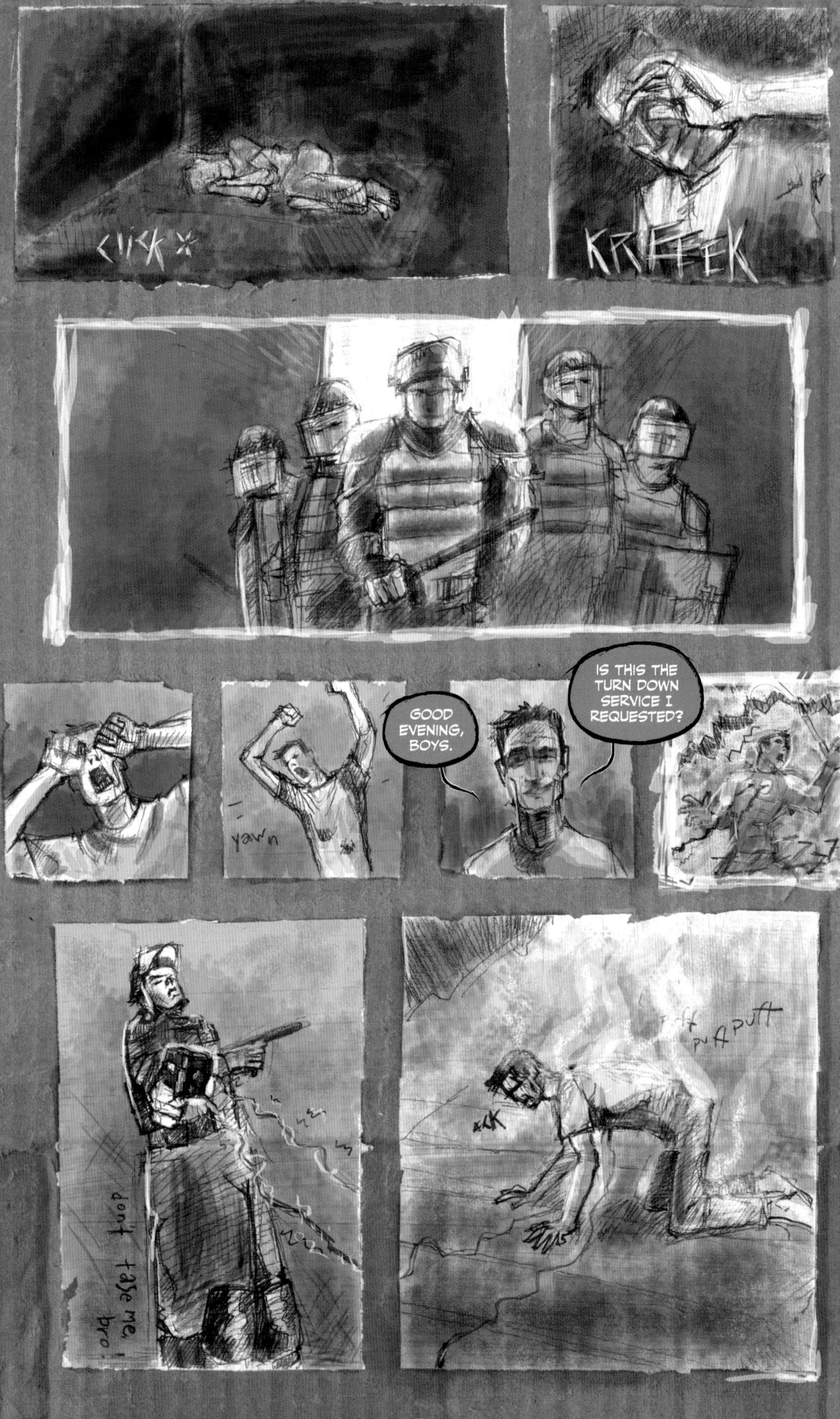
CLICK
GOOD EVENING, BOYS.
IS THIS THE TURN DOWN SERVICE I REQUESTED?
yawn
don't tase me, bro!
puff puff puff

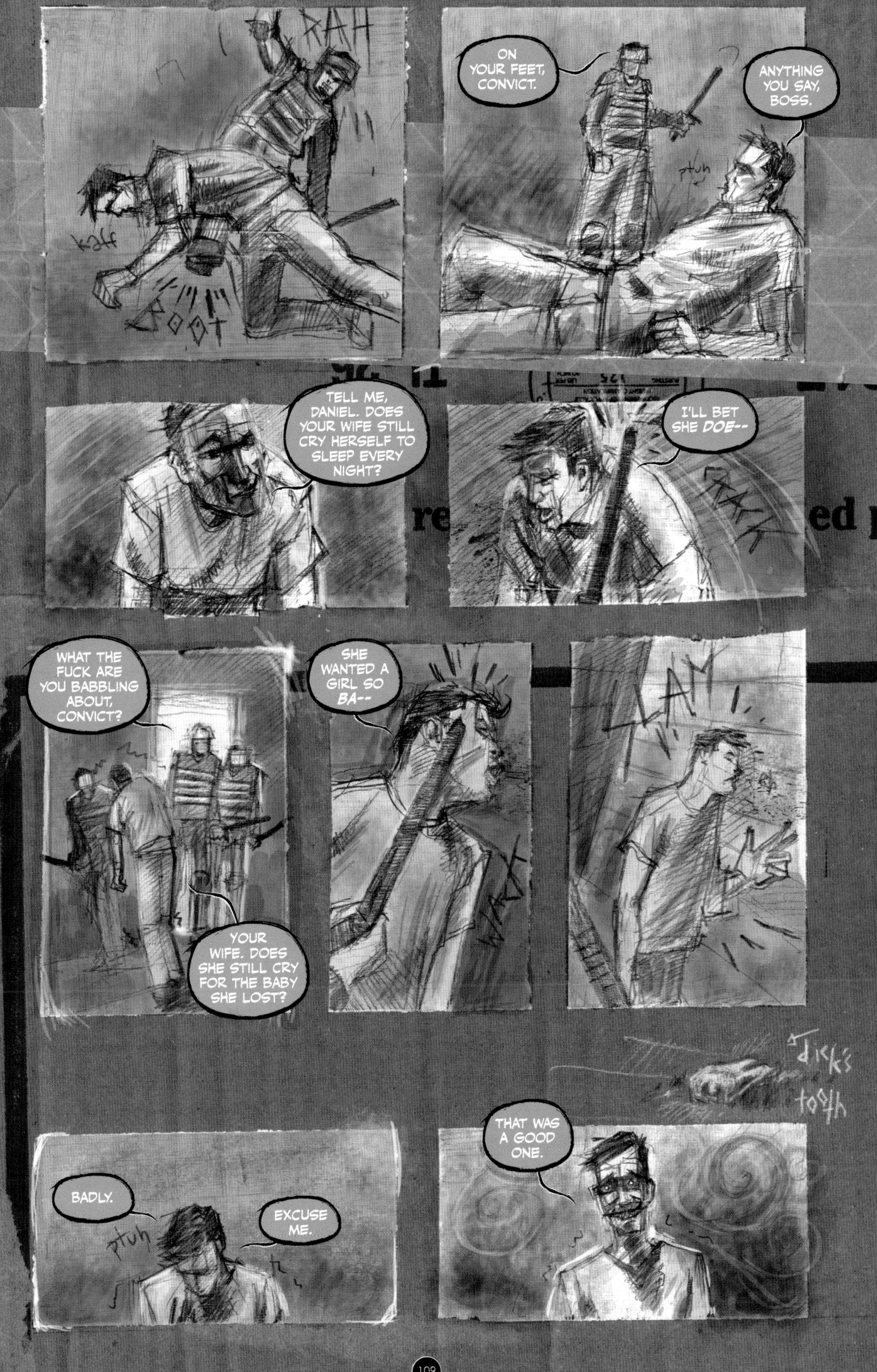
RAH
kaff
BOOT
ON YOUR FEET, CONVICT.
ANYTHING YOU SAY, BOSS.
ptuh
TELL ME, DANIEL. DOES YOUR WIFE STILL CRY HERSELF TO SLEEP EVERY NIGHT?
I'LL BET SHE DOE--
CRACK
WHAT THE FUCK ARE YOU BABBLING ABOUT, CONVICT?
YOUR WIFE. DOES SHE STILL CRY FOR THE BABY SHE LOST?
SHE WANTED A GIRL SO BA--
LAM
dick's tooth
BADLY.
ptuh
EXCUSE ME.
THAT WAS A GOOD ONE.

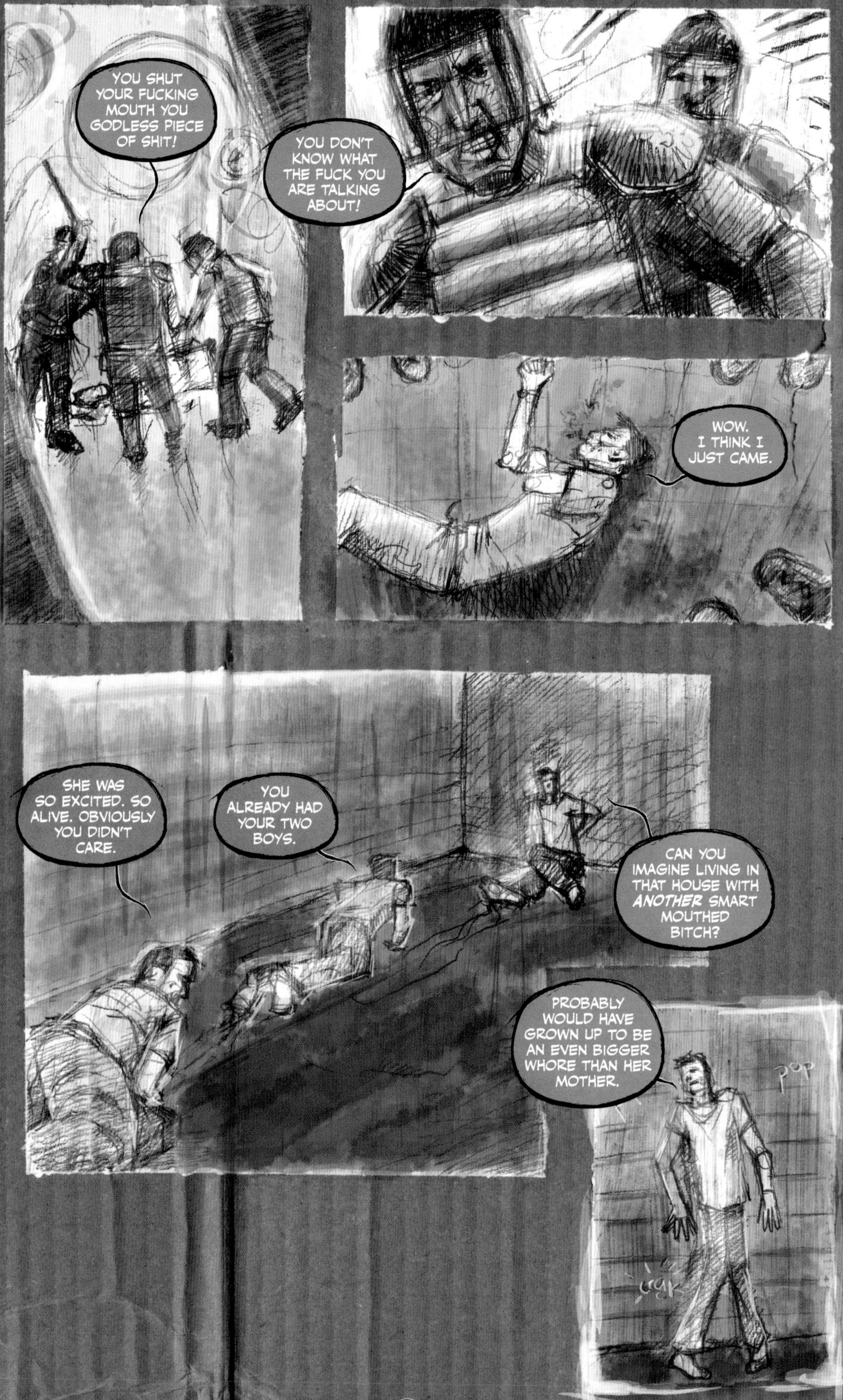
YOU SHUT YOUR FUCKING MOUTH YOU GODLESS PIECE OF SHIT!
YOU DON'T KNOW WHAT THE FUCK YOU ARE TALKING ABOUT!
WOW. I THINK I JUST CAME.
SHE WAS SO EXCITED. SO ALIVE. OBVIOUSLY YOU DIDN'T CARE.
YOU ALREADY HAD YOUR TWO BOYS.
CAN YOU IMAGINE LIVING IN THAT HOUSE WITH *ANOTHER* SMART MOUTHED BITCH?
PROBABLY WOULD HAVE GROWN UP TO BE AN EVEN BIGGER WHORE THAN HER MOTHER.
pop

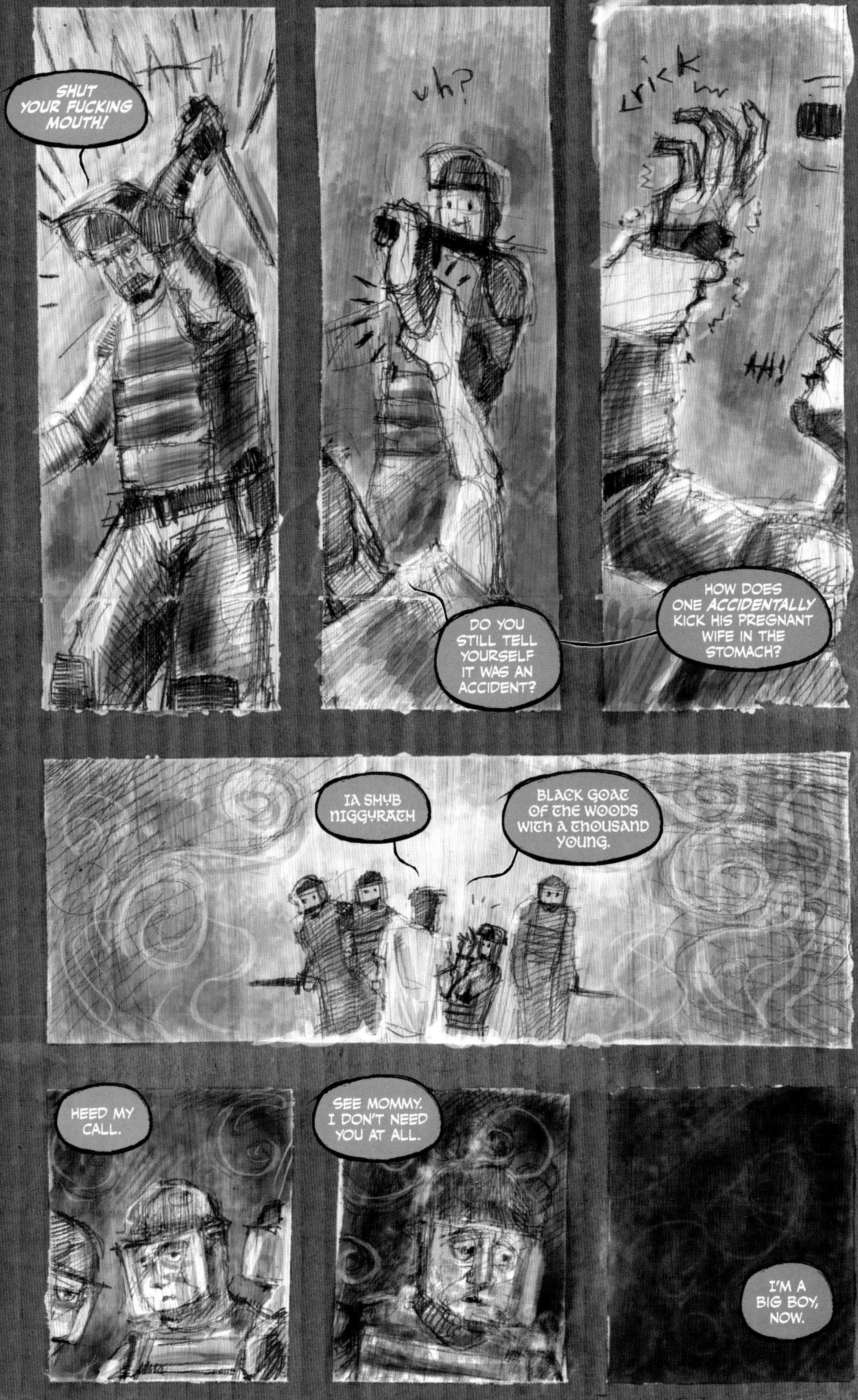
SHUT YOUR FUCKING MOUTH!
uh?
AH!
DO YOU STILL TELL YOURSELF IT WAS AN ACCIDENT?
HOW DOES ONE *ACCIDENTALLY* KICK HIS PREGNANT WIFE IN THE STOMACH?
IA SHUB NIGGURATH
BLACK GOAT OF THE WOODS WITH A THOUSAND YOUNG.
HEED MY CALL.
SEE MOMMY. I DON'T NEED YOU AT ALL.
I'M A BIG BOY, NOW.

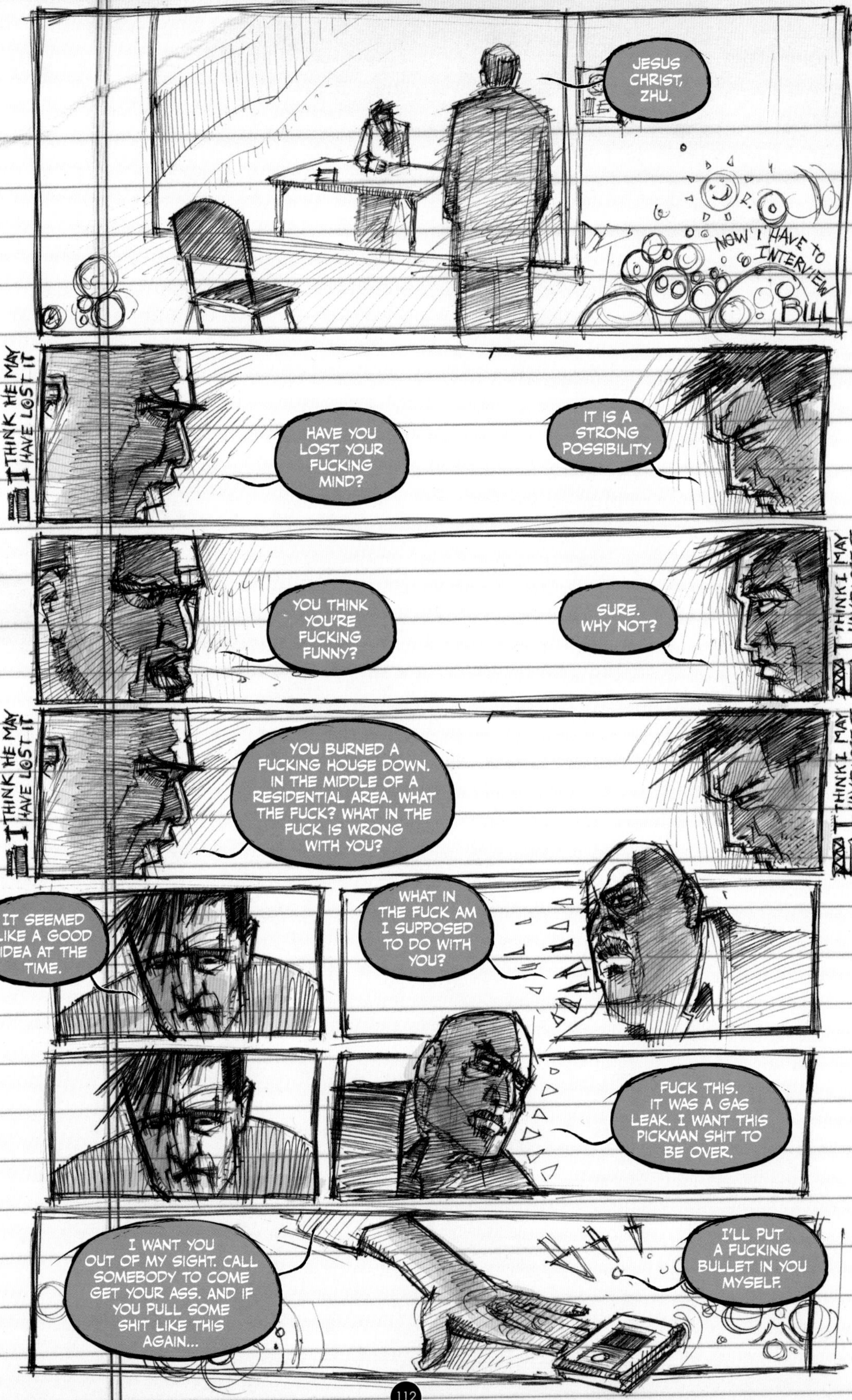
JESUS CHRIST, ZHU.
NOW I HAVE TO INTERVIEW BILL
I THINK HE MAY HAVE LOST IT
HAVE YOU LOST YOUR FUCKING MIND?
IT IS A STRONG POSSIBILITY.
YOU THINK YOU'RE FUCKING FUNNY?
SURE. WHY NOT?
I THINK I MAY HAVE LOST IT
I THINK HE MAY HAVE LOST IT
YOU BURNED A FUCKING HOUSE DOWN. IN THE MIDDLE OF A RESIDENTIAL AREA. WHAT THE FUCK? WHAT IN THE FUCK IS WRONG WITH YOU?
I THINK I MAY HAVE LOST IT
IT SEEMED LIKE A GOOD IDEA AT THE TIME.
WHAT IN THE FUCK AM I SUPPOSED TO DO WITH YOU?
FUCK THIS. IT WAS A GAS LEAK. I WANT THIS PICKMAN SHIT TO BE OVER.
I WANT YOU OUT OF MY SIGHT. CALL SOMEBODY TO COME GET YOUR ASS. AND IF YOU PULL SOME SHIT LIKE THIS AGAIN...
I'LL PUT A FUCKING BULLET IN YOU MYSELF.

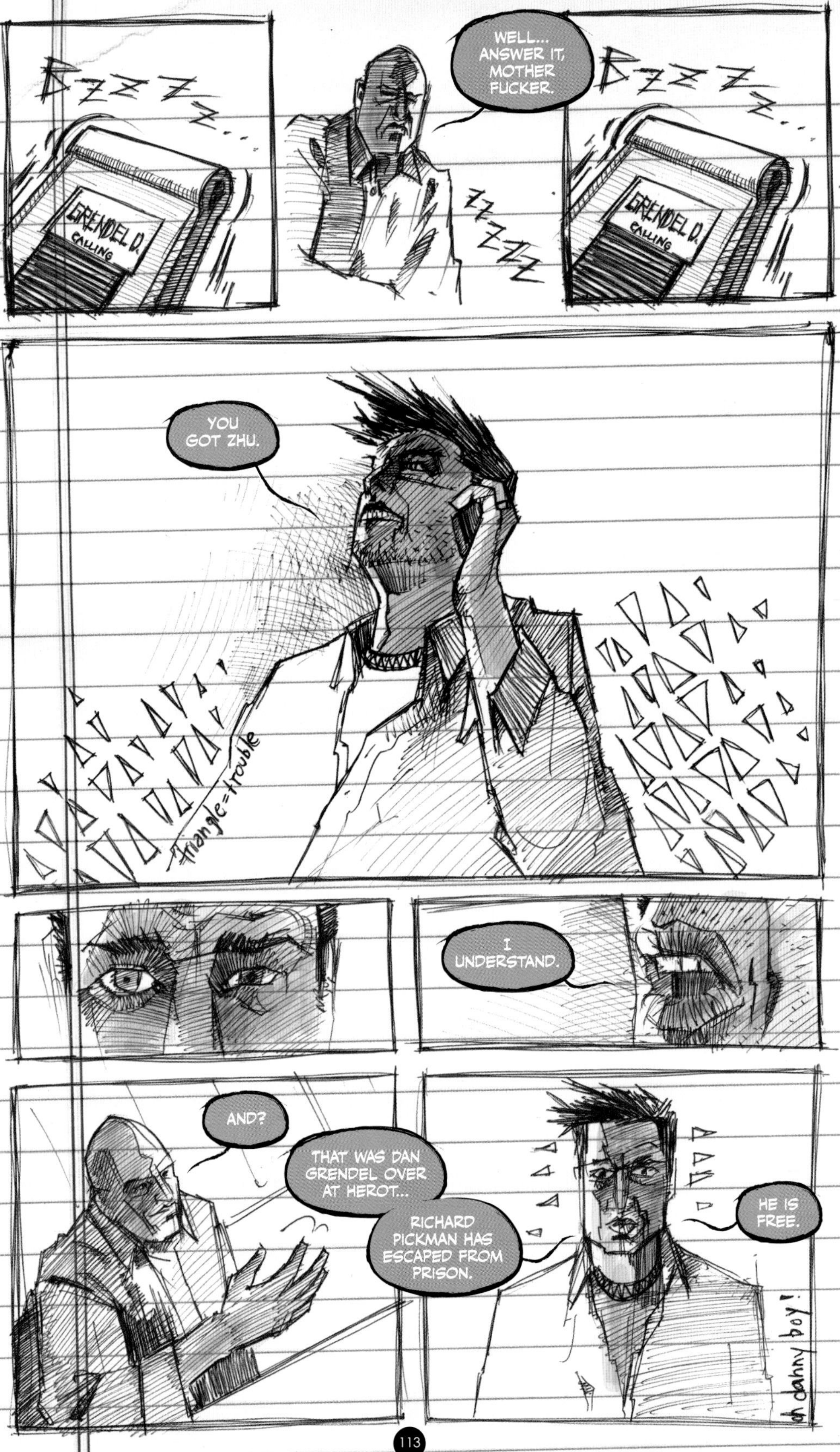
GRENDEL D.
CALLING
WELL... ANSWER IT, MOTHER FUCKER.
GRENDEL D.
CALLING
YOU GOT ZHU.
triangle=trouble
I UNDERSTAND.
AND?
THAT WAS DAN GRENDEL OVER AT HEROT...
RICHARD PICKMAN HAS ESCAPED FROM PRISON.
HE IS FREE.
oh danny boy!

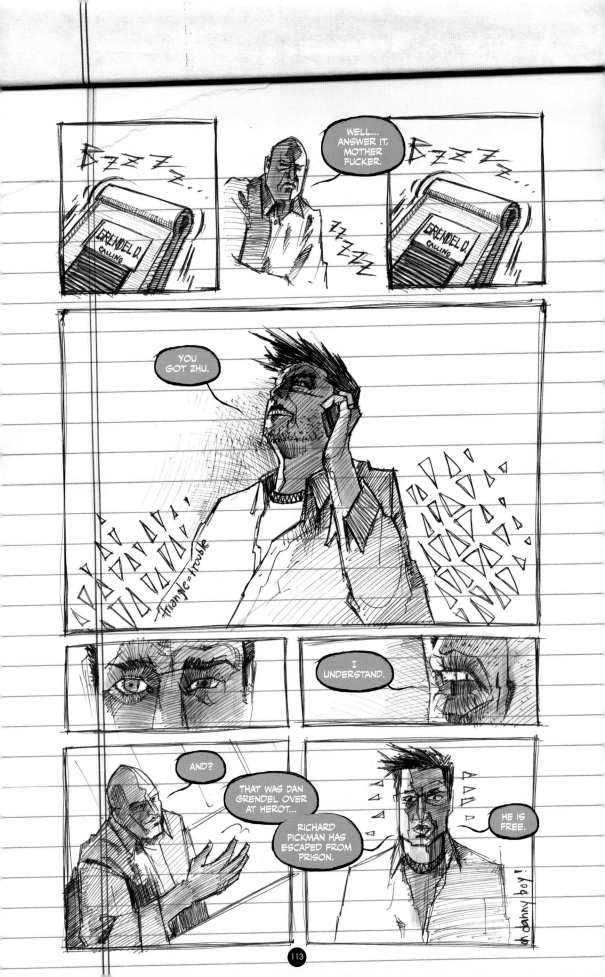

chapter six

DOOM OF GLORY

"I seek doom of glory, or
Death shall take me."
—Beowulf

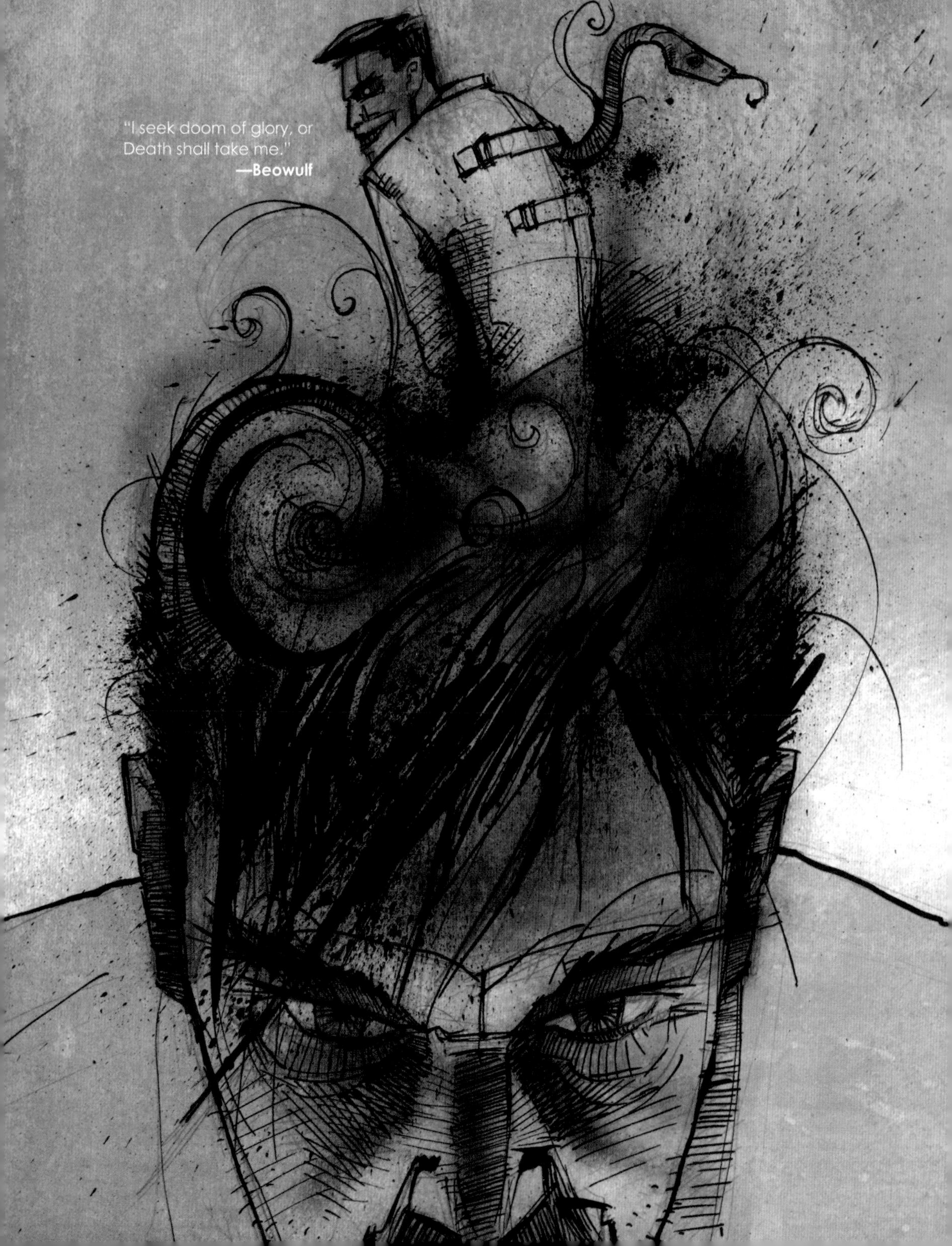

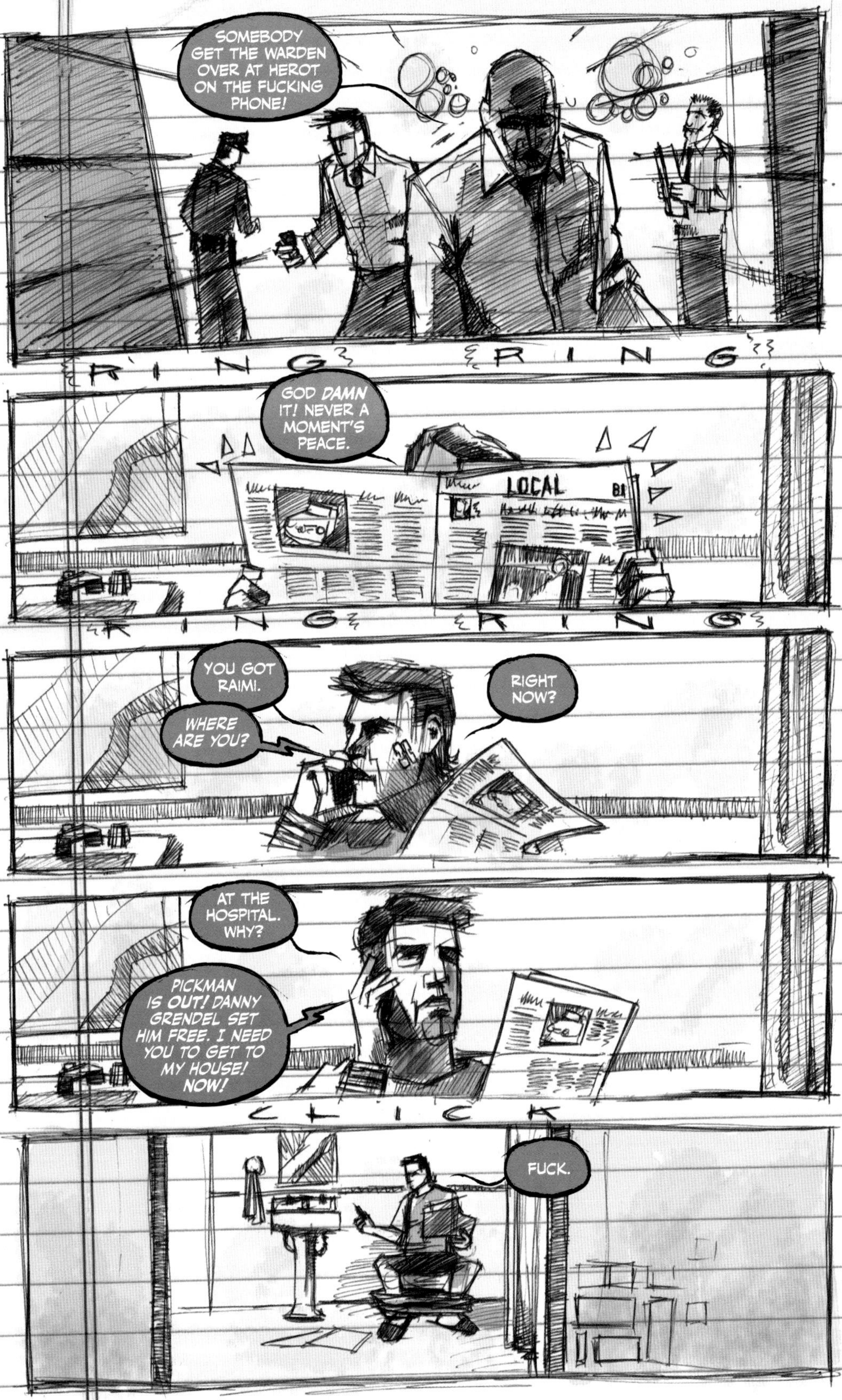

SOMEBODY GET THE WARDEN OVER AT HEROT ON THE FUCKING PHONE!
RING RING
GOD DAMN IT! NEVER A MOMENT'S PEACE.
LOCAL
RING RING
YOU GOT RAIMI.
WHERE ARE YOU?
RIGHT NOW?
AT THE HOSPITAL. WHY?
PICKMAN IS OUT! DANNY GRENDEL SET HIM FREE. I NEED YOU TO GET TO MY HOUSE! NOW!
CLICK
FUCK.

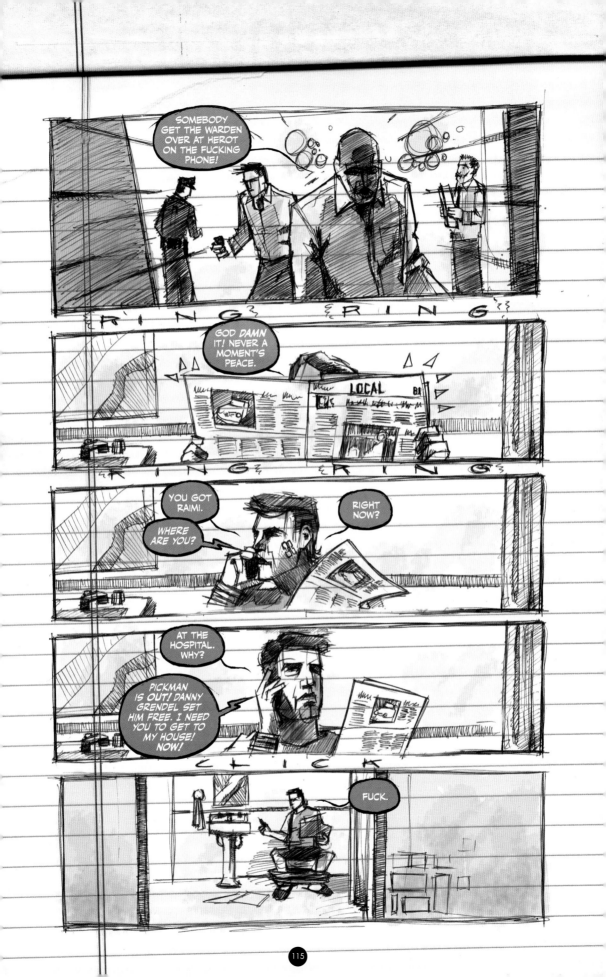

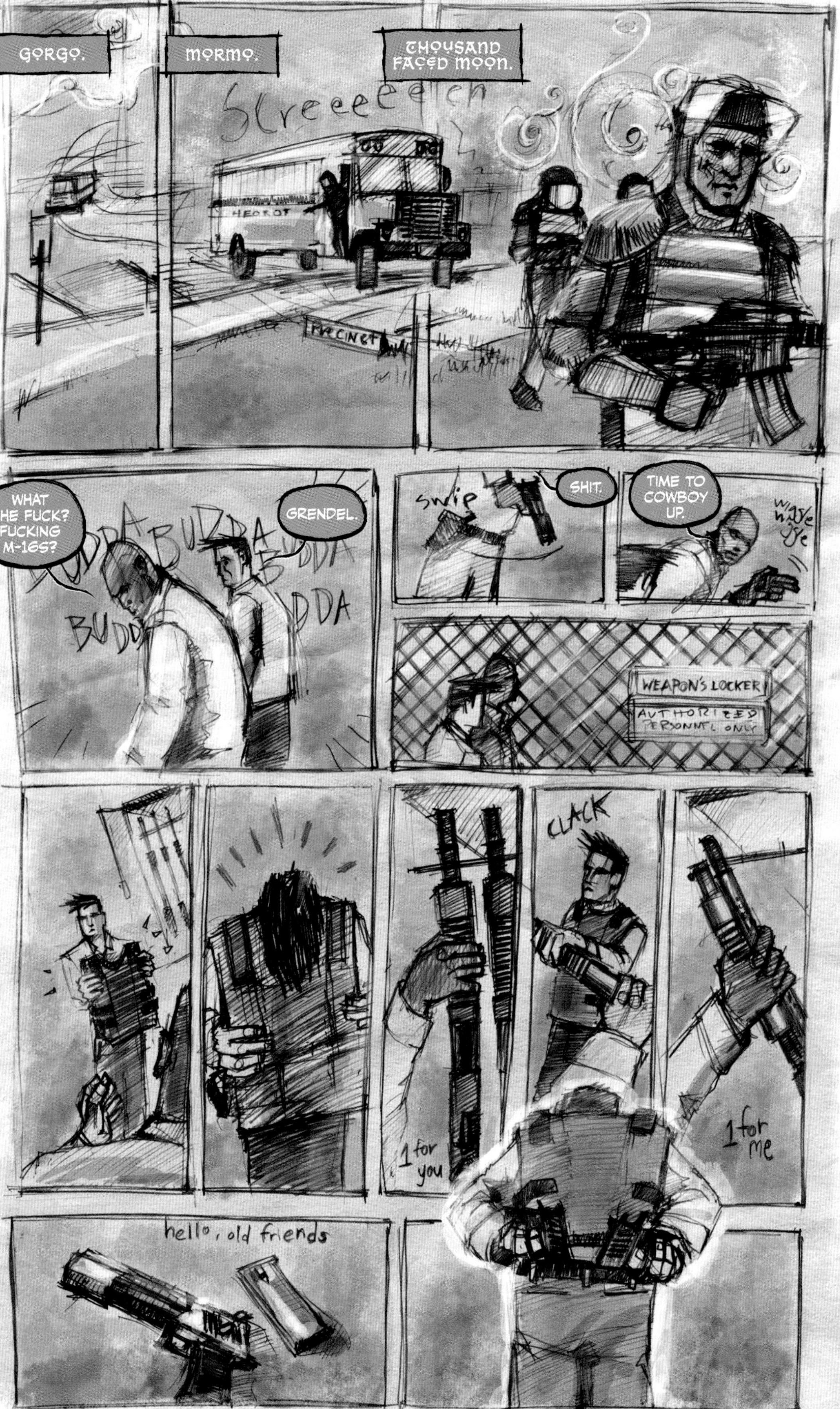
GORGO.
MORMO.
THOUSAND FACED MOON.
HEOROT
PRECINCT
WHAT THE FUCK? FUCKING M-16S?
GRENDEL.
BUDDA BUDDA BUDDA BUDDA
swip
SHIT.
TIME TO COWBOY UP.
WEAPON'S LOCKER
AUTHORIZED PERSONNEL ONLY
CLACK
1 for you
1 for me
hello, old friends

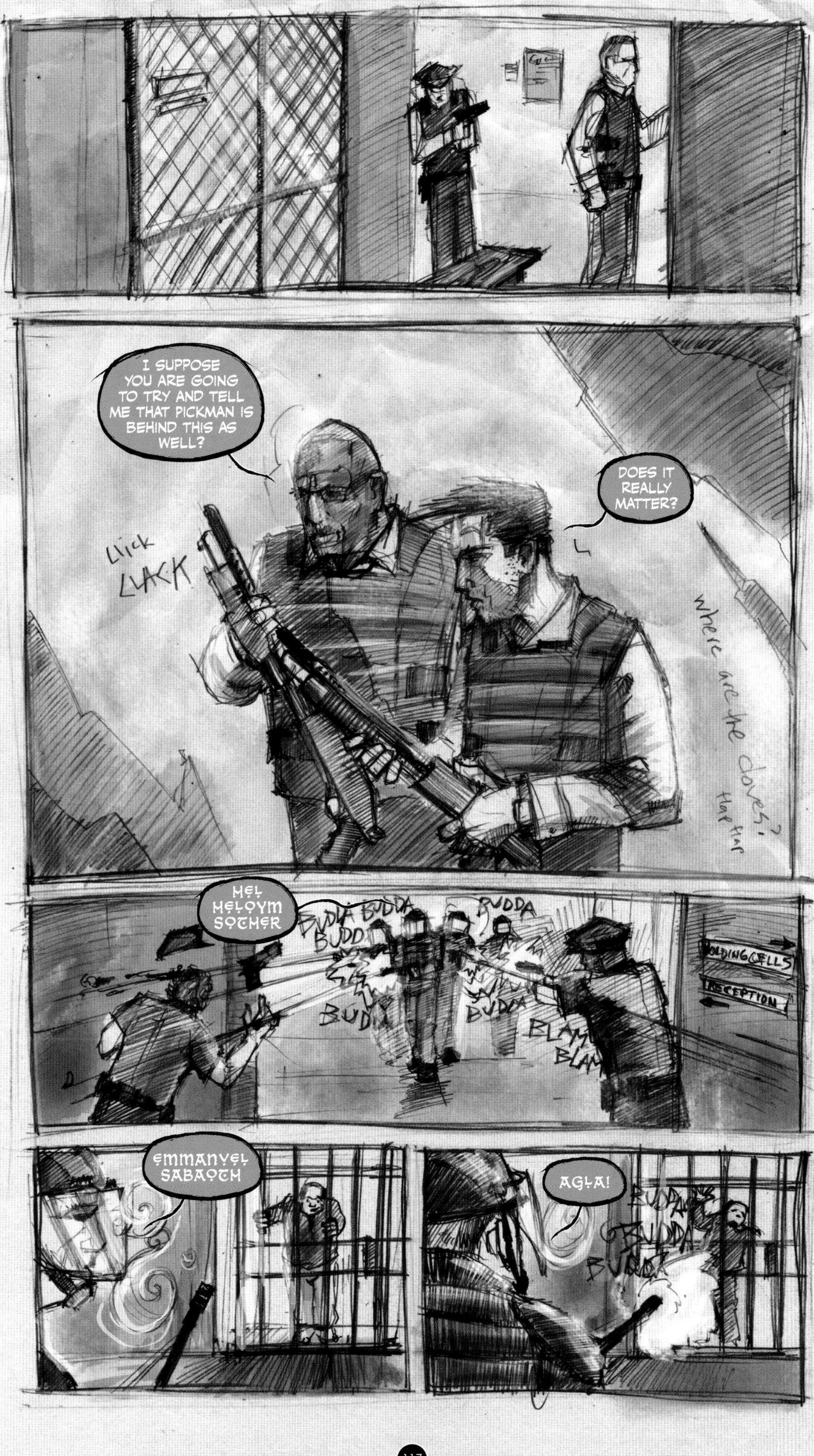

I SUPPOSE YOU ARE GOING TO TRY AND TELL ME THAT PICKMAN IS BEHIND THIS AS WELL?
Click CLACK
DOES IT REALLY MATTER?
HEL HELOYM SOTHER
BUDDA BUDDA BUDDA
BUDDA
BLAM BLAM
HOLDING CELLS
RECEPTION
EMMANUEL SABAOTH
AGLA!

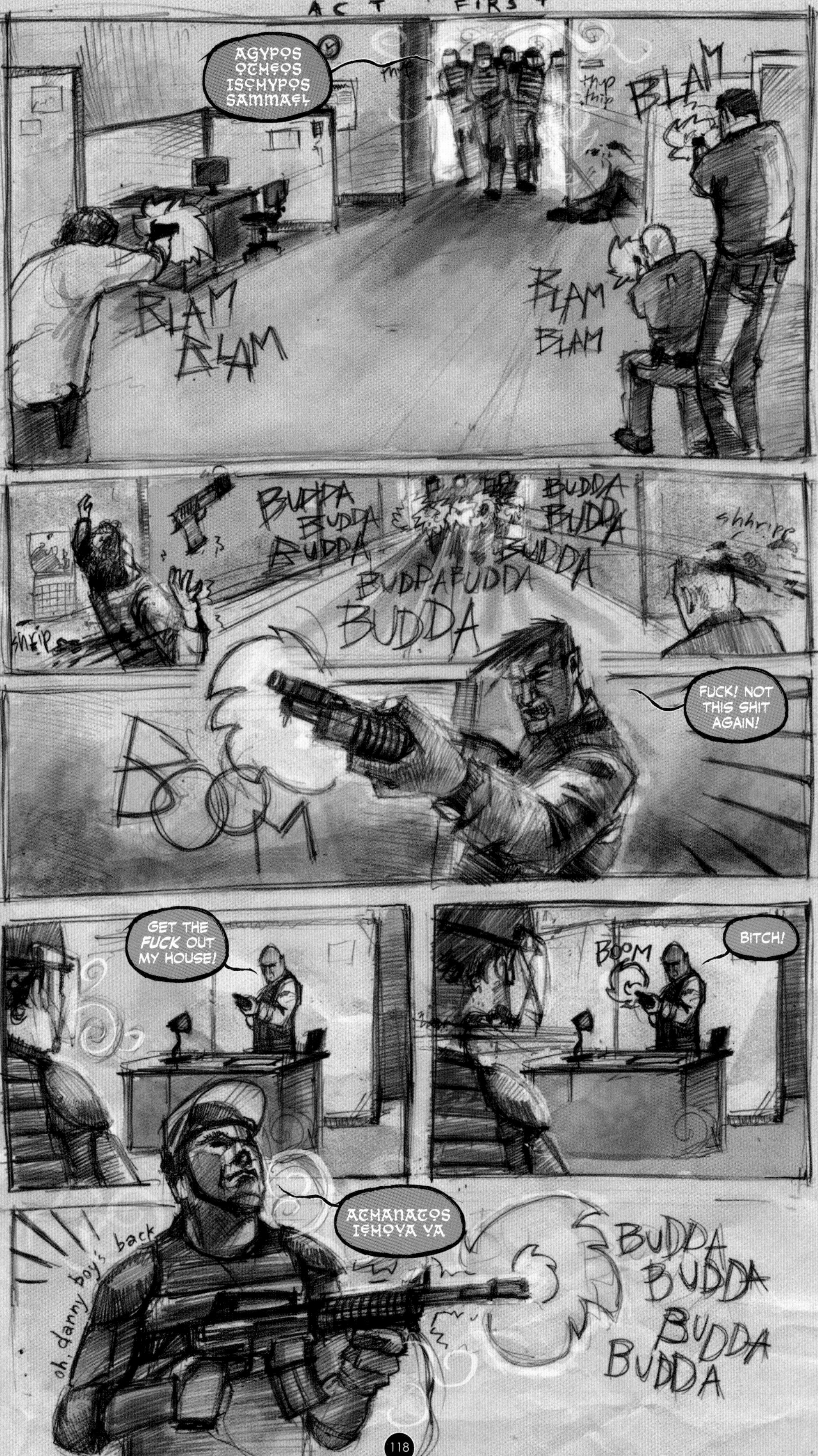
AGYPOS OTHEOS ISCHYPOS SAMMAEL
thip
thip thip
BLAM
BLAM BLAM
BLAM BLAM
BUDDA BUDDA BUDDA
BUDDA BUDDA BUDDA
BUDDABUDDA
BUDDA
shhrip
shrip
BOOM
FUCK! NOT THIS SHIT AGAIN!
GET THE FUCK OUT MY HOUSE!
BOOM
BITCH!
oh, danny boy's back
ATHANATOS IEHOYA YA
BUDDA BUDDA BUDDA BUDDA

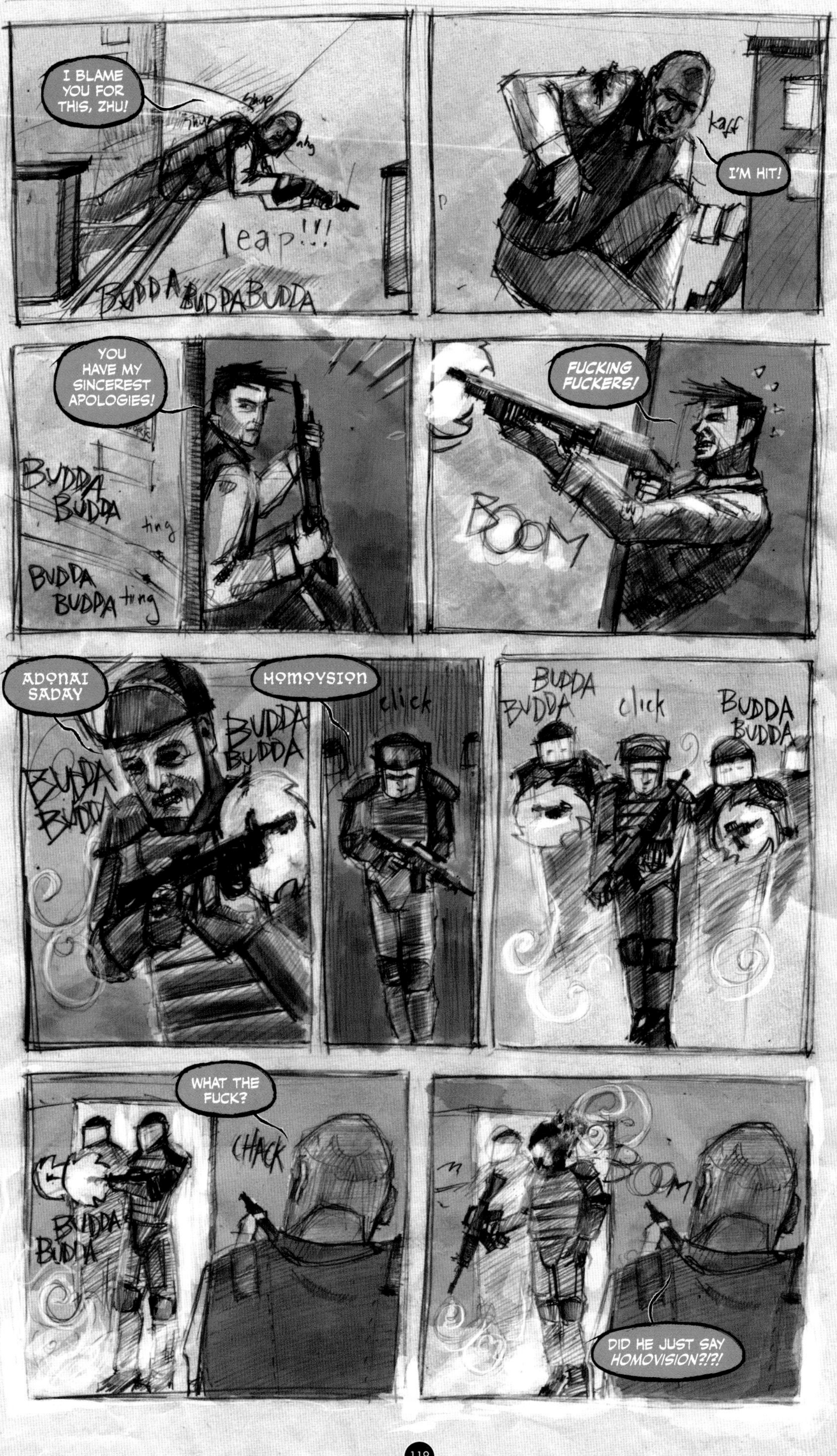
I BLAME YOU FOR THIS, ZHU!
leap!!!
BUDDA BUDDA BUDDA
kaff
I'M HIT!
YOU HAVE MY SINCEREST APOLOGIES!
BUDDA BUDDA
ting
BUDDA BUDDA
ting
FUCKING FUCKERS!
BOOM
ADONAI SADAY
BUDDA BUDDA
BUDDA BUDDA
HOMOVSION
click
BUDDA BUDDA
click
BUDDA BUDDA
WHAT THE FUCK?
CHACK
BUDDA BUDDA
BOOM
DID HE JUST SAY HOMOVISION?!?!

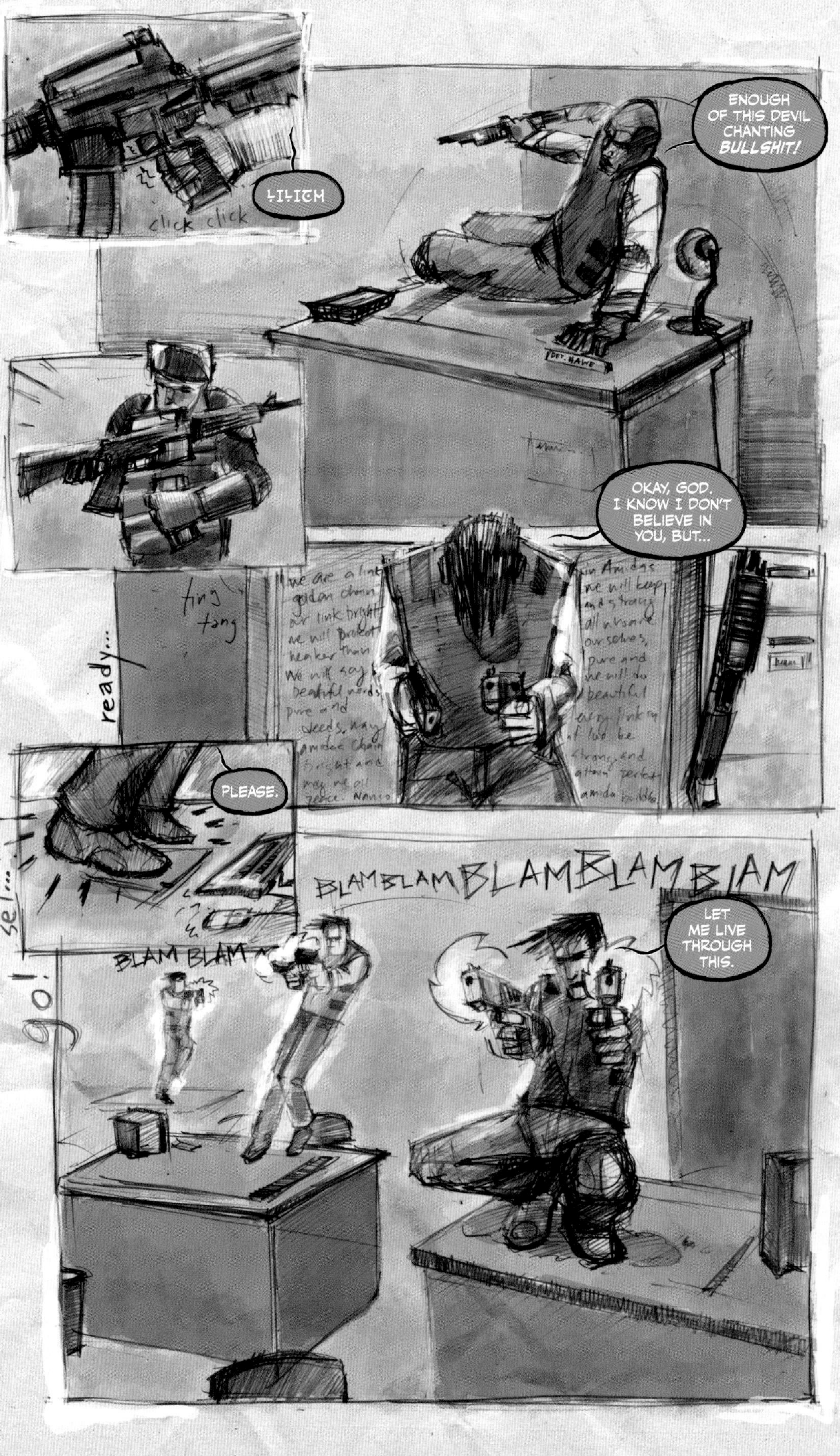
click click
ENOUGH OF THIS DEVIL CHANTING *BULLSHIT!*
OKAY, GOD. I KNOW I DON'T BELIEVE IN YOU, BUT...
ting tang
ready...
PLEASE.
set...
go!
BLAMBLAMBLAMBLAMBLAM
BLAM BLAM
LET ME LIVE THROUGH THIS.

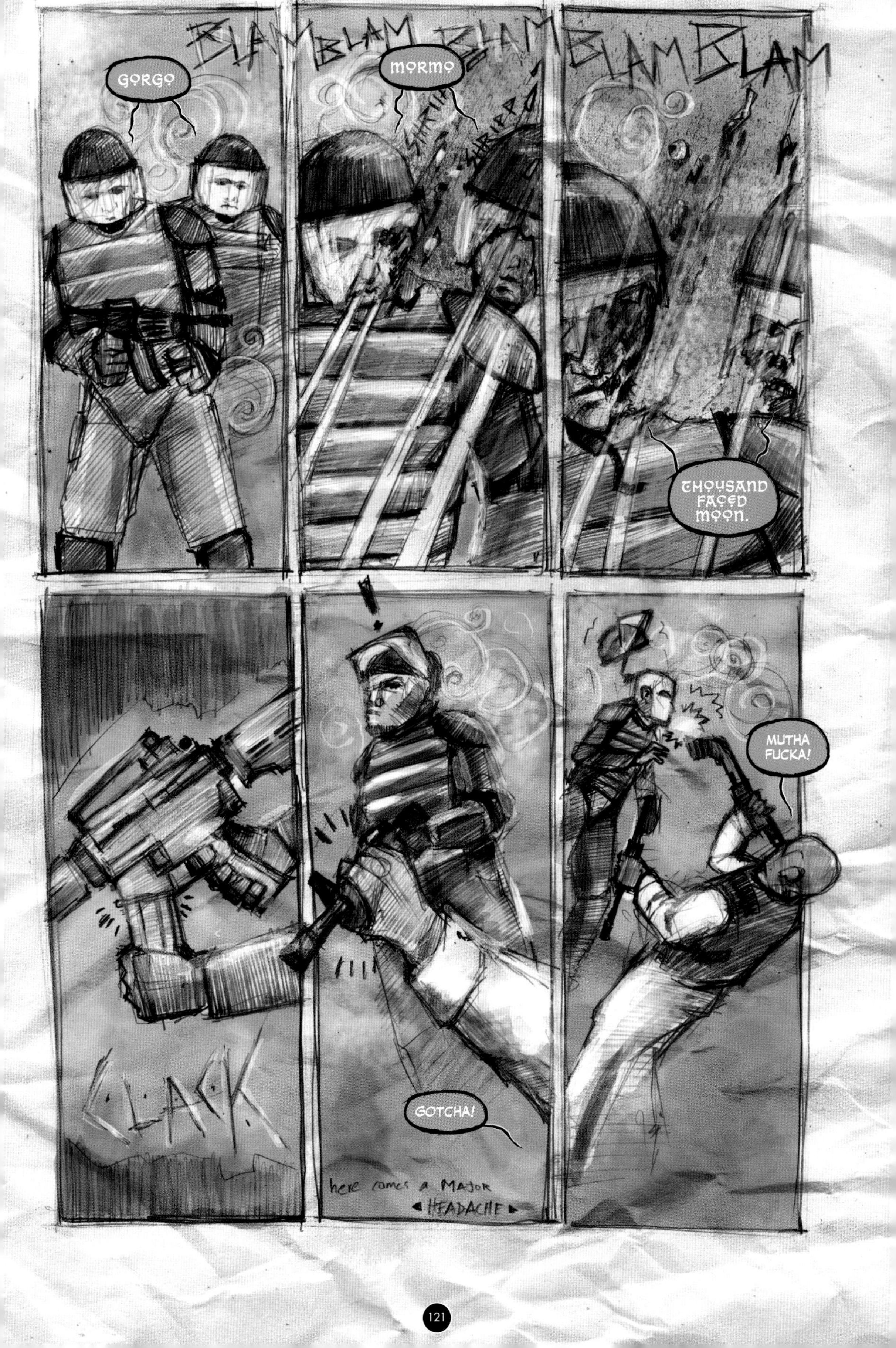
BLAM
GORGO
BLAM BLAM
MORMO
BLAM BLAM
THOUSAND FACED MOON.
CLACK
GOTCHA!
here comes a MAJOR HEADACHE
MUTHA FUCKA!

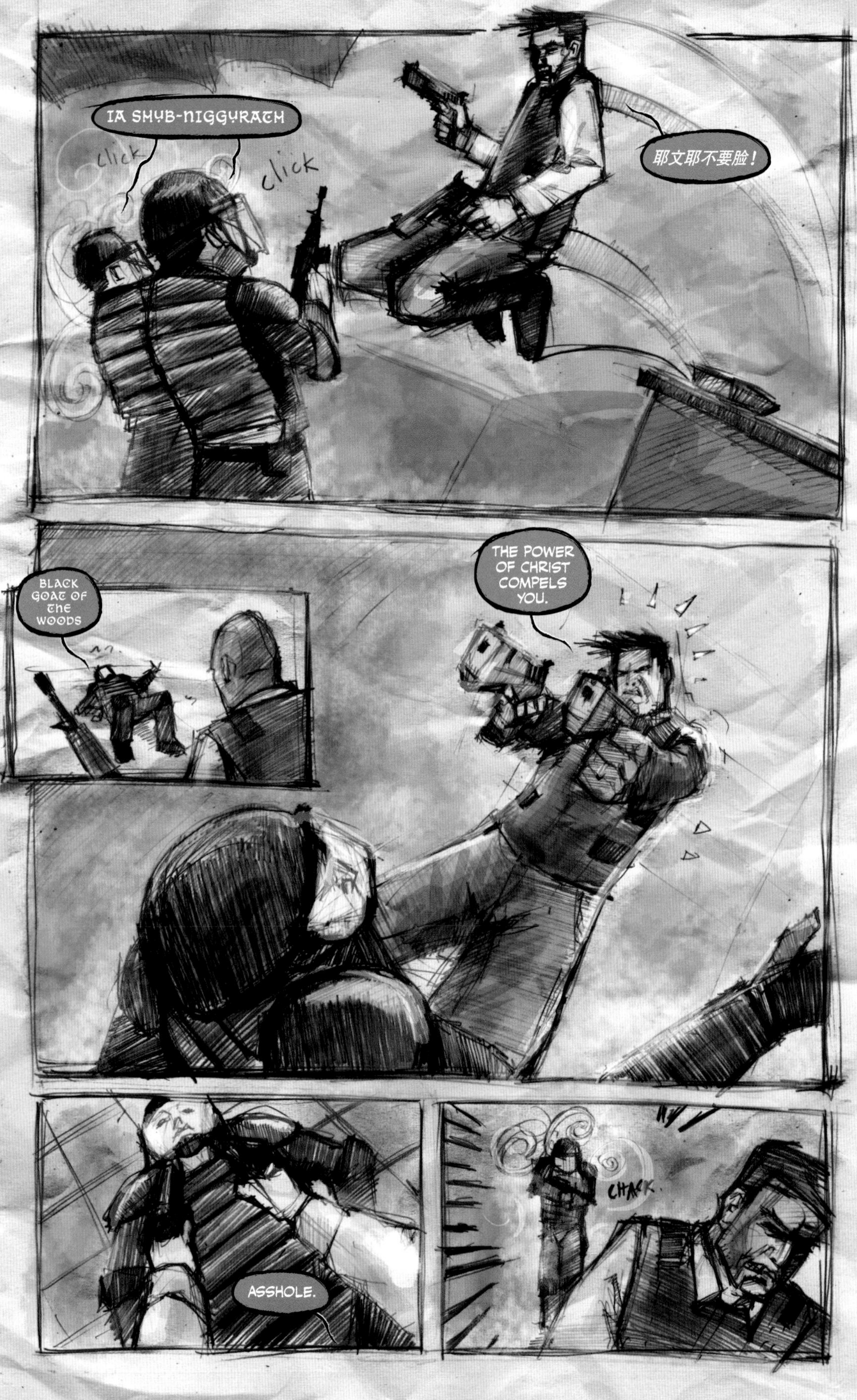
IA SHUB-NIGGURATH
click
click
耶文耶不要脸！
BLACK GOAT OF THE WOODS
THE POWER OF CHRIST COMPELS YOU.
ASSHOLE.
CHACK.

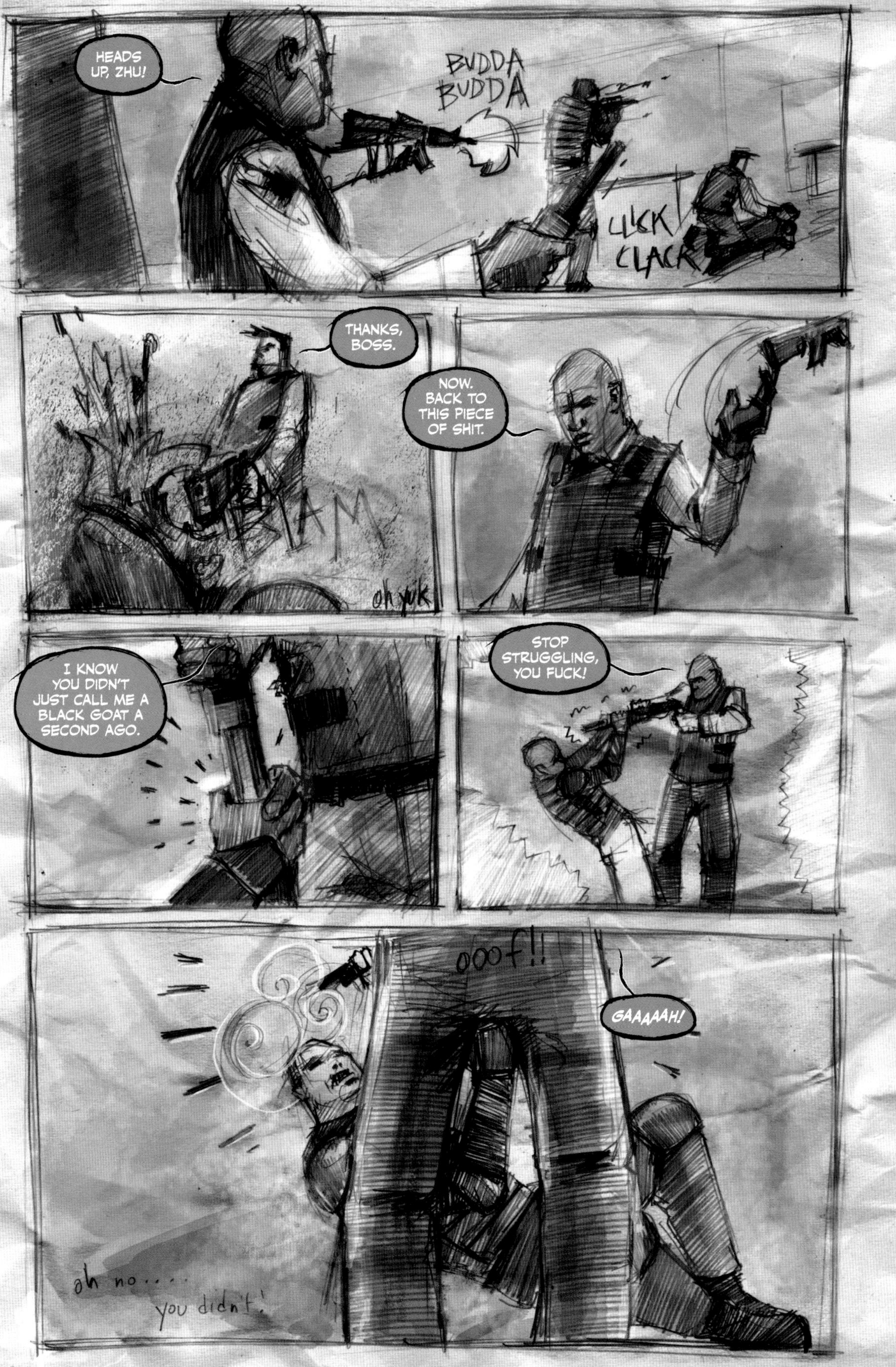
HEADS UP, ZHU!
BUDDA BUDDA
CLICK CLACK
THANKS, BOSS.
BLAM
oh yuk
NOW. BACK TO THIS PIECE OF SHIT.
I KNOW YOU DIDN'T JUST CALL ME A BLACK GOAT A SECOND AGO.
STOP STRUGGLING, YOU FUCK!
ooof!!
GAAAAAH!
oh no....
you didn't!

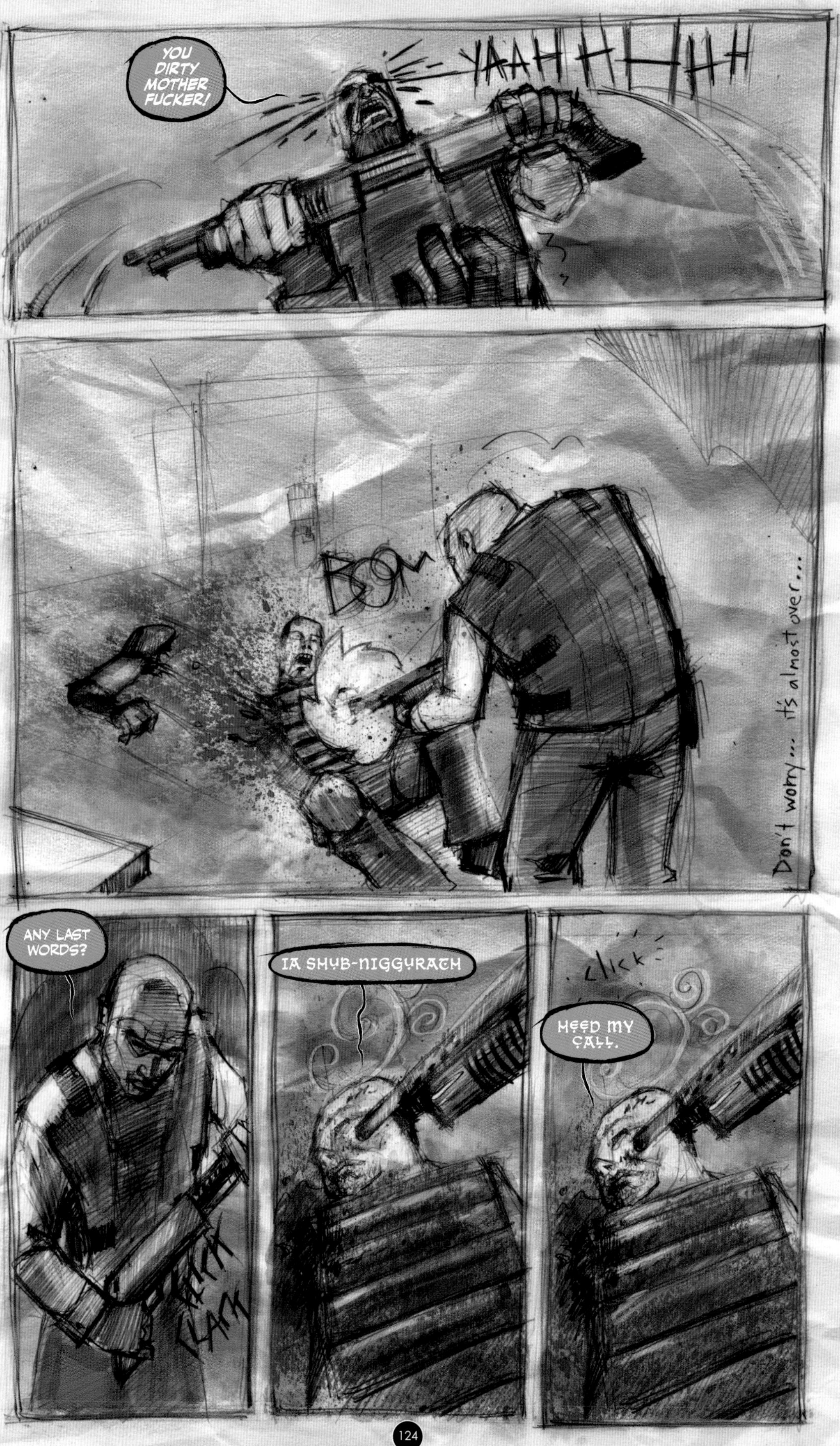

YOU DIRTY MOTHER FUCKER!
YAAHHHHHH
BOOM
Don't worry... it's almost over...
ANY LAST WORDS?
CLACK
IA SHUB-NIGGURATH
click
HEED MY CALL.

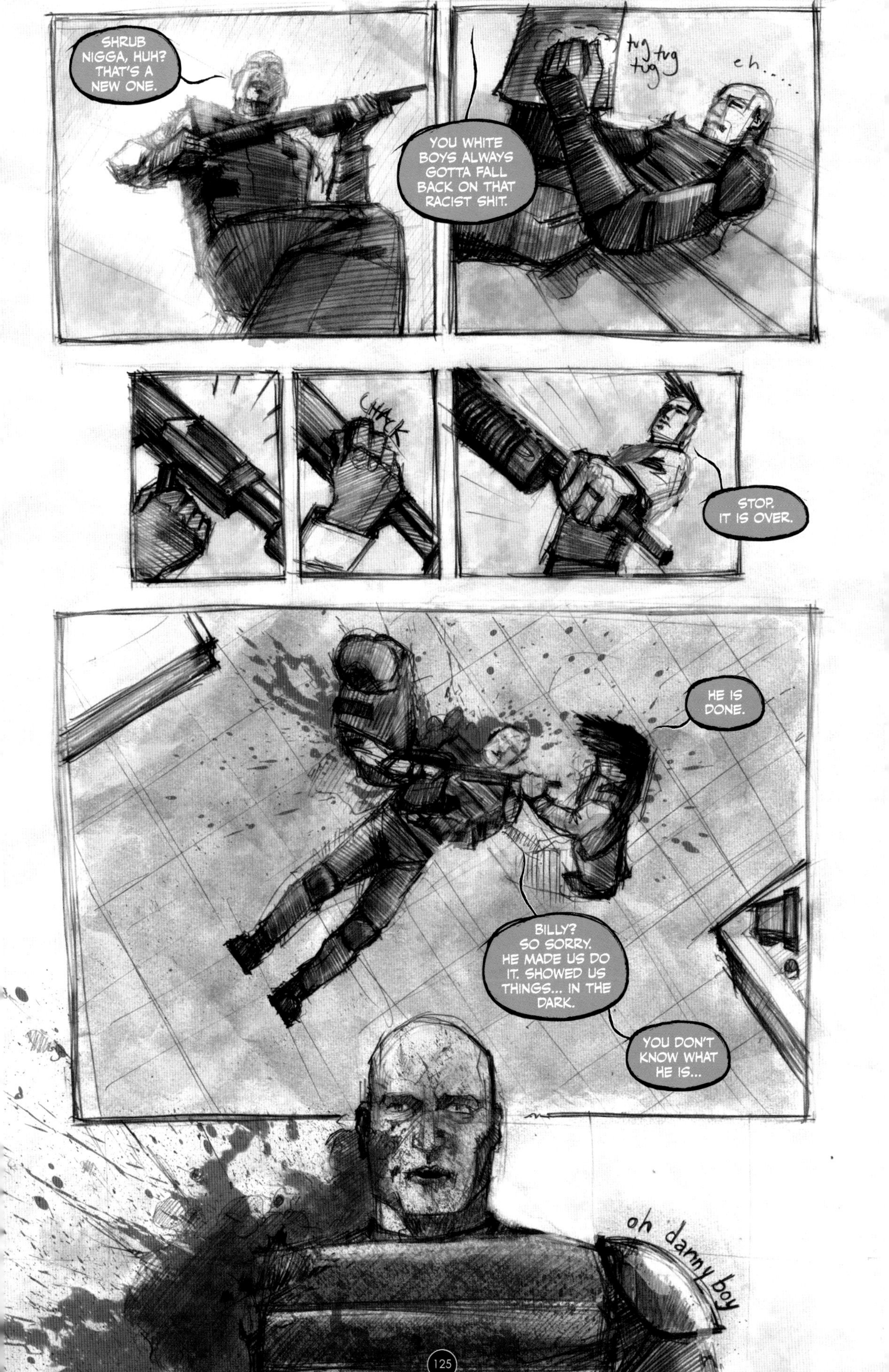
SHRUB NIGGA, HUH? THAT'S A NEW ONE.
YOU WHITE BOYS ALWAYS GOTTA FALL BACK ON THAT RACIST SHIT.
tug tug tug
eh.....
STOP. IT IS OVER.
HE IS DONE.
BILLY? SO SORRY. HE MADE US DO IT. SHOWED US THINGS... IN THE DARK.
YOU DON'T KNOW WHAT HE IS...
oh danny boy

ACT THE SECOND

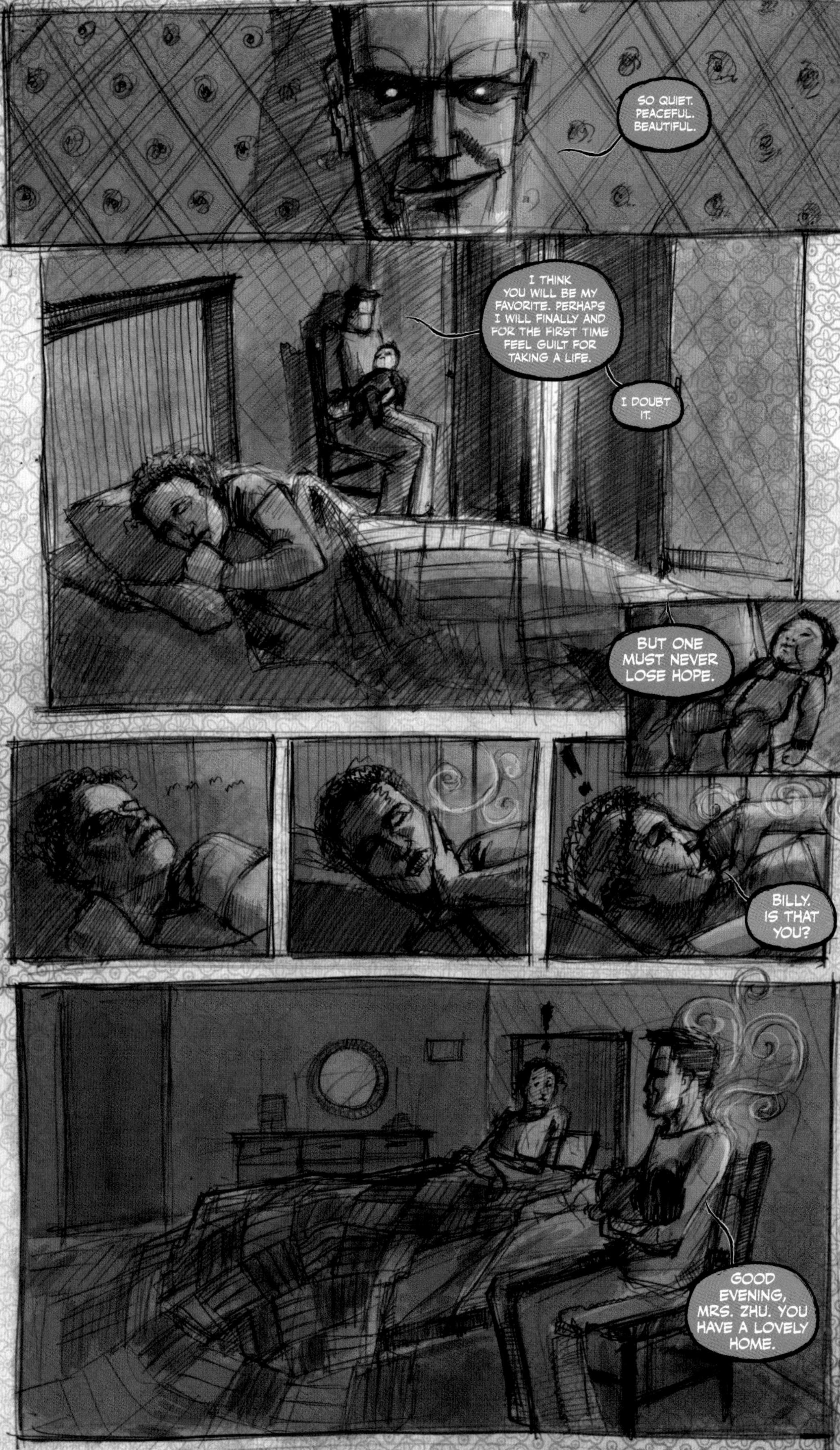
SO QUIET. PEACEFUL. BEAUTIFUL.
I THINK YOU WILL BE MY FAVORITE. PERHAPS I WILL FINALLY AND FOR THE FIRST TIME FEEL GUILT FOR TAKING A LIFE.
I DOUBT IT.
BUT ONE MUST NEVER LOSE HOPE.
sleepy little dragon
BILLY. IS THAT YOU?
GOOD EVENING, MRS. ZHU. YOU HAVE A LOVELY HOME.

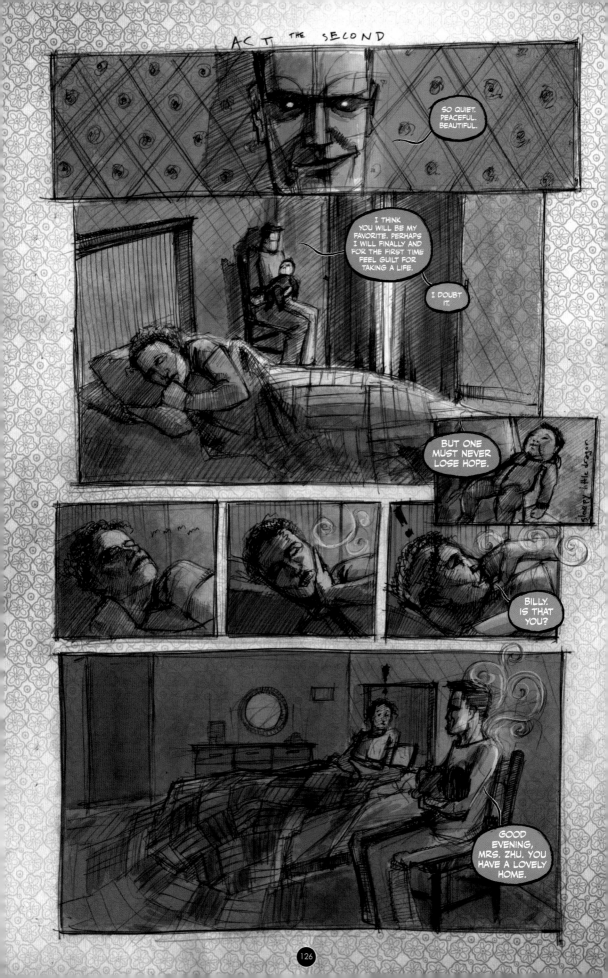

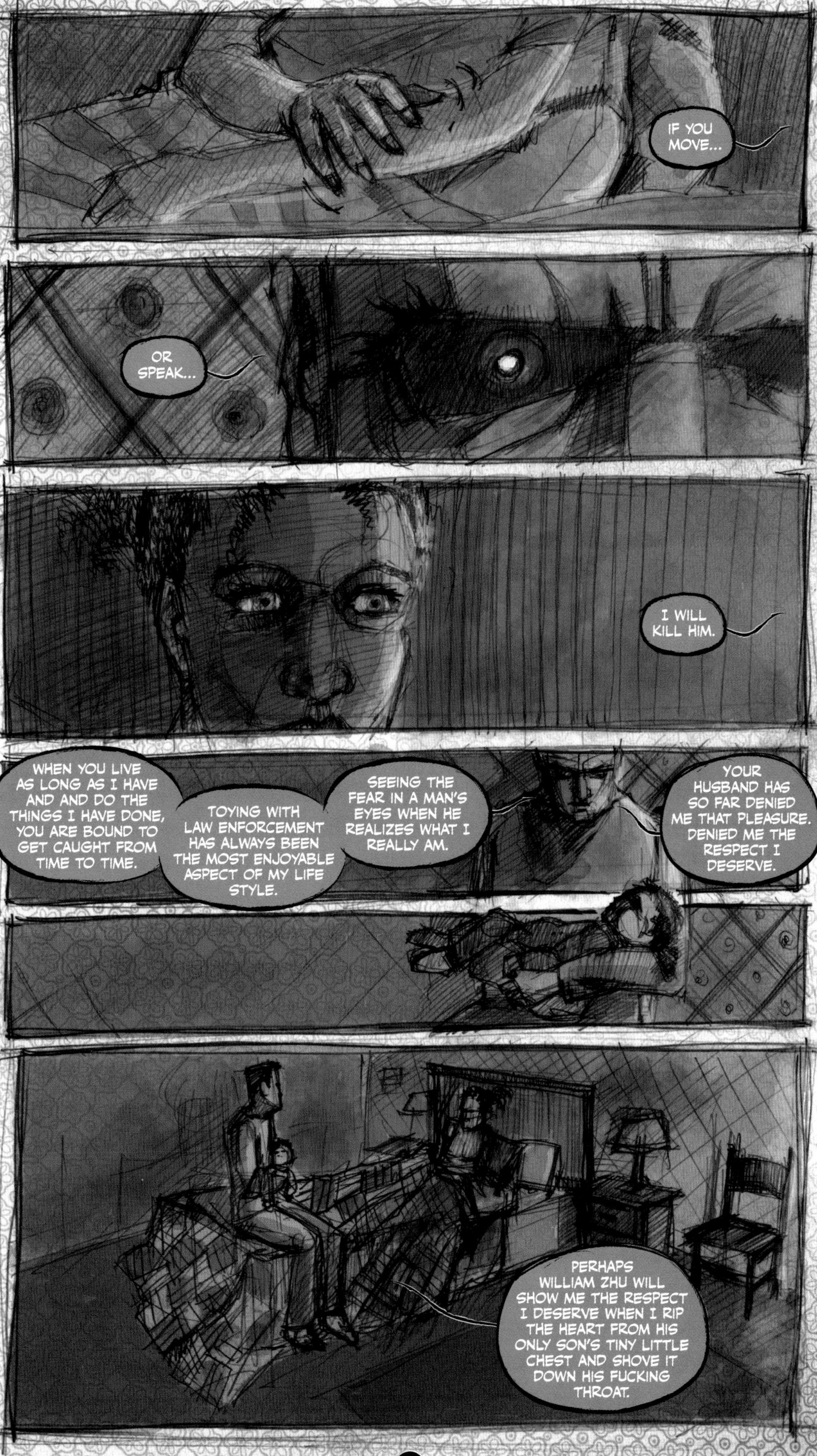
IF YOU MOVE...
OR SPEAK...
I WILL KILL HIM.
WHEN YOU LIVE AS LONG AS I HAVE AND AND DO THE THINGS I HAVE DONE, YOU ARE BOUND TO GET CAUGHT FROM TIME TO TIME.
TOYING WITH LAW ENFORCEMENT HAS ALWAYS BEEN THE MOST ENJOYABLE ASPECT OF MY LIFE STYLE.
SEEING THE FEAR IN A MAN'S EYES WHEN HE REALIZES WHAT I REALLY AM.
YOUR HUSBAND HAS SO FAR DENIED ME THAT PLEASURE. DENIED ME THE RESPECT I DESERVE.
PERHAPS WILLIAM ZHU WILL SHOW ME THE RESPECT I DESERVE WHEN I RIP THE HEART FROM HIS ONLY SON'S TINY LITTLE CHEST AND SHOVE IT DOWN HIS FUCKING THROAT.

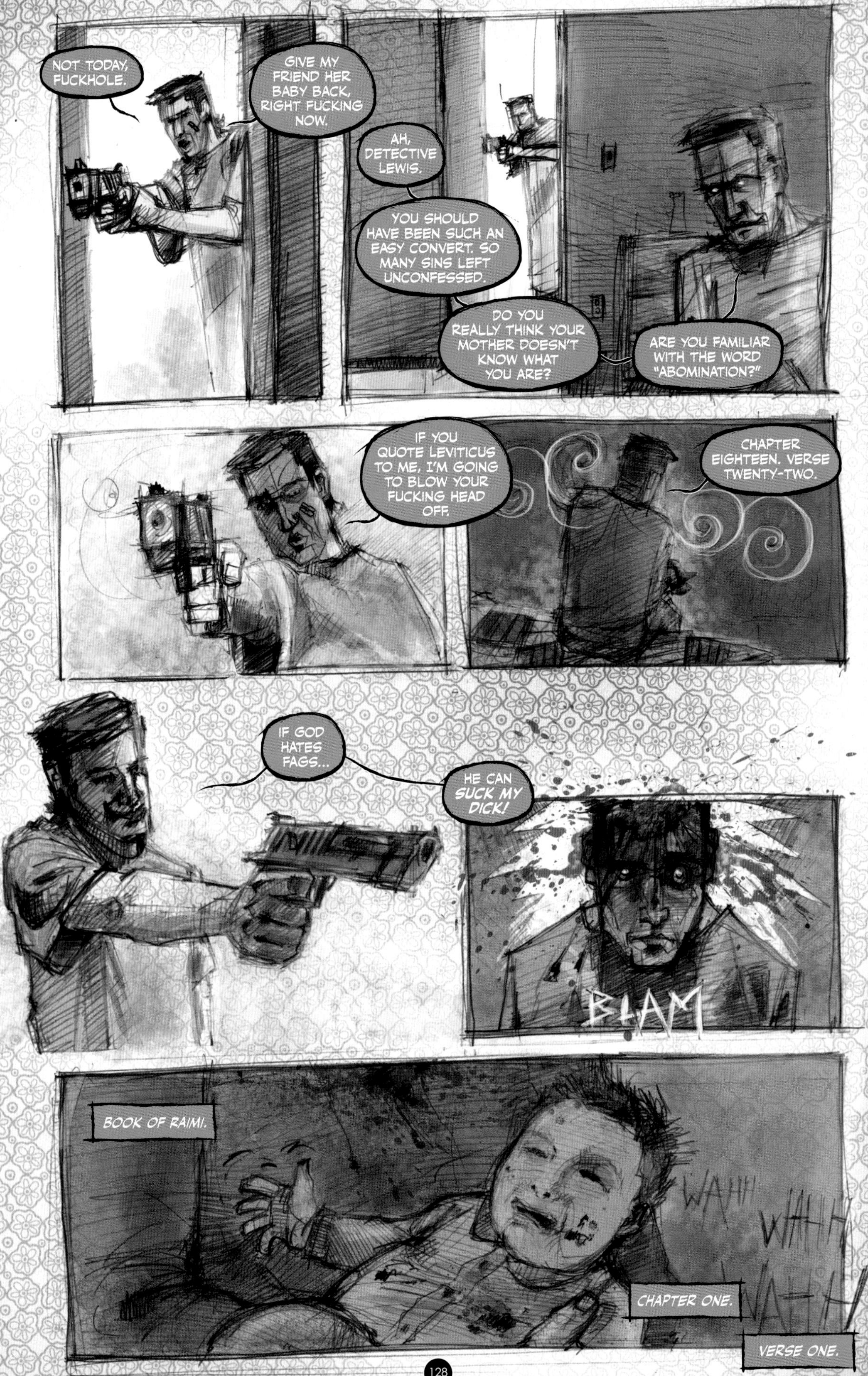
NOT TODAY, FUCKHOLE.
GIVE MY FRIEND HER BABY BACK, RIGHT FUCKING NOW.
AH, DETECTIVE LEWIS.
YOU SHOULD HAVE BEEN SUCH AN EASY CONVERT. SO MANY SINS LEFT UNCONFESSED.
DO YOU REALLY THINK YOUR MOTHER DOESN'T KNOW WHAT YOU ARE?
ARE YOU FAMILIAR WITH THE WORD "ABOMINATION?"
IF YOU QUOTE LEVITICUS TO ME, I'M GOING TO BLOW YOUR FUCKING HEAD OFF.
CHAPTER EIGHTEEN. VERSE TWENTY-TWO.
IF GOD HATES FAGS...
HE CAN *SUCK MY DICK!*
BLAM
BOOK OF RAIMI.
WAH WAHH WAHH
CHAPTER ONE.
VERSE ONE.

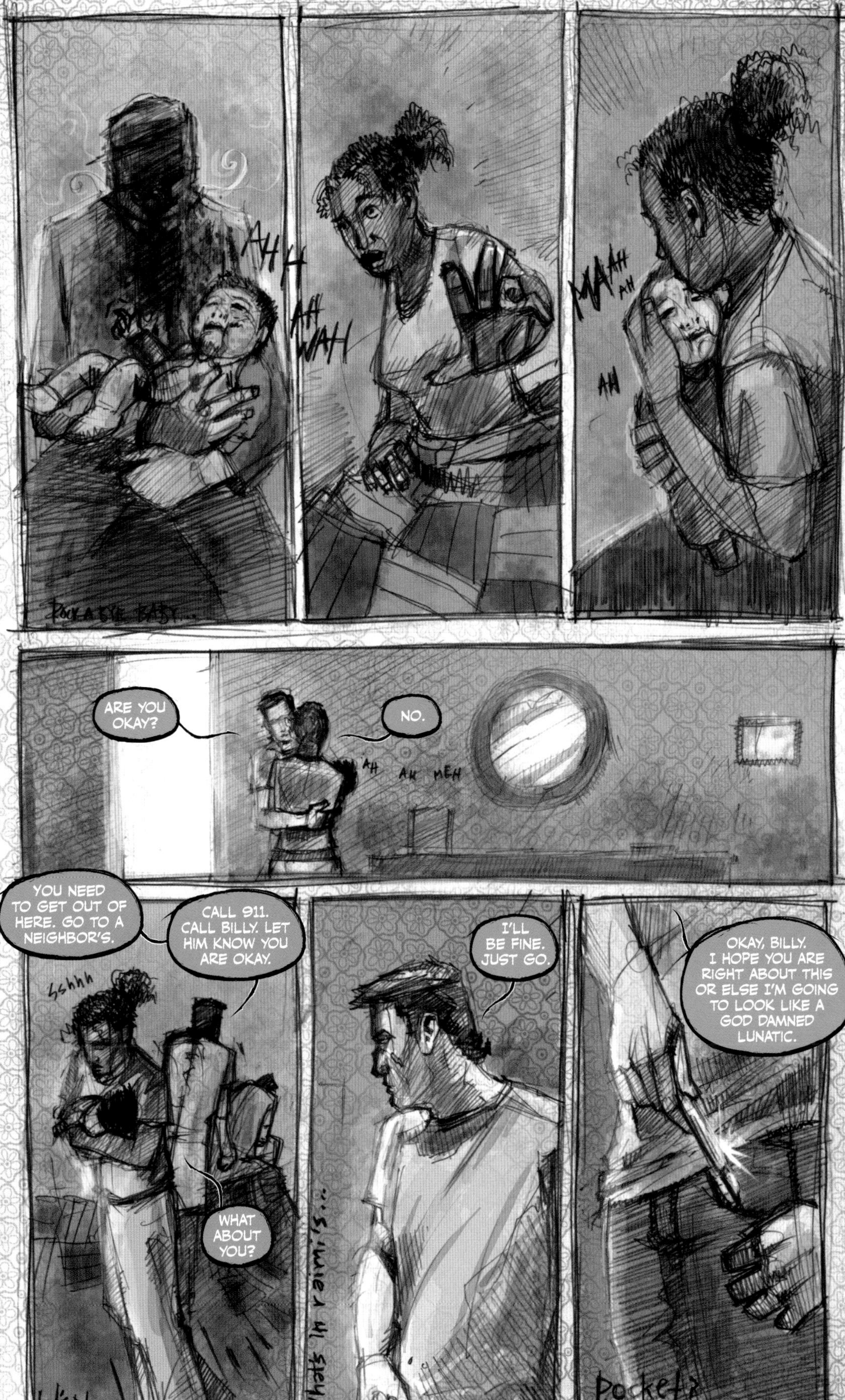
AHH
AH WAH
ROCK A BYE BABY...
MAAH AH
AH
ARE YOU OKAY?
NO.
AH AH MEH
YOU NEED TO GET OUT OF HERE. GO TO A NEIGHBOR'S.
CALL 911. CALL BILLY. LET HIM KNOW YOU ARE OKAY.
Sshhh
WHAT ABOUT YOU?
Let's play...
I'LL BE FINE. JUST GO.
Whats in raimi's...
OKAY, BILLY. I HOPE YOU ARE RIGHT ABOUT THIS OR ELSE I'M GOING TO LOOK LIKE A GOD DAMNED LUNATIC.
Pocket?

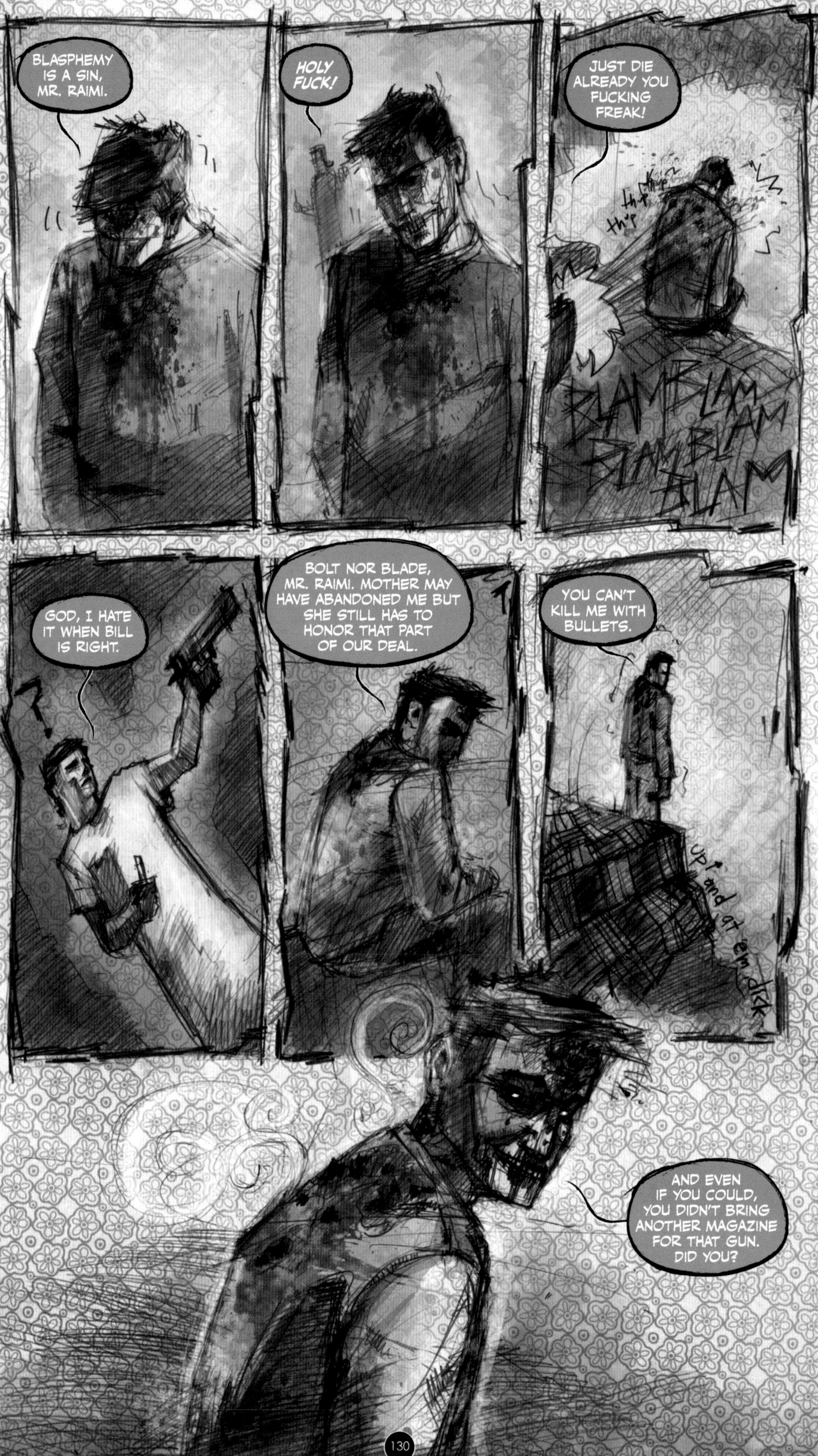
BLASPHEMY IS A SIN, MR. RAIMI.
HOLY FUCK!
JUST DIE ALREADY YOU FUCKING FREAK!
BLAM BLAM BLAM BLAM BLAM
GOD, I HATE IT WHEN BILL IS RIGHT.
BOLT NOR BLADE, MR. RAIMI. MOTHER MAY HAVE ABANDONED ME BUT SHE STILL HAS TO HONOR THAT PART OF OUR DEAL.
YOU CAN'T KILL ME WITH BULLETS.
up and at 'em dick
AND EVEN IF YOU COULD, YOU DIDN'T BRING ANOTHER MAGAZINE FOR THAT GUN. DID YOU?

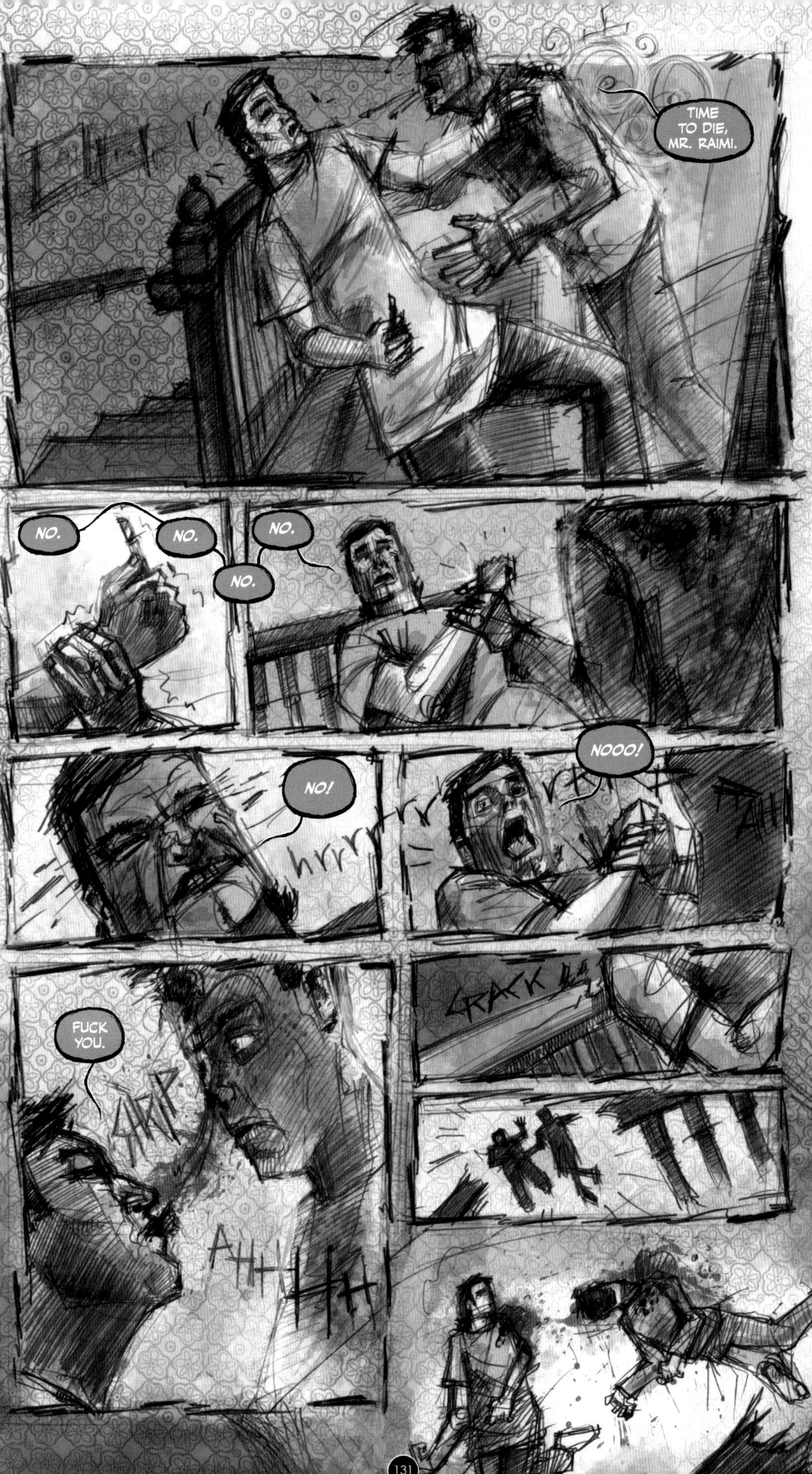
TIME TO DIE, MR. RAIMI.
NO.
NO.
NO.
NO.
NO!
NOOO!
FUCK YOU.
CRACK

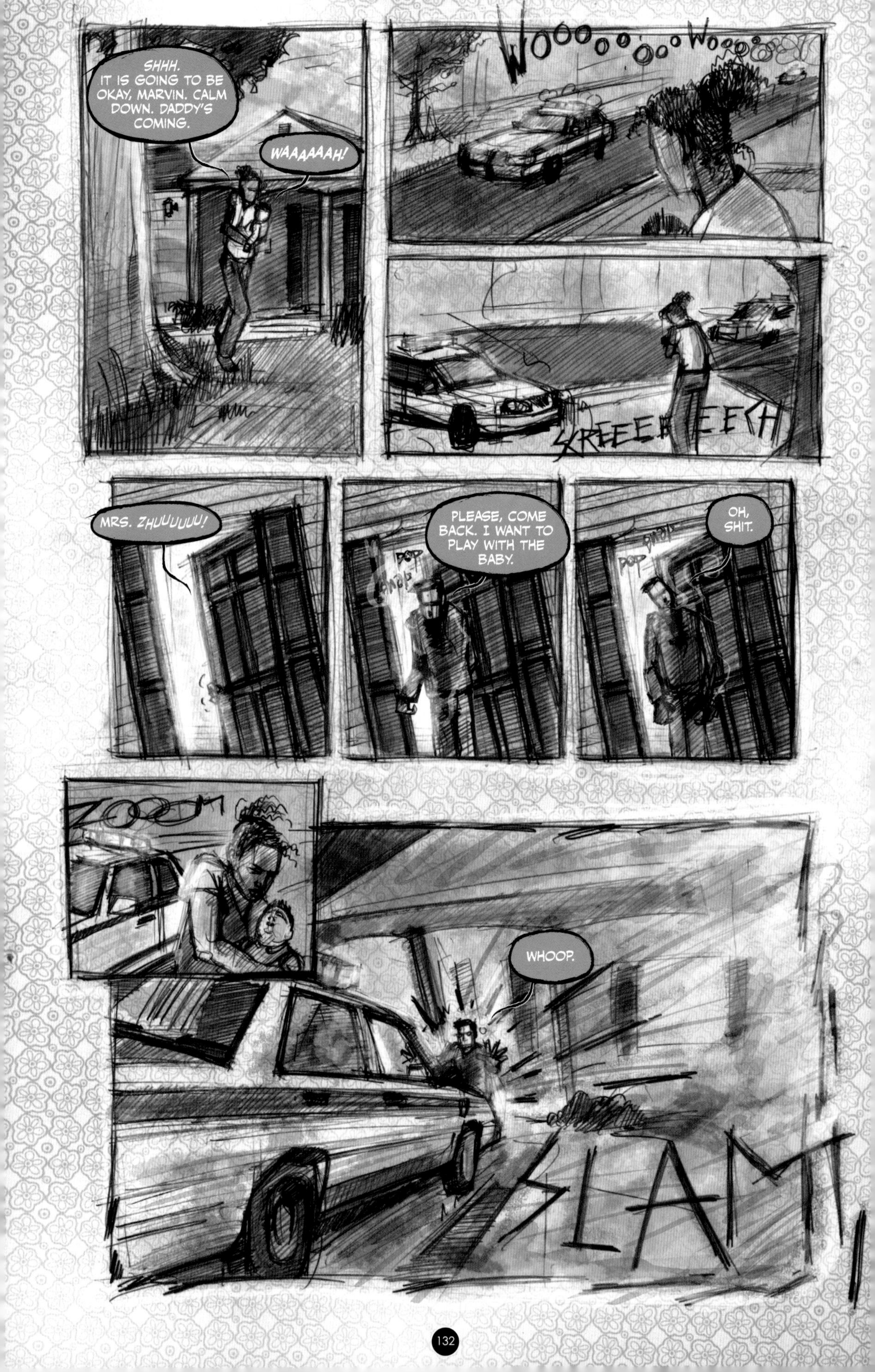

SHHH. IT IS GOING TO BE OKAY, MARVIN. CALM DOWN. DADDY'S COMING.
WAAAAAAH!
SKREEEEEEECH
MRS. ZHUUUUUU!
PLEASE, COME BACK. I WANT TO PLAY WITH THE BABY.
OH, SHIT.
ZOOOM
WHOOP.
SLAM!

ACT THE THIRD

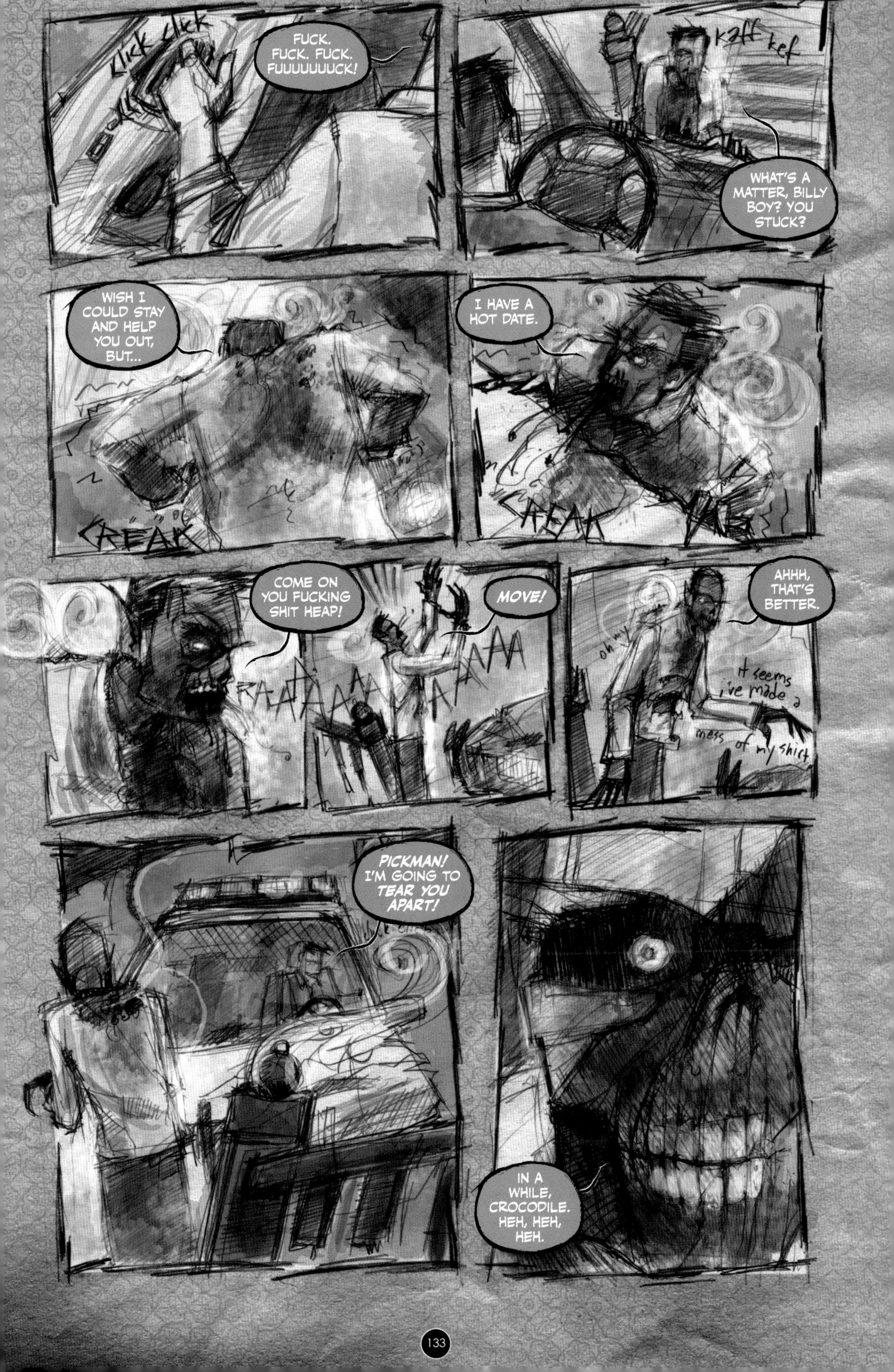

klick click
FUCK. FUCK. FUCK. FUUUUUUUCK!
kaff kef
WHAT'S A MATTER, BILLY BOY? YOU STUCK?
WISH I COULD STAY AND HELP YOU OUT, BUT...
CREAK
I HAVE A HOT DATE.
CREAK
COME ON YOU FUCKING SHIT HEAP!
MOVE!
AHHH, THAT'S BETTER.
oh my
it seems i've made a mess of my shirt
PICKMAN! I'M GOING TO TEAR YOU APART!
IN A WHILE, CROCODILE. HEH, HEH, HEH.

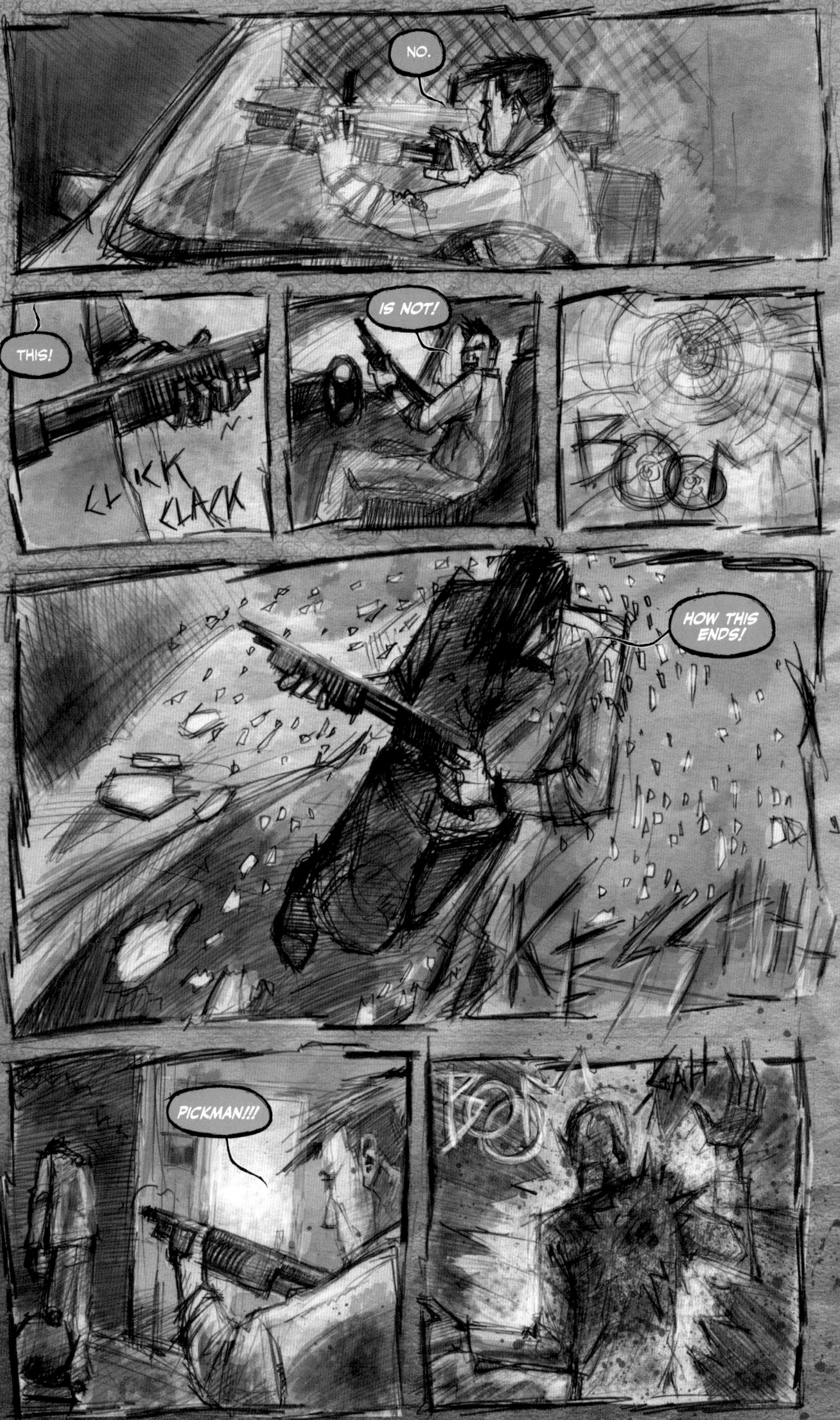

NO.
THIS!
CLICK
CLACK
IS NOT!
HOW THIS ENDS!
PICKMAN!!!
GAH

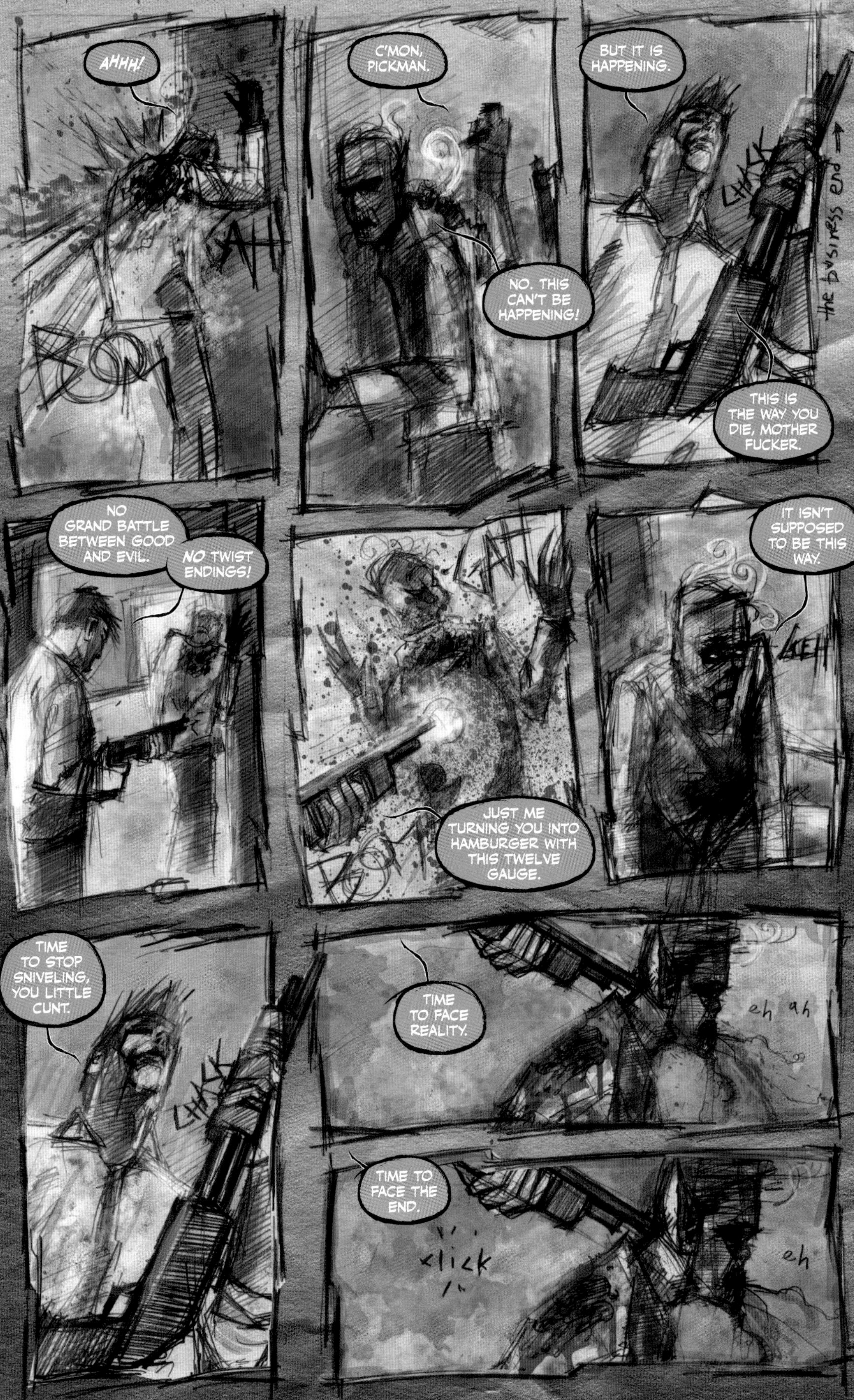

AHHH!
C'MON, PICKMAN.
NO. THIS CAN'T BE HAPPENING!
BUT IT IS HAPPENING.
the business end
THIS IS THE WAY YOU DIE, MOTHER FUCKER.
NO GRAND BATTLE BETWEEN GOOD AND EVIL.
NO TWIST ENDINGS!
JUST ME TURNING YOU INTO HAMBURGER WITH THIS TWELVE GAUGE.
IT ISN'T SUPPOSED TO BE THIS WAY.
TIME TO STOP SNIVELING, YOU LITTLE CUNT.
TIME TO FACE REALITY.
eh ah
TIME TO FACE THE END.
click
eh

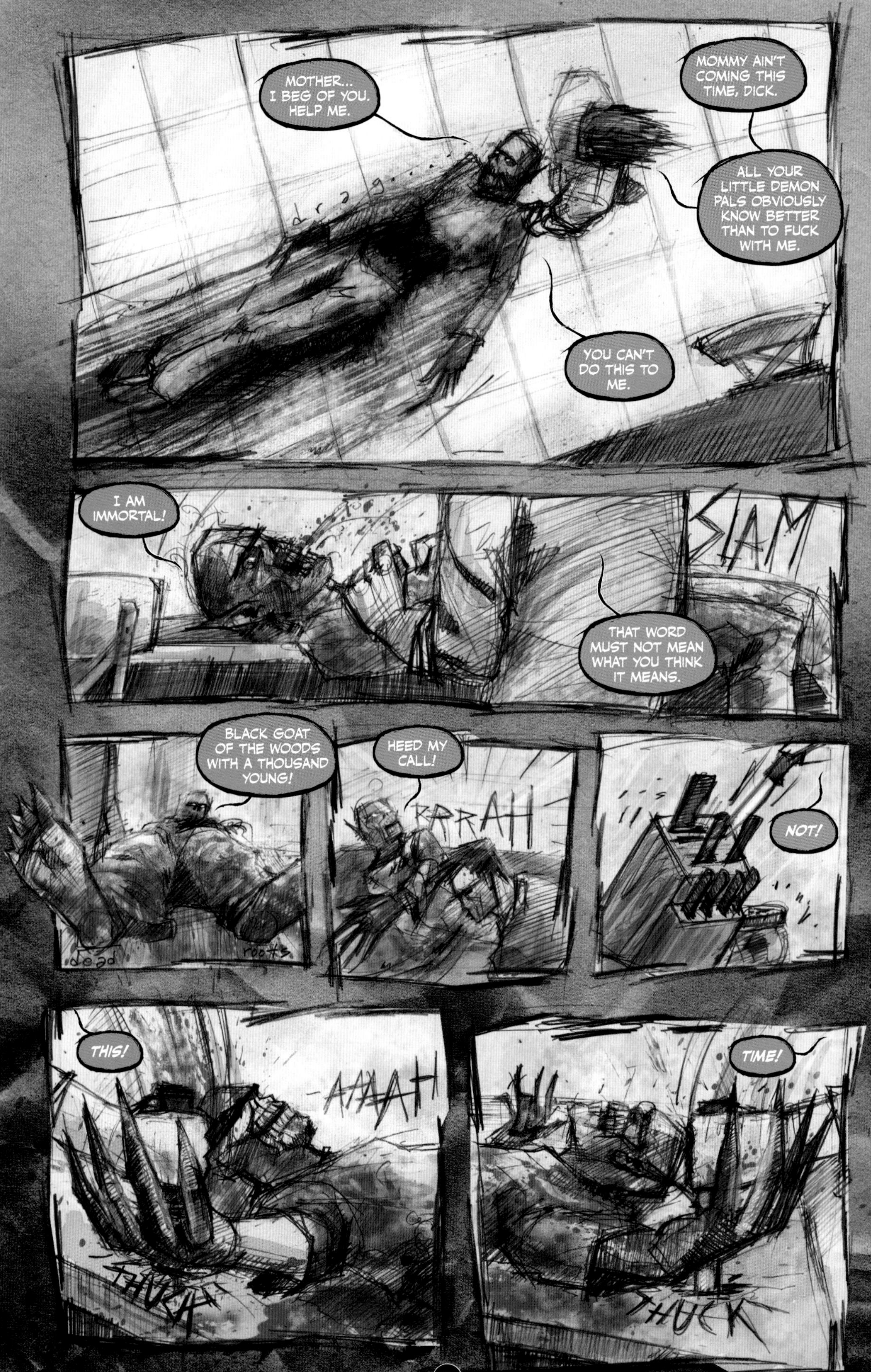
MOTHER... I BEG OF YOU. HELP ME.
drag...
MOMMY AIN'T COMING THIS TIME, DICK.
ALL YOUR LITTLE DEMON PALS OBVIOUSLY KNOW BETTER THAN TO FUCK WITH ME.
YOU CAN'T DO THIS TO ME.
I AM IMMORTAL!
SLAM
THAT WORD MUST NOT MEAN WHAT YOU THINK IT MEANS.
BLACK GOAT OF THE WOODS WITH A THOUSAND YOUNG!
dead
roots
HEED MY CALL!
RRRAH
NOT!
THIS!
AAAAH
THUCK
TIME!
THUCK

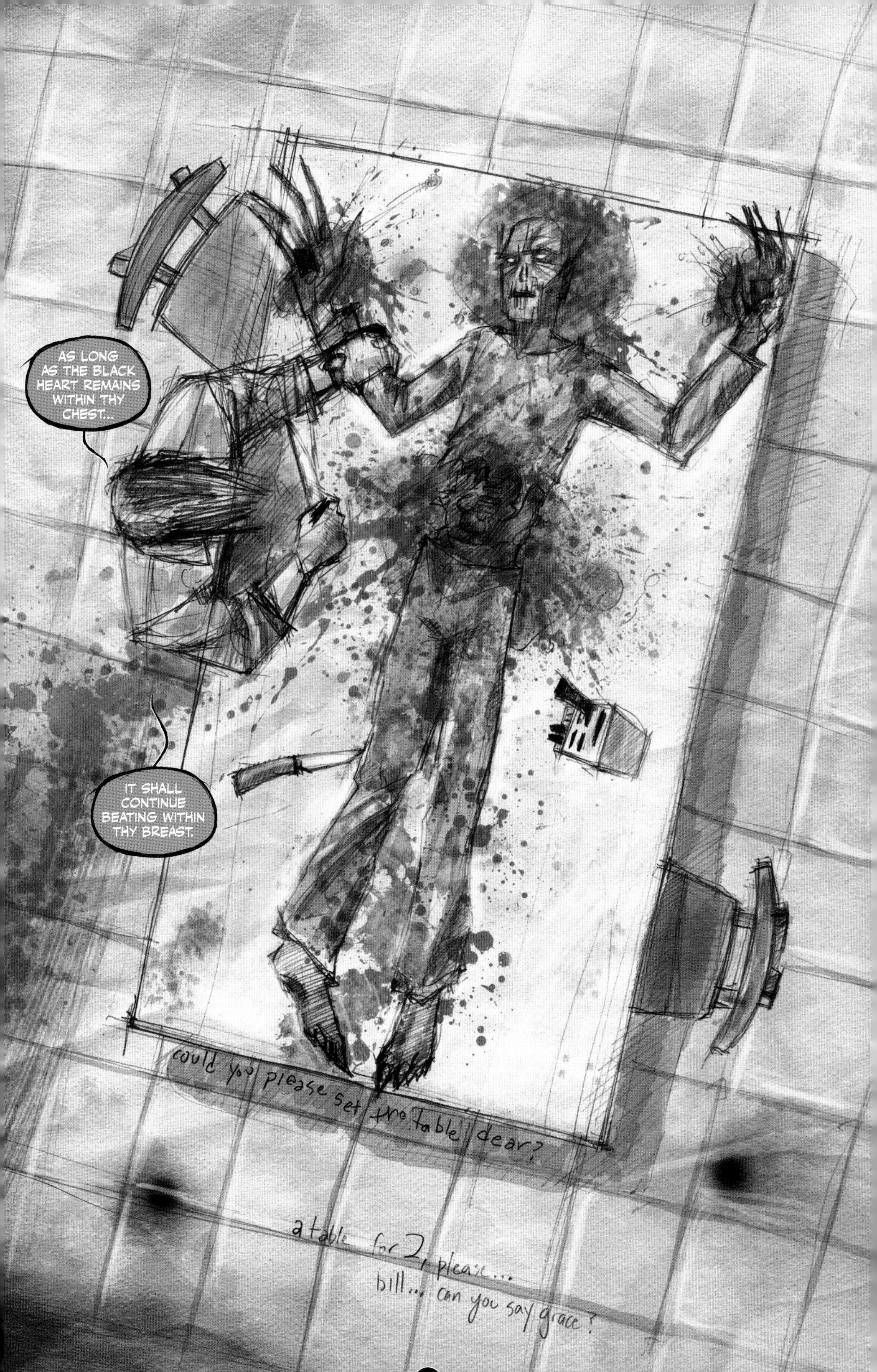
AS LONG AS THE BLACK HEART REMAINS WITHIN THY CHEST...
IT SHALL CONTINUE BEATING WITHIN THY BREAST.
could you please set the table dear?
a table for 2, please...
bill... can you say grace?

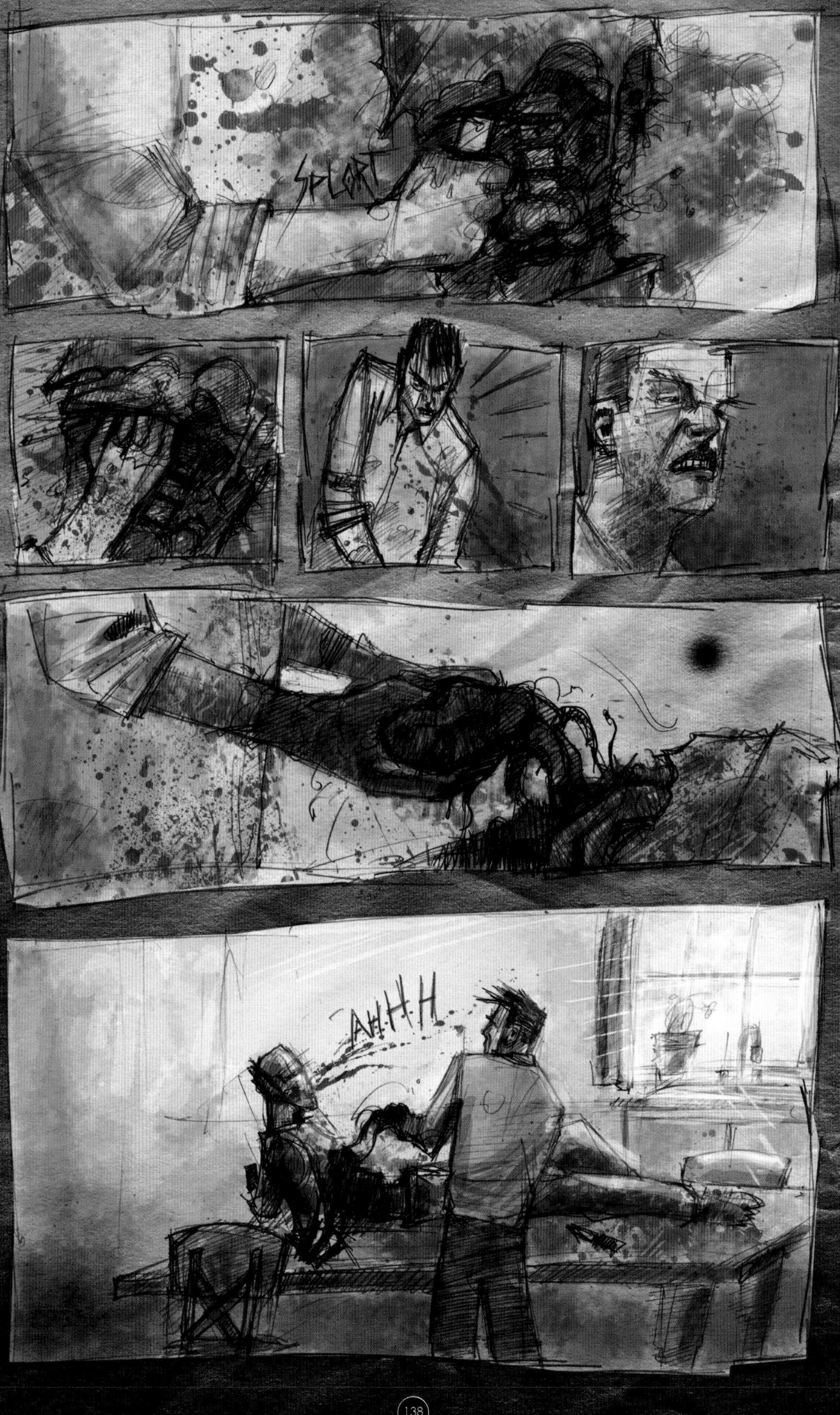
SPLORT
AHHH

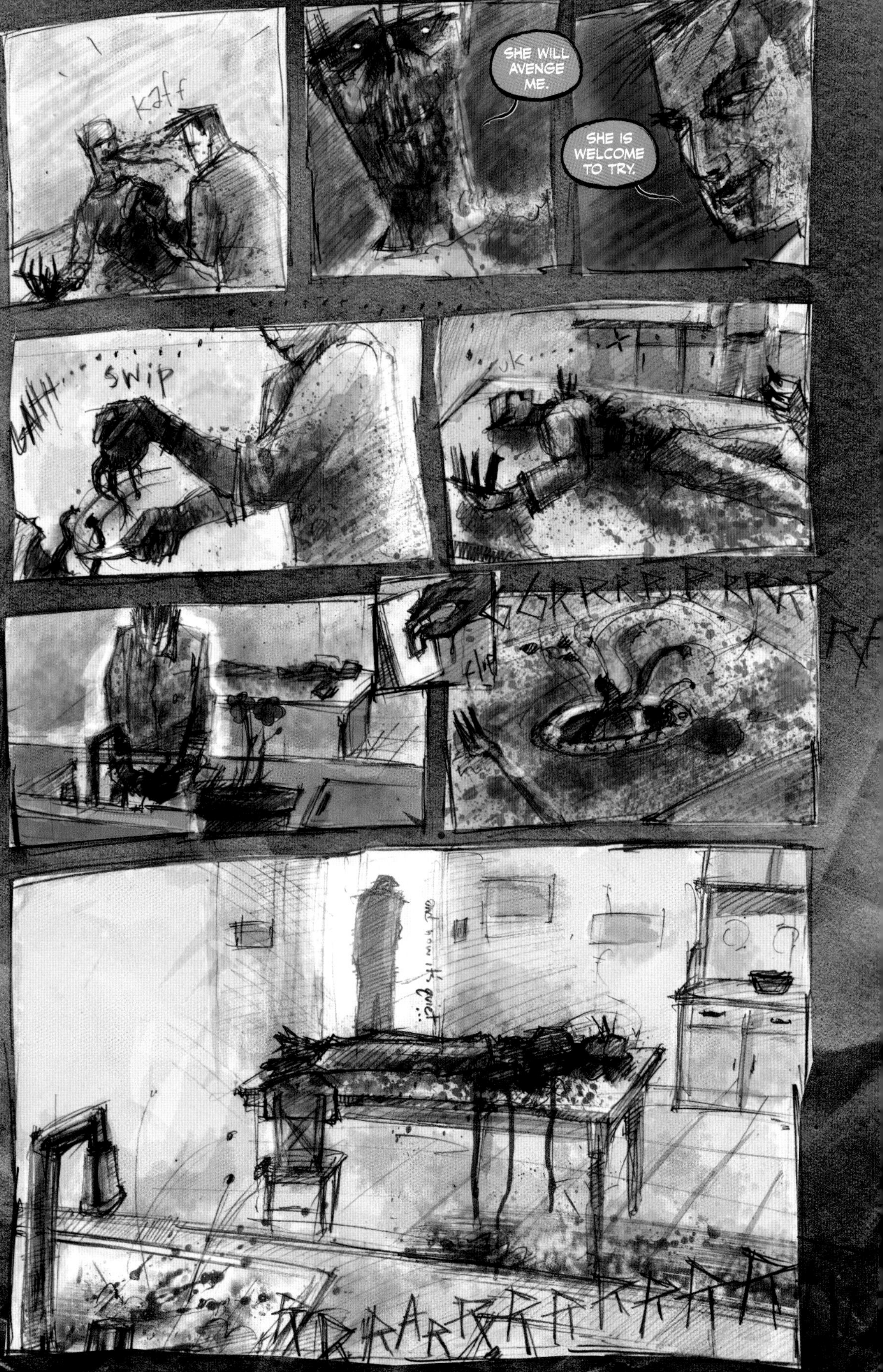
kaff
SHE WILL AVENGE ME.
SHE IS WELCOME TO TRY.
swip
uk
and now it's quiet...

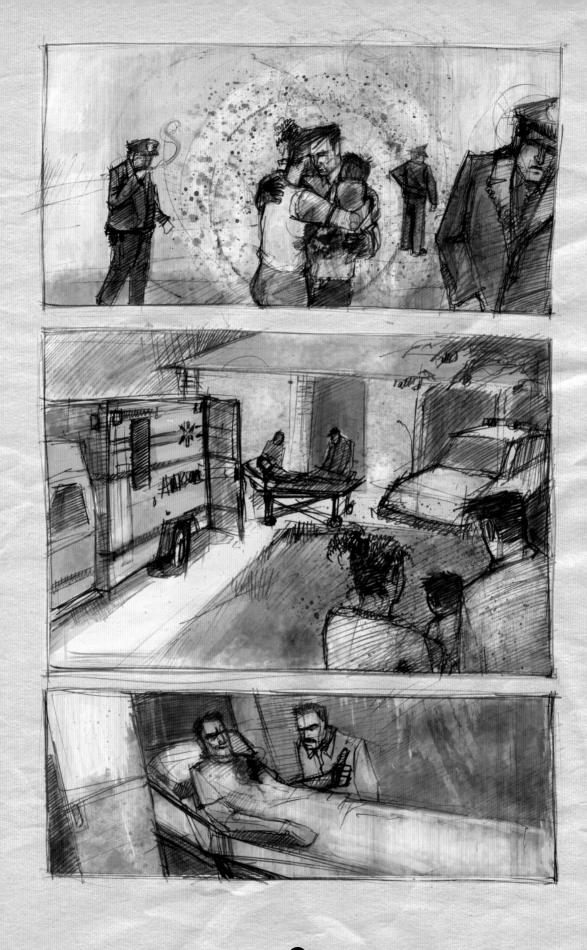

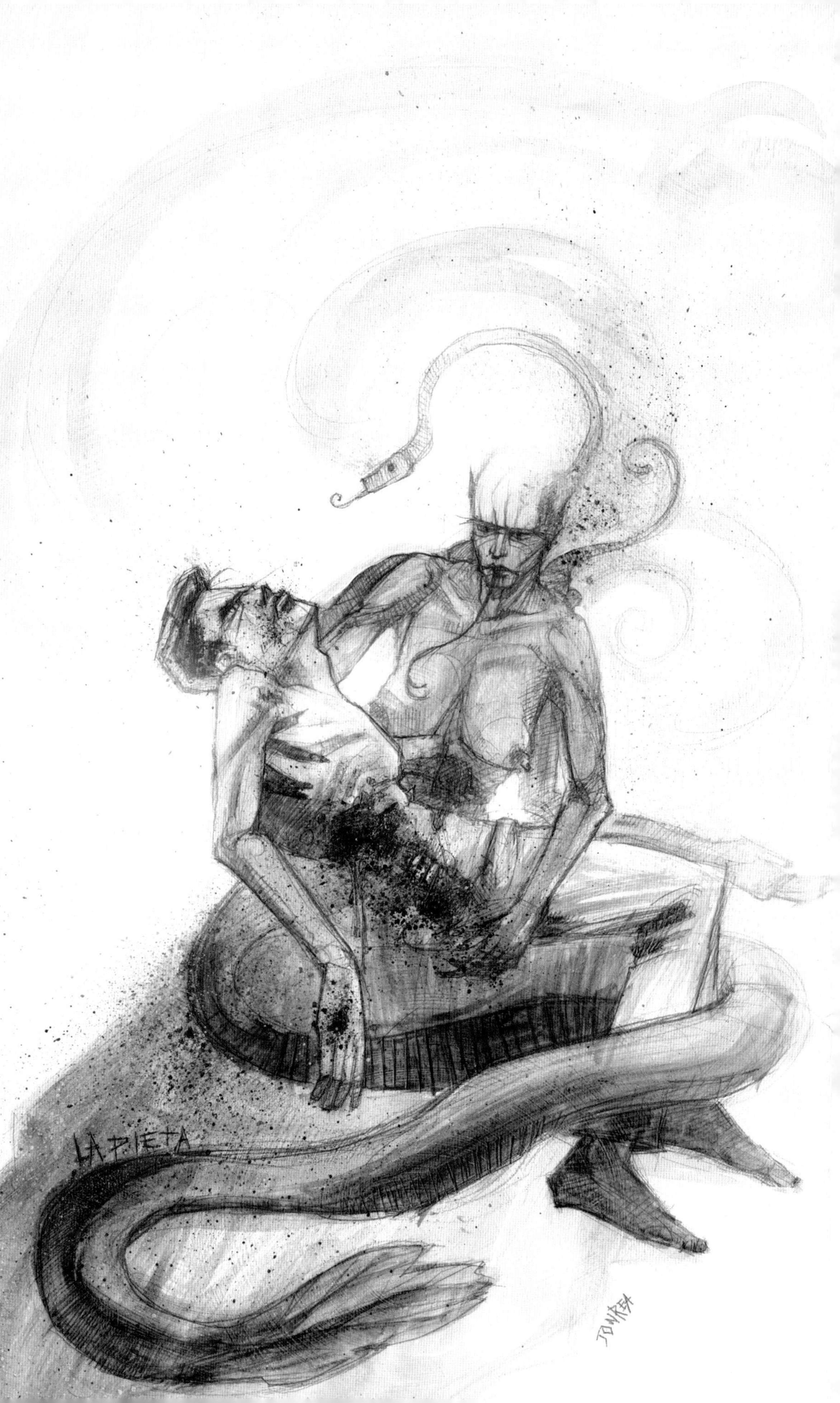
LA PIETA
JON REA

behind the scenes

A CRIMINAL MIND

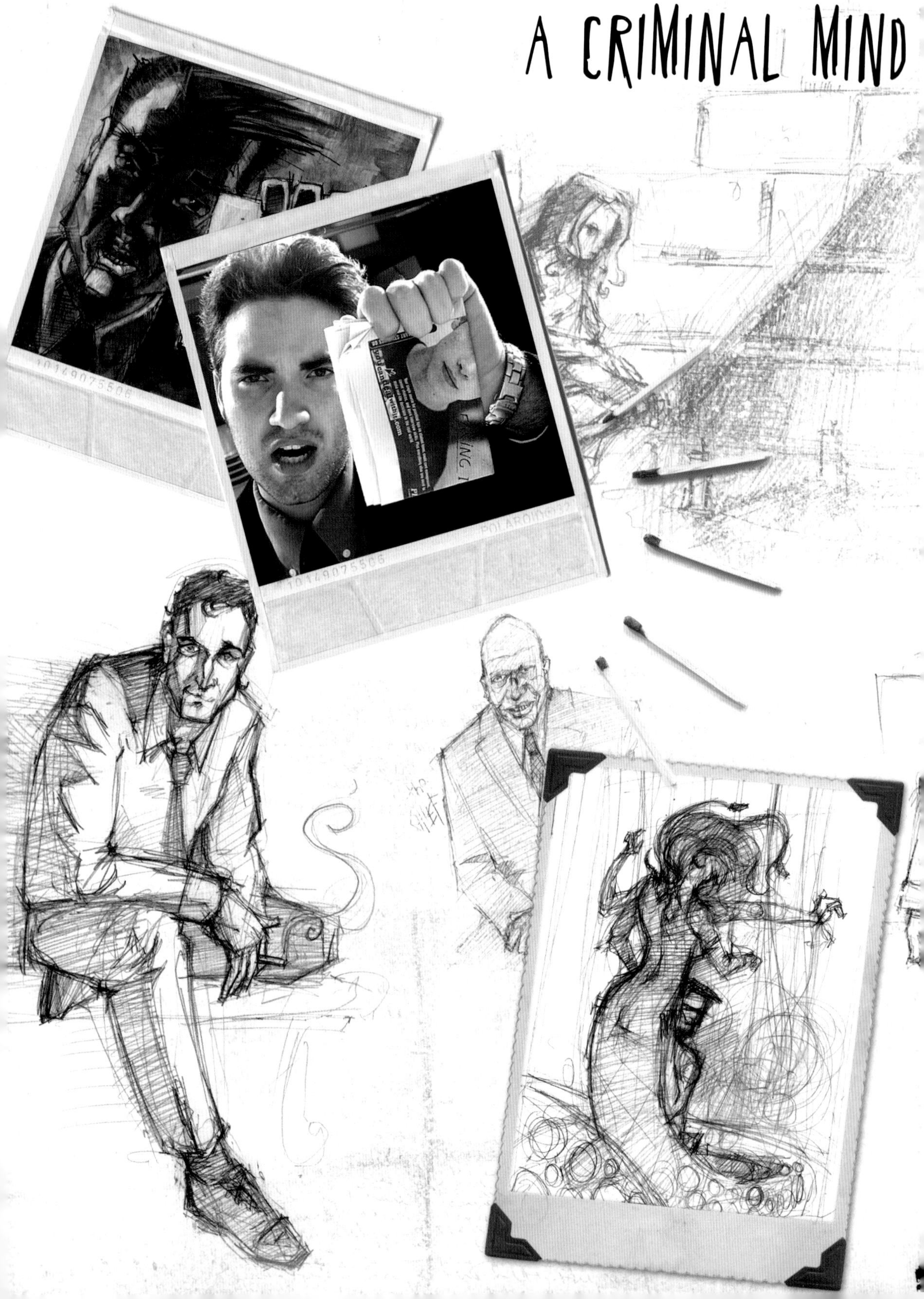

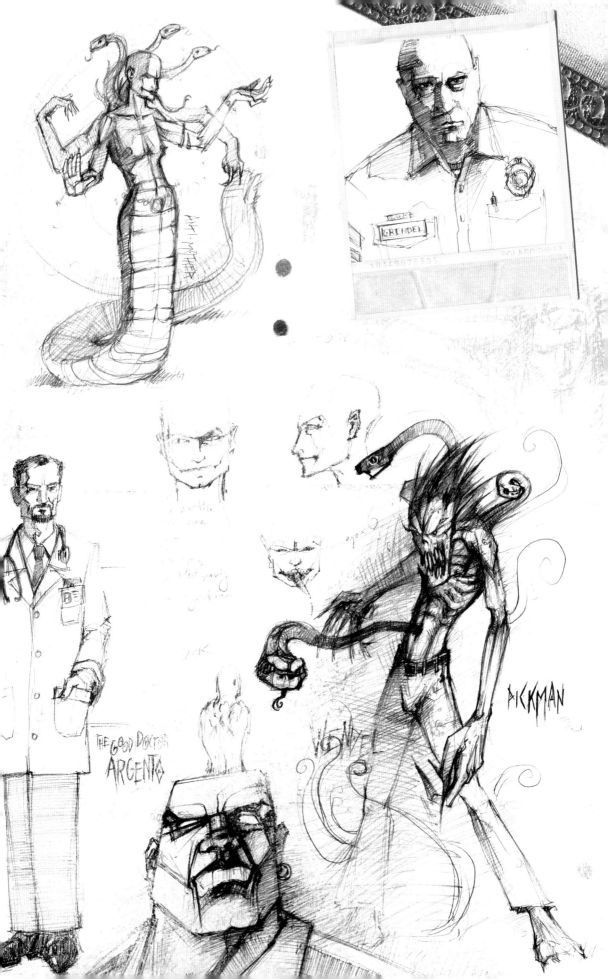

GRENDEL

THE GOOD DOCTOR ARGENTO

PICKMAN

about the authors

JASON E BECKER

See that picture right there beside these words? THAT is Jason Becker. At some point in the recent past he was born. He probably isn't homeless or dead yet. He wrote this book and another one called **Hero Corps: The Rookie**. He might write another book at some point in the future. That is about it. If you are brave

Photo by Amby Jordan

and Twitter is still a thing follow him there. *@JasonEBecker*

JON REA

Jon has been working on **Killing Pickman** for what seems like forever and now you are holding it in your precious little hands. Jon is a graduate of Syracuse University with a BFA in Illustration and lives and works from his home in Bucks County, Pennsylvania, with his wife, Jill and two dark seedlings, Jacob and

Illustration by Jon Rea

Madeline. He is an adjunct professor at Cabrini College in Radnor, Pennsylvania in the Graphic Design Department where he prides himself on discouraging bright-eyed youth and telling them to switch to major in business. Don't let Jon's dour, gloomy artwork fool you, he generally has a sunny disposition and sings loudly with the car radio, usually but not exclusively to embarrass his family members.